W9-ACY-263

SIBERIA

PERM

HELSINKI

ST PETERSBURG

RUSSIA

PRESSBURG

VIENNA

BADEN

NGARY

ROUMANIA

CRIMEA

ZUGDIDI

KUTAISI

BAKU

RVIA

BULGARIA

TURKEY

GREECE

CYPRUS

ALFRED NOBEL

THE LONELIEST MILLIONAIRE

Alfred Nobel about 1890

ALFRED NOBEL
The Loneliest Millionaire

By Michael Evlanoff *and* Marjorie Fluor
Foreword by Simon Ramo
Commentaries by Arnold O. Beckman *and*
Henry T. Mudd

The Ward Ritchie Press

To the Fluor Family
WHOSE HIGH IDEALS AND LOYAL FRIENDSHIP HAVE GUIDED ME
IN MY SEARCH FOR TRUTH AND BEAUTY.
CONFUCIUS SAID,
"IT IS NOT TRUTH THAT MAKES MAN GREAT,
BUT MAN THAT MAKES TRUTH GREAT."

To Youka and Marcia
Prince and Princess Troubetzkoy
THIS BOOK WOULD NOT HAVE BEEN STARTED
WITHOUT THEIR MOST GRACIOUS INTEREST,
INSPIRATION AND ENCOURAGEMENT
AND I OWE THEM MY DEEPEST GRATITUDE.

Copyright © 1969 by Michael Evlanoff and Marjorie Fluor
Library of Congress Catalog Card Number 77-96732
Printed in the United States of America by Anderson, Ritchie & Simon
Map end sheets by Daniel R. DeChaine
Designed by Joseph Simon

Foreword

This is an age of conflict—of philosophies and ideologies, of ways of life, of disparate goals, of the new with the old, of advancement with backwardness. It is a good time to ponder the life and works and prizes of Alfred Nobel. For it is also a period of mismatch between accelerating scientific discovery and technological development, on the one hand, and lagging social maturing and change, on the other. Nobel seems to have understood this phenomenon of imbalance between the technological and social worlds. Moreover, he reacted as one might expect an especially intelligent, active, sensitive, practical visionary to react. The symbols and influences of Nobel's contributions remain available to provide guidance, if we are inclined to want to work at solving our problems rather than merely to despair of them.

In his time, chemical phenomena could be used for either war-making or enhancing man's material requirements and comforts. Today, nuclear phenomena can either destroy our whole society or make more of the earth's resources available to man, give him more power for useful purposes, even prolong his life. But the problem is the same. Science and technology, advanced though they are today, are still but tools of man. They do not lead him to evil or force him into a technological society inevitably so constructed as not to be to his liking. Neither does the availability of the scientific approach and engineering expertise guarantee that mankind will benefit itself no matter how it applies the knowledge and methodologies. The new tools offer opportunities, but the choices and decisions are man's.

Nobel's approaches and insights, exemplified by the prizes for which he is now so well remembered, stand in answer to a rather prevalent line of thought which is growing today—a point of view that is blindly antiscience and antitechnology. Sometimes it is antagonistic to scientists and engineers. It loosely identifies the tool, science, with the bad uses to which the tool had been put rather than with the science that wields it. It reasons that we want peace, but instead have science to make war more efficient, more horrible; that technology has given us color TV and the automobile, hence it is to be blamed for the vapid programs and noisy commercials that issue from our sets and the painful traffic congestion that plagues our cities; that science has given us the pill, therefore it is a devil that steers our young people towards an immoral sex life; that science was behind the industrial revolution which drove us from the good life of the land into the ills of city life.

Many act as though we really ought to legislate against further scientific discovery and technological development but, since we can't, we are at liberty to default. The myth is growing that we are certain to have a robotlike, technological society in which man becomes a docile, instructed, disinterested participant in a network of rapidly clicking gears, transistors, signals, satellites, cables, and moving vehicles, all preset and run by a computer—that it is only a matter of time. We will not easily be able to distinguish man from machine, and there is nothing we can do about it.

This reasoning goes on to separate the scientific and technological world from the rest of society, from humanity. It assumes two cultures which cannot mix, one or the other having to win in a competition critical to man. Perhaps it is not surprising that the more one who accepts this assumption ponders the relationship of science to society (all the while realizing that science and technology are here to stay and will be stronger elements in determining the pattern of civilization) the surer he becomes that humanity will be the loser.

But this popular line of contemplation, from the concept that technology is bad to the notion that there are two inharmonious cultures, is wrong. Man can control his destiny. But he won't do it without effort and understanding. The relationship of science to society is not easy to unravel and reweave; however, the reward of fuller utilization of technology on behalf of humanity makes the task worth while, and the penalty of default is correspondingly too high to accept. Alfred Nobel understood this. Anyone who in a serious way wants to get to know the nature of, and help to influence, the future impact of science on society would benefit greatly by studying the life of Alfred Nobel.

SIMON RAMO

Contents

List of Illustrations

A Word to the Reader

My first book on Alfred Nobel, entitled "Nobel-Prize Donor," was published in 1944. Under war regulations on conservation of paper and materials, the book had to be abridged to less than half of its original content.

This book, now long overdue, concerns not only Alfred Nobel, the inventor of dynamite and advocate of peace, but also his fascinating family. Good fortune gave me the opportunity to become an intimate friend of the large Nobel family, and I shall present them all to my reader. Much to my regret, I did not know nor could have known Alfred Nobel. He was beyond the barrier of my time.

The attempt to write biography is notoriously beset with the difficulties of understanding the motives and judgments of the man or woman a writer attempts to put on paper. What can one do, but probe and sift and sort, until he feels he has found the kernel of truth? The person or fact or event has its own integrity and the writer seeks to avoid distortion of it.

Alfred Nobel is presented here as man and scientist moving in a world of indignity and ruthlessness. In the analysis of his complicated nature nothing has been invented. Great people are human beings and combine hopes, fears, strengths and failings.

Alfred Nobel had a complex personality. He was a mass of contradictions. Nobel lived all his life as a tormented person.

In the early years of his career, he believed civilized nations would abandon war, if the methods of warfare threatened the annihilation of those nations. He did not idealize humanity and, at first, attached no importance to the pacifist movement. Ever with sober and pensive mood he declared, "Resolution and more resolution will not secure peace," and concluded with melancholy, "If only they had listened to me."

But wars grew progressively more disastrous and his torment never ceased. At last, he realized dynamite would not prevent wars through the fears of its destruction. Man would always be a beast, ready to attack and kill. He then admitted the failure of his first belief and reconciled his philosophy with the pacifist movement. In his will he designated his great fortune to be used as annual prizes for "the greatest services to mankind" in the fields of chemistry, physics, medicine, literature and international peace. Thus, he chose to award the areas of advancement he considered most beneficial to the forward progress of mankind.

In an effort to serve all, one takes the risk of fully satisfying none, but the advantage of this multiple approach seems worth the danger. Therefore combined for you in this book are Alfred Nobel's scientific achievements, his pathetically sad life, the great service he rendered world culture in establishing the prizes which bear his name and link him to all of the humanities. Here too is presented the vast Nobel oil industry in the Caucasus with Emmanuel Nobel, his nephew, at the helm. His name has been spelled both *Emanuel* and *Emmanuel* by various biographers. In this book, the spelling *Emmanuel* has been used consistently.

Through happy coincidence I met and grew close to Emmanuel Nobel, the directing genius of the tremendous oil enterprises of the Russian Caucasus. He was then the most prominent and influential member of the family. His clarity, wit, charm, the drama of his actions and the human simplicity of his passions made him an outstanding man.

Since I became a participant, instead of an outside observer, there is obligation on my part to see that my story has no filled-in places. To the best of my knowledge and belief, I have made no significant statement that has not been covered in a contemporary document. Where dialogue or incident has been improvised it has been minor and has been based on available letters or other material.

Despite Nobel's abhorrence of biographers and newspaper chroniclers, his life is better known than the lives of other members of the Nobel clan. Much research was done on books by: Ragnar Sohlman and Henri Schuck, Herta Pauli, Erik Bergengren, Richard Hennig, Bertha von Suttner, Henri de Mosenthal and Nicholas Halasz, and I found their records to be indispensable.

I want to express my gratitude to Lilly and Mark Millard, whose friendship has been an inspiration and guiding light. I also owe much to the kindness of my friends the late Mrs. George Butler and her daughter Gloria Butler for their unfailing devotion.

To express my appreciation of my collaborator, Marjorie Fluor, would take pages of copy and words beyond my grasp. Mrs. Fluor's organization and sensitive additions to my discourse, her inspiration and enthusiasm for my appraisal of Alfred Nobel and his family, urged me on again and again to completion of this book.

And since I am not a man who underestimates the perception and aesthetic intuition of a woman, I rejoiced when Mrs. Fluor took command of the complexities of Alfred Nobel's love affairs. She delineates with understanding the lovely Bertha von Suttner who passionately adored her younger husband, yet remained the devoted and affectionate feminine influence of Alfred's life, and probes into the true nature of that frivolous child, Sofie Hess, whose ravishing beauty was an obsession with Alfred for eighteen years.

So, to Marjorie Fluor my love and gratitude; to Richard D. Lewis, that generous and splendid publisher, my fervent thanks; to Alice Wellman Harris, for her thoughtful assistance in editing and consultation, I send warm appreciation.

MICHAEL EVLANOFF

PART I

HIS LIFE

The Loneliest Man in the World

It was nearing the twilight hour and a man walked alone through the bustling throngs of Christmas shoppers on Copenhagen's winding *Stroget*, "The Stretch." He did not glance at the gaily decorated shops, or the flag-draped booths of Danish craftsmen, that bordered the sides of the thoroughfare. He seemed unaware of curious stares from laughing folk who passed him and then turned to watch him make his way toward Town Hall Square. No wonder they stared, for the lonely man emanated distinction in his appearance, his bearing, his very presence.

The furred collar of his sombre black greatcoat shielded his neat bearded cheeks and chin from the chill December wind; his black hat shadowed eyes as deeply blue as the Baltic Sea; his gold-headed cane struck the age-smoothed cobbles of the *Stroget* with rhythmical beat. His steps held determination, but his face was drawn and anguished.

Suddenly, a bright yellow ball banged against the man's knee. He turned his head to look into the apprehensive face of a small boy, standing in the roadway. The boy pulled off his red-knit cap, bowed his apology. The man lifted his cane and, using its gold knobbed head for a bat, sent the ball into the child's outstretched hands. Then the man smiled and the boy smiled back.

Just ahead, Town Hall Square opened up. The boy tucked his yellow ball under his arm and kept pace with the man, as they entered the great square together. They passed the red-bricked Town Hall with its crown of the city's coat-of-arms and, still without exchanging a word, turned into the soft turf beside it. At the bronze statue of the immortal Dane, Hans Christian Andersen, they halted.

The huge statue was evidently the child's destination, for he seated himself on a jutting corner by Andersen's great bronze foot. He would wait there for an adult to fetch him away. He looked up at the man shyly and lifted his hand in farewell.

Alfred Nobel—for the man was Alfred Nobel, giant of wealth, genius of chemistry, one of the most noted and notorious figures of the time—lifted his hat in solemn courtesy to the small boy with the yellow ball, then saluted the facsimile of that spinner of children's tales, towering above the lad's head. He swung his cane beneath his arm and walked on, alone.

Back in his hotel suite, Alfred Nobel stood at the window, looking down upon the passing merry-makers, their arms loaded with gay-wrapped packages, their voices rising in excited greetings through the still, cold air to his ears. There remained only a week until the Christmas of 1889 and Alfred Nobel who had many times before called himself, "the loneliest man in the world," knew this night a loneliness more poignant, more unbearable than any he had known before.

Ten days ago he had buried his mother, Caroline Nobel, who even in her aging years remained his close companion and most understanding confidante. Following the funeral had come the arrangements to be made in accordance with will, the choice of grave memorial, all the sorrowful duties of a devoted son.

Only a year and nine months before in the April of 1888, Alfred had watched his brother, Ludwig, meet a tortured death. The strong-bodied, ebullient Ludwig who had never kept still a moment of his waking hours had grown gaunt and frail with suffering from an incurable throat disease. The two brothers sat on a bench at a resort on the French Riviera, silently watching the movement of the opal-hued ocean, each thinking his own thoughts. Only the pressure

4

of the sick man's hand on Alfred's arm told of Ludwig's gratitude at having his brother near him.

When Ludwig died and Alfred read the obituary, written by a French journalist, he received a psychic wound so deep, so mortal, that he could never recover from it. The journalist had mistaken the death of Ludwig for that of Alfred and had reviewed Alfred's life, proclaiming him "the merchant of death."

This label shocked and saddened Alfred. For the first time he realized the civilized world must regard him only in the light of his well publicized inventions: dynamite and blasting gelatine. He wondered whether in truth he deserved any other recognition. Had he done anything for suffering humanity, except to bequeath it these weapons of destruction? Certainly, he had hoped the explosives he created would serve valuable purposes, but the leaders of warfare had quickly adapted them for devastation of enemy countries. "The merchant of death"—this title haunted his days and tortured his nights.

Now, on this night in Copenhagen with Christmas gaiety resounding in the streets below him, Alfred pondered his life and knew he had missed the very things he had most longed for.

All his life he had longed for love. His mother's care and love during his childhood had nurtured the hope that he would experience a great absorbing love and that he, too, would have a home with children in it. If a man begets children, rears them with the inspiration of his love, imbues them with knowledges gained from joys and sorrows of his own life, he leaves to the world the most precious and valuable part of himself, when he dies. So Alfred had felt.

But Alfred had no children. The two women he might have married had failed him. First, there was lovely and brilliant Bertha Kinsky, but she chose to join a life far away from him. Then there was breathtakingly beautiful Sofie Hess whose simple ways and childlike innocence attracted him, but who had become a distasteful responsibility. He could not bear to think of her voluptuous bed tonight.

Since Angina Pectoris dogged his footsteps he knew he had not many years of traveling left. When death would call him, he had nothing of his abundance of love to leave behind him. Only an hour ago, he had saluted the statue of Hans Christian Andersen who left much of love, much of imagination and joy he gave children all over the world. But Alfred Nobel's gifts of love—must they die with him?

With love, he had always longed for learning. Without cessation he had searched for knowledge, not only in his particular inventive fields, but in all sciences, in literature, in arts, in people of the far corners of the earth. What of his devotion to learning would he leave the world? Dynamite? Blasting gelatine? Explosive destroyers? Dealers of death? Must his dedication to all avenues of knowledge die with him?

That depth of compassion for the sufferings of mankind that had ever filled his heart—would even his few intimates remember it for long? What could he do to make his compassion known to the world? To those who would call him "the merchant of death?"

"But, cease these sorrowful meanderings, Alfred," he commanded himself, and he turned from the window to go to the desk to take up pen and paper. He did have at hand one powerful tool that could build a framework for his memorial-gift to mankind. He had wealth, tremendous wealth, for the times in which he lived. He would draw up a plan that would convince the nations of the world that the real Alfred Nobel cherished above all things these three: Love, learning and compassion.

By means of his immense fortune, he would leave an estate that could ease the sufferings of humanity. He would arrange a system of commendations, of rewards to be given to the selfless humanitarians, the dedicated researchers for

6

knowledge to benefit their fellow men, the courageous champions of world peace.

Through this bequest to the world, all human beings would inherit the love, the devotion to learning and the compassion of Alfred Nobel.

He began to write hurriedly, urgently. He must tell his beloved Baroness Bertha von Suttner of his plan for his estate, for Bertha had lent her brilliant mind and unremitting efforts to the prayed-for coming of world peace ever since her return to Austria. Then, too, with her usual kindness she had invited Alfred to spend the Christmas holidays with the Baron and herself. In courtesy he must refuse them, for the burden of the tragic loss of his mother had made him an unfit guest of these gracious friends.

He wrote: "... I am just here from Stockholm where I have been to conduct to her last home my poor dear mother...." He expressed his regret at refusing the holiday invitation, and then the words poured onto the paper, his thoughts too fast for his flowing script to put them down. His plan had as yet no organization, no exactitude, but that would come—Bertha von Suttner would understand the plan could not spring full-fledged from a weary brain. And she would rejoice with him at knowing that when he was gone, his fortune would honor before all the world the champions humanity and peace. The page was filled. He finished.

"I press your two hands—the little hands of a dear kind sister who wishes me well just as I wish her and hers well.

A. NOBEL"

He sealed the letter and addressed it. On this night of Copenhagen's Christmas season in 1889, the framework for the Nobel Prizes had come into being.

The portrayal of Alfred Nobel in the scene above required little embellishment to come to life. It introduces this great man whose complexities of nature, curiously enough, were never revealed to the world until his death.

7

A Genius Is Born

Caroline Andriette Nobel had plenty of courage and resourcefulness, but when she saw her new-born son on October 21, 1833, her heart sank in despair. His body was so frail, it seemed scarcely to rest in her arms; his drawn face and weak mewing cries wrung her heart.

The child's birth had been difficult, as were those of her first three babes. She had lost her first-born, though four year old Robert-Hjalmar and the two-year toddler, Ludwig-Immanuel, were now healthy, energetic small boys. But this delicate baby, would he survive?

As she rocked the too-quiet infant in her arms, she vowed she would rear this boy. She would protect his every moment, nurse him to health. Erik Bergengren writes, it took "all her love and tender care to keep his flickering life flame burning. She alone believed and succeeded when all others had given up hope."

Caroline gave Alfred-Bernhard her continuous, watchful care for eight years. The boy's weak spine brought on convulsions; he had difficulty in breathing; his digestion was inadequate.

Alfred grew into a studious, thoughtful child, though always pale and undersized. When he was still trotting unsteadily at Caroline's heels, she discovered his probing, insatiable mind. She must often have wished Alfred's body could gain the strength and vitality of his mind, as ever with patience and understanding, she sought to feed that mind and give it the sturdiest kind of nourishment. The boy studied with his two older brothers, had no difficulty in matching their pace of learning, if not exceeding it.

When he was eight, Caroline permitted him to attend school, but he could not exercise or play the energetic games of other children. He never enjoyed the freedom and romping of childhood.

In his autobiographic poem, written at eighteen in English, he told of his babyhood in:

> My cradle looked a death-bed, and for years
>   a mother watched with ever anxious care,
>   so little chance, to save the flickering light.
> I scarce could muster strength to drain the breast,
>   and then convulsions followed, till I gasped
>   upon the brink of nothingness—my frame
>   a school for agony with death for goal.

Of his two school terms at St. Jakob's Higher Apologist School, he wrote with the same longing he must have felt in watching his schoolmates at their games:

> We find him now a boy. His weakness still
>   makes him a stranger in the little world
>   wherein he moves. When fellow-boys are playing
>   he joins them not, a pensive looker-on;
>   and thus debarred the pleasures of his age
>   his mind keeps brooding over those to come.

These two terms at St. Jakob's were the only real schooling received by Alfred, according to Bergengren. "His reports there show that in all subjects . . . he gained the highest marks, which were given to only two others of the school's eighty-two pupils."

Reared by an ambitious and brilliant father and a mother whose good humor and balance countered the temperamental moods of her husband, the three Nobel brothers experienced a home-life of immeasurable value in the development of their characters.

Through Immanuel Nobel, their father, they gained inventive and ingenious minds, plus a sense of logic and painstaking industry. Through Caroline Andriette Ahlsell, their mother, they learned the necessity for patience and stamina in pursuing any project. She was the most unassuming of women, and none of her sons could tolerate pretense or vanity in themselves or others. Caroline was even-tempered, controlled in emergency, and serene in her manner and in her influence on her children.

Unfortunately, Alfred did not receive his mother's even disposition. He said in later years, "...the Nobel blood surges up, there is no lack of my own explosiveness, I get so angry the sparks fly, but it lasts for only half an hour." From anger, he could drop into a deep depression. He told a friend to consider him "a worthless instrument of cogitation, alone in the world and with thoughts heavier than anyone can imagine."

The natural genius and spirited inventiveness of Immanuel Nobel seem to have been his birthright, and he must have passed his gifts on to his sons, since Robert and Ludwig had initiative and resourcefulness as well as Alfred. The generations that preceded Immanuel date back to the seventeenth century to the province of Skane that thrusts out into the Baltic Sea on the southern tip of Sweden.

In Scandinavian countries the concept of aristocracy is relative. In the sense of purity of blood, the peasantry of Sweden, as in most European countries, may be deemed the purest social class. Mixed marriages among them are practically unknown, owing to the manner and customs of their lives. It is to this peasantry that the first Nobels belonged.

About the year 1655, a peasant by the name of Petrus Olaffson was born in the Nobbellov community of the province of Skane. He possessed some means and sought to work himself up. He managed to matriculate at the University of Uppsala. At that time students customarily had Latinized names, so Petrus, abiding by the tradition, Latinized his

10

name and called himself Petrus Olavi Nobelius after the place of his birth. In the university he studied law and, being very musical, his taste in music won him entrance into the distinguished circle of Professor Olaf Rudbeck. Petrus made a brilliant match by marrying Professor Olaf Rudbeck's daughter, Vendela.

Olaf Rudbeck was a famous intellectual figure of the time, well-known throughout Europe. A man of many gifts, he could be labeled the Swedish Leonardo da Vinci, on a somewhat lesser scale. At the age of twenty-three, while still studying at the University, he made the important contribution to anatomical science of discovery of the lymphatic vessels. His particular specialty was botany and it was Rudbeck who laid out the first botanical garden in Sweden. He gave instruction in physiology, astronomy, physics, zoology, mathematics, architecture, chemistry and mechanics. After drawing up plans of canals for the Swedish Government, he did much for the architectural development and beautification of Uppsala and—at the same time became a patron of music, painting, sculpture, and all the fine arts.

Incongruously, he acquired European prominence as the author of a work that in our day possesses merely a curiousity interest. Professor Rudbeck published a voluminous work, *Atland,* in which he sought to prove that the site of the Garden of Eden was in Sweden and that the Paradise of the Bible and the Atlantis of Plato were an extension of the Scandinavian peninsula. His fellow-scientists were less disposed to laugh at his theories than to marvel at his extraordinary erudition in the fields of history and archeology. Even so, his book was pooh-poohed, and provoked bitter controversies.

Rudbeck came from a family of position. His father was a well-known archbishop who coupled a profound knowledge of theology with great ability in debate. The whole Rudbeck family possessed passionate temperaments, together with erudition, versatility, and a patriotism that in Olaf, reached the point of narrow nationalism. Perhaps it was this which prompted him to conceive the bold idea of annexing Paradise and the Atlantis to his barren homeland.

For Petrus Olavi Nobelius, a humble peasant youth, his marriage into the Rudbeck family meant tremendous social advancement. Though none of his descendants were peasants, nevertheless, up to the nineteenth century, they were never admitted to the exclusive circles of the Belgravians. Olaf, the son of Nobelius, taught the art of engraving and painted miniatures.

Immanuel, the son of Olaf, became a surgeon and served as physician to the Swedish army during the Russo-Swedish War (1700-1721). Scandinavian officers opposed the pedantry which affixed an "ius" to family names, so Immanuel Nobelius became plain Nobel, when he joined the army.

The son of Immanuel, also called Immanuel Nobel, was Alfred's father. He could be called the actual founder of the Nobel dynasty, for in fact his sons created a dynasty of wealth and power that their father, [Immanuel I] could never have foretold in his fondest dreams.

Immanuel, himself had great ability, and was never idle. There was never enough time to develop the schemes and ideas that came into his inventive mind. He had no bent for study in his youth, so he made certain his sons had as much education and training as he could afford to give them. Perhaps his greatest bequest to them was to imbue them with the same kind of faith in whatever they planned and the industry to carry out their plans, that he had had in himself.

Though Immanuel attended school in Gavle, the town where he was born in 1801 and where he grew up, he was never able to overcome the poverty of his education. Herta Pauli said, "all his life, his handwriting remained unformed, his spelling poor, his style and grammar deplorable." His inborn gifts were for drawing and solving mechanical problems.

12

From childhood he craved adventure and envisioned becoming an important, influential man. He had an exploring mind and an ambitious will. At fourteen he signed as cabin boy on a ship in the Mediterranean service, with a monthly salary of four riksdalers. During his three years at sea, he visited the Mediterranean countries and the Near East, but shipping was not his interest, so he returned to Sweden and became apprenticed to a builder.

Glimmerings of inventive genius stirred early in Immanuel. When he was six he contrived an incendiary glass he used to light his father's pipe. A story went that whenever he was locked into a dark room for misbehavior, young Immanuel spent his time inventing items that were entirely usable.

In Stockholm he matriculated at the Royal Academy of Arts for courses in architecture, but later entered the Mekanikskola to study mechanical engineering under Frederik Blom, a noted architect and inventor. He won scholarships, awards of medals, was a designer and instructor in the Academy's mechanical projects. Eventually, he broke away to set up his own business as architect and builder. He then built houses, bridges and made involved machine tools that brought him considerable recognition.

His inventive powers did not stop with building problems; he set up the first rubber factory in Sweden to supply rubberized supplies to the military, the medical profession and industry. The man's innovations brought him enemies, and he had not the economic judgment to match his creative ability. Times grew hard for him and he had to move his bride, Caroline, to successively cheaper, poorer sections of the city to reduce their home expenses.

A child was born in each temporary home they occupied— eight children in all. Only Robert, Ludwig and Alfred lived to reach their twenty-first birthdays. Caroline's life was filled with hard work and much sorrow, but she bore her burdens all in a kind of stoic way and tried to give her sons the happiest life possible. Only the year before Alfred's birth, when fire swept through their home, she managed to save her children by quick, courageous action. Their loss of the house and everything in it brought the family finances to the point of poverty.

Immanuel was in the midst of designing a suspension bridge, but the fire wiped out his small capital. His liabilities totalled less than five thousand dollars; his assets were perhaps two thousand. From the twentieth century viewpoint the deficit seems small, but at that time it was enough to break a man. Immanuel hit bottom. His patent ventures failed; his business terminated abruptly; he was declared bankrupt. With the financial assistance of Ludwig Ahlsell, Caroline's brother, the bankruptcy ended in July 1834, the year after Alfred's birth. It took Immanuel seventeen years to pay off the indebtedness, but he paid every farthing of it.

Once more he began to invent. He created rubber bags, holding life-saving devices and a mattress, for army men. When an explosion occurred in his factory, he lost confidence in his efforts. Fortunately there were no casualties in the blow-up, but the accident did not increase public respect for the young inventor and industrialist.

Disheartened and defeated, Immanuel did not know where to turn to establish himself again. His sons were growing fast, his family needed a decent home and a peaceful existence. His beloved wife, Caroline, seemed scarcely able to smile these days.

He had listened to stories, for a long time, of the energetic and industrious men who had emigrated from the west to Russia. Europe had been rife with tales of tremendous wealth and fabulous luxury that the Russians and those foreigners who had dared fate, to go to the fabled land, now enjoyed. Always Immanuel's life had abounded in drastic change and adventure; he feared few things. Sweden now represented the scene of his bankruptcy and business losses, so he decided to leave his native land and search for his "pot of gold" in Russia.

Rumor had it that a Baron von Hartman invited Immanuel to come to St. Petersburg. However a stop in Finland, where Immanuel tried to find a business opportunity, does not seem in accord with such a report. Actually, his journey to Russia was more like a haphazard adventure, the desperate try of a defeated man.

Not until October 21, 1842, was Immanuel able to send for Caroline and his sons to join him. His family got their passports to Russia, tried to look their best in shabby, oft-mended clothes. Caroline was still a striking woman nearing 30, her great blue eyes as clear and bright as ever and her hair, a crowning mass of dark gold. But she was tired; the years since Immanuel left for Russia had been hard ones. Her sons had depended upon her, alone, for their simple food and meagre living, so that her chief role had become that of intercessor with her husband for her sons, as well as the other way round.

This journey to Russia determined the future of the whole Nobel family. The Nobel's destiny was forever to be bound to Russia.

The Formative Years

Few men discourse equally well in more than one language. Their acquired languages are supposed to travel through a roundabout kind of mental pattern that translates them into use from the man's native tongue. Nobel spent his childhood years in Sweden, but from his ninth year when the family joined father Immanuel in Russia, his most important period of boyhood and adolescent development was with the Russian background and education. Bertha von Suttner called Russian Alfred's "second native tongue."* Alfred attained the "thinking basis" in both languages.

According to Henri de Mosenthal, one of Alfred's close friends, the Nobel sons attended a St. Petersburg school for a time, but ill health compelled Alfred to leave it, particularly because of the weakness of his spinal column. Alfred often spoke of himself as a privately educated man. Since his father had gained a foothold in his Russian iron mills, he could afford tutors for his sons. They were privileged in having instruction from the renowned professor of chemistry, Nikolai Zinin, and the Swedish language and history professor, B. Lars Satesson.

From the time Alfred's mother taught him to read, for she tutored him in his early years, he read constantly—everything at hand. Perhaps, the only way to explain the breadth and profundity of Alfred's knowledge is to call him largely self-taught. He treated no subject superficially. His proficiency in languages did not limit him to conversing in them for he wrote six (Swedish, Russian, French, German, English and Italian) in polished, grammatical prose. One critic,

Caroline Andriette Nobel, née Ahlsell, Alfred Nobel's mother

Immanuel Nobel, Jr., Alfred Nobel's father

Alfred Nobel, c. 1853

Alfred Nobel's house in Paris, avenue Malakoff 53
where he lived for many years

Alfred Nobel's writing desk with personal belongings, from the Nobel rooms in the Nobel library of the Swedish Academy

Alfred Nobel's travelling bag

Alfred Nobel, c. 1880

Emmanuel Nobel II, son of Alfred's brother Ludvig Nobel

Sir Winston Churchill's Nobel Diploma Literature

Nobel Medals (left) obverse and (right) reverse of the medal for peace. (Left) obverse of the Swedish medals and (right) reverse of the medals for Physics and Chemistry. (Left) reverse of the medal for Literature and (right) reverse of the medal for Physiology/Medicine

on reading his youthful poetry in English, exclaimed, "What a poet he could have been in his native tongue!"

Alfred was born during the most difficult financial time of his father's life, eighteen months after Immanuel's bankruptcy was declared. The family endured extreme poverty. When the father left to make a place for the family in Russia, Caroline took charge of a small shop that sold dairy products and vegetables. It brought in a small income that allowed her to feed and clothe her boys.

Two stories reported by Bergengren that showed how meagre was their living, were told by Alfred's brothers. Robert wrote that "one of my most painful memories is a little episode from this time, when I had been sent out by my mother to buy food for dinner with a threepenny bit and had lost the pitiful little coin." Ludwig described a time when he and Robert stood on the street corner selling matches to get a few coins to help their mother.

Caroline Andriette Nobel had been brought up in the province of Smaland in southern Sweden. She came from a large family, the Ahlsells, who reared their children to be industrious and self sufficient. Hers and Immanuel's match was rich in love for each other and the children they brought into the world. Always in spite of problems and the lack of money, their home held the good things of affection, respect and ambition.

The bankruptcy proceedings entailed both grave and petty humiliations. Alfred's childhood, burdened by illness and poverty, brought him few joys, and this left an imprint on his character. In his mature years he gained the reputation of being gloomy, sarcastic and misanthropic in disposition.

He received, along with his brothers, the full benefit of their father's mechanical and technical knowledges. Their home always kept an atmosphere of discovery and invention, which instilled in Alfred, from his earliest years, a respect for science and a fascinated interest in all scientific problems. When their home was established in Russia in the militaristic environment of the St. Petersburg of that epoch, it must have seemed like a bit of Paris in the era of the French Encyclopaedia. The future inventor of dynamite, in his mental make-up, was close to the encyclopaedists.

Alfred-Bernhard studied the same subjects at the same level as did his brothers, though Robert-Hjalmar was four years older than Alfred, and Ludwig-Immanuel, two years older. Their youngest brother Oscar-Emil ten years younger than Alfred was born in 1843 in Russia.

Immanuel, the father, devoted much attention to the mental development of his children whom he tenderly loved. Readers who have enjoyed Emile Zola's novel, *Paris,* are struck by the close analogy between the Nobel family and that of the idealistic, friendly and attractive family of the French chemist, Froman, whom Zola described as being engaged in the invention of some dreadful explosive.

It was at this time that Alfred began his study of foreign languages. He had a real gift for them, so when the family funds again hit a low point, Alfred was the member delegated to seek credit in European banks. When at seventeen, he left Russia for a study and training trip that was to take him to Germany, France, Italy and North America, his father wrote Ludwig Ahlsell, Caroline's brother: "My good and industrious Alfred . . . is held in high esteem by his parents and brothers, both for his knowledge and for his untiring capacity for work, which is excelled by no one."

Alfred's facility in languages also intensified his broad world outlook. For people of the nineteenth century, cosmopolitanism depended on their knowledge of languages, particularly of French, which was considered the language of the civilized world.

Alfred lived in Paris a while and spent time in the United States. His was not a merely educational journey, such as the wealthy grandees of Russia afforded for their sons; he was expected to find a profession for himself, or to learn some trade. He studied engineering in America under the guidance of the Swedish engineer, Ericsson, but he did not stay long in the United States and never acquired the status of engineer.

Engineering could never have suited Alfred. He was no automaton of science, no robot duplicating technical operations of other men. Even at this time of his youth, his scientific interests lay in working out his original ideas and schemes. He had an abundance of animation, an interest in everything and everybody, and a poet's way of seeing the world about him, as was shown in this bit of poetry that tells of his first sight of the Atlantic. Not even this great ocean could equal the one he had imagined:

... Thus confident I left in early youth my home for distant lands beyond the sea; but strange to say, e'en when the Ocean spread its grandeur round, it struck me not as new—my mind had pictured Oceans far more wide ...

His stay in Italy, a country that was not visited in those days for scientific or technical learning, might have included a chance for him to walk the same paths that his most admired English poets, Shelley and Byron, had trod a quarter of a century before.

By the end of the 1840's, his father's business had improved, so Immanuel could afford to provide Alfred with funds for additional foreign travels and for the "cures" his health had made necessary since his early years. On his return to Paris, it is probable that he worked in the laboratory of Professor Pelouze. Chemistry had already become Alfred's dedicated interest. Since the noted Pelouze had established a free laboratory in Paris in the year 1846, it was less difficult to obtain entrance there than in the university laboratories, where a young foreigner without diplomas would

27

hardly have been admitted. In Pelouze's laboratory special studies in explosive substances were pursued at this time.

1854 found him in Berlin where he wrote this letter to his parents:

Finally, I begin to hope that my nomadic existence will soon come to an end and that I shall be able to turn to a more active life. Verily, it is time. Life begins to grow tedious because of its monotony, to which, however, sooner or later, one may become accustomed; but aside from that, I feel I am a burden to my parents and my brothers, instead of being a help to them.

Even though I did not succeed in improving my physical condition, as I have been hoping (my sojourn in Stockholm and Dalar was more beneficial than the time I spent at Franzensbad), nevertheless I will return home as soon as I manage to complete the business which remains to be done in Berlin. I would like to return by the 21st of this month, when I shall reach the age of twenty-one.

This letter reveals the serious, dutiful nature of young Nobel. Instead of being eager to prolong an exciting journey in fascinating places, he longed intensely to return home. Given an opportunity to lead an independent life and be free from his parents' tutelage, he chose the bonds of love that united his whole family.

Alfred's desire to return to St. Petersburg on his twenty-first birthday, October 21, 1854 revealed his hope of beginning active life. He had learned so much, he was ready to put it to use.

Since the Crimean War had begun in the preceding year, his father and brothers were busily engaged in the manufacture of sea mines, much in demand by the Russian Tzar, Nicholas I, for destroying enemy ships. This explosive product undoubtedly created great interest in Alfred. He had received thorough and advanced training in the chemistry that held such great attraction for him, but he would study it and laboriously experiment in it all his life. He must have longed to work on his father's mines, for he was certain even at that time that the 500-year-old gunpowder, used for all explosive purposes, could be improved upon.

"It is plain ..." wrote his distinguished biographer, Henrik Schuck, "that Alfred Nobel was already head and shoulders above his age group, both, in knowledge and mental maturity. He was a scientifically trained chemist, he was an excellent linguist with a mastery of German, English and French as well as Swedish and Russian, he had a strong literary bent, being particularly interested in English Literature, and the basic features of his outlook on life were already fully developed. Letters from this period give a picture of a precocious, intelligent, but sickly, dreamy, and introspective young man who preferred solititude."

Back in Russia, Nobel had the opportunity to work under Professor Zinin in 1855, where, as Sohlman and Schück mention, he "became initiated into the problem of nitroglycerine by a Professor Zinin in St. Peterburg." Zinin played an enormous role in the history of Russian science and exercised a pronounced influence over his pupils. Only the archives of the St. Petersburg University could answer the questions of when and how long Nobel worked in Zinin's laboratory. One thing is undeniable: the invention of dynamite was the outgrowth of the combined efforts of many minds: of the Frenchmen, Braconneau, Pelouze, Chevreul and Berthelot; the Swede, Scheele; the Italian, Sobrero; and the Russian, Zinin. All these men paved the way for the work of Alfred Nobel.

Among these, Sobrero's part is most prominent, for it was he who actually discovered nitro-glycerine, but, as his biographers Molinari and Quartieri observe, he did not know how to make practical use of his discovery. Ascanio Sobrero was not lucky. In his youthful years he wrote a dissertation on the subject of surgery and had a good chance of being appointed a professor on the medical faculty of a university but, through intrigues of several jealous physicians, his candidacy was rejected. When at the age of thirty-five he discovered nitro-glycerine, he decided that it was too dangerous a substance for industrial purposes and that it should be applied only in medicine. In his later years when he learned about the industrial success of Nobel, he planned a factory of his own but again nothing materialized.

Alfred Nobel always had a high opinion of Sobrero and fully recognized that Sobrero had discovered the compound from which Nobel derived his millions. However, people were inclined to underestimate Sobrero's contribution to chemistry and by the seventies he had been forgotten. The discovery of nitro-glycerine was attributed either to Nobel or to Pelouze, yet these men made no such claim and Pelouze was fond of his Italian pupil. Pelouze wrote from Paris to Sobrero's father: "Never have I had in my laboratory a more assiduous, hardworking and capable young man." Alfred Nobel offered Sobrero the position of consultant in his company, granted him a large salary, and after his death Nobel paid a pension to his widow. A remarkable bust of Sobrero stood in one of Nobel's factories and, in its laboratory in a bottle filled with water, was preserved the first-glycerine produced by the Italian scientist.

Sobrero did not gain world fame, nor did he make millions; yet it is to him that the merit and responsibility must be given the chemical reaction producing the formation of nitro-glycerine:

$$C_3H_5(OH)_3 \ 3HNO_3 \ C_3H_5(NO_3)_3 \ SH_2O$$

In 1855 Professor Zinin suggested to Alfred Nobel that he experiment with nitro-glycerine as a possible explosive for his father's sea mines.

During the Crimean War, both Alfred and his father experimented with explosive substances for the sea mines, but had had to retain the old stand-by black gunpowder. The war ended with the Treaty of Paris in 1856, and the frenzied pace of Immanuel Nobel's factory came to an abrupt halt. Nicholas I died, the new government broke contracts, the military severed all relations with the Nobel business. From sea mines and war weapons, Immanuel tried to convert quickly to the production of steam machinery, but the family took a tremendous loss.

This was the time when Alfred, because of his gift for languages, went to London and Paris to attempt to raise credit for his desperate father. But bankers had no idea of loaning funds to an insecure factory in Russia. Alfred returned in disconsolate failure.

Immanuel and Caroline determined it was best for them to return to Sweden. Oscar-Emil, the youngest boy, went with his parents. Robert, Ludwig and Alfred remained at the St. Petersburg factory to salvage whatever could be saved from the collapsed enterprise that only two years before had boasted more than a thousand workers on full-scale production.

The two older brothers battled to set the firm's finances in order, while Alfred spent his time in the laboratory tussling with technical problems that required his chemistry knowledge, though not of a strictly chemical character. He received a British patent on a special gasometer, two other patents on a water meter and an improved barometer. These comparatively unimportant items put the lure of creation into his blood. From that time on, his passionate love was invention.

The Heleneborg Disaster

Sweden called to Alfred for his return. Robert and Ludwig would remain in Russia where they had started up the factory on a small scale, turning out machinery and armaments, But Alfred wished to join his father, mother and Oscar-Emil in Stockholm.

He had collaborated for a long time with his father—though not without friction—and he knew Sweden would be more suitable for the international production of his invention results. Also there would be the possibility there of securing financing for his first experiments in the industrial manufacture of nitro-glycerine.

Hennig stated that Alfred's experimental funds (100,000 francs) were contributed by Napoleon III. He later states that this sum, at the suggestion of Napoleon, came from the Paris banker, J. Pereire.

At that time Alfred Nobel had not yet given serious thought to dynamite. He busied himself with an idea of a different character which had enormous practical significance. This was the detonator for the explosion of nitro-glycerine. The idea consisted of devising a method by which a sudden discharge of energy within a nitro-glycerine mass would cause the strong percussion required for the explosion.

He conducted not less than fifty experiments and, finally, he conceived an altogether novel idea from a technical standpoint. He inserted into a mass of explosive substance a copper case filled with mercury fulminate. Its combustion automatically caused the explosion of the nitro-glycerine. This was a new principle expressed thus: by means of a primary, easily-produced explosion, a secondary, or main, detonation is caused.

This device caused a revolution in the technique of explosive substances. Hennig called it ingenious and maintained that, since the invention of gun powder, nothing more important had been developed in either the technique or science dealing with explosives. Sohlman and Schuck regarded this principle, insofar as its scientific value was concerned, to be of more value than the invention of dynamite itself.

Nobel started the complicated patent procedure on his detonator at once, but only gradually, in what he termed *"das Prinzip der Inizialzundung"* (the principle of primary inflammation) that underlay the patent on his detonator, was Nobel's priority universally recognized. He pursued the patent in different countries and, without doubt more time had to be devoted to legal procedures than he spent on the invention. Patent laws have always been notoriously involved, especially in those countries where it is necessary to prove one's priority in regard to an invention, but Nobels' patience and health were exhausted long before the legalities ended.

Since Immanuel and Alfred Nobel had determined to proceed at once with the manufacture of nitro-glycerine in considerable quantities, Immanuel rented premises at Heleneborg.

Oscar-Emil was then attending the university. Emil was a chemist of great promise and Immanuel asked him to participate in the work. Money was so scarce that the Nobels sought by every possible means to curtail on labor. They did practically everything themselves, probably working in shifts.

Could it have been possible that the Nobels did not realize the extreme danger of this work? Sobrero, the inventor of nitro-glycerine, had considered it too dangerous for in-

33

dustrial development, since the liquid could not be relied upon to react twice in the same way. The father, Immanuel, should have borne the responsibility for safety in handling the treacherous substance, but he was not a chemist and it is doubtful that he was even well read in chemical literature. His work in Russia with submarine mines had undoubtedly developed in him a certain insouciance—"See, I was not blown up by that!"—or fatalism. Had he realized he was embarking on the manufacture of an explosive substance with a terrific, and yet undreamed-of force, he would certainly not have drawn into this work his youngest son who, notwithstanding his exceptional ability, had not yet had proper training for such techniques.

On the 3rd day of September, 1864, during the hours of Emil Nobel's shift, a horrendous explosion blew up the plant. The twenty-one year old Emil, the three employees, and a casual caller who had dropped in—all perished in the disaster. Everything was lost; the ramshackle building was scattered in shreds. This fearful catastrophe that robbed Immanuel of his young, brilliant son haunted the old man for the remainder of his days. The causes of the explosion remained unknown, because not one of the potential witnesses of the disaster survived.

There is a Russian proverb: "Misfortune never comes singly." The Nobels suffered intense grief over the death of Emil, the boyish favorite of the family, and over the deaths of their employees. Public opinion in Sweden was aroused against the family. To make things worse, the Nobels had neglected to advise the authorities in advance as to just what they were manufacturing.

A bitter campaign against the Nobels ensued. Nevertheless, the Swedish authorities acted with wisdom and moderation on the case. In any other country the consequences to the ill-fated owners of the Heleneborg enterprise could have ruined their lives.

34

At the trial Immanuel Nobel defended himself. At first, he testified that nitro-glycerine is a harmless substance! Then he stated that, in his opinion, the explosion was caused by the fact that his young son Emil sought to simplify the methods of its manufacture. His judgment of Emil might have been correct, although the Nobels manufactured nitro-glycerine in the way Sobrero originally suggested and as it is produced today by the action of glycerine on a mixture of nitric and sulphuric acids. But to say that nitro-glycerine was harmless was so fantastic an error that it must have been overlooked by the authorities, because of the mental and physical condition of the old inventor. The horror of the Helenborg disaster had brought on a stroke five weeks later. Immanuel suffered paralysis, though in his case the paralysis passed. He recovered part of his faculties, but his former personality had disappeared forever. He regained strength enough to work, and brain power enough to continue his constant schemes, even though he could not bring them to a logical conclusion.

His condition must have stirred sympathy in the Stockholm court officials, for he was not called to trial under criminal procedure, but was instead ordered to transfer the manufacture of nitro-glycerine to some uninhabited locality.

The disaster left a lasting and sad impress upon Alfred Nobel. In a case such as this he could not have denied all responsibility. His father was a mere dilettante, while he, the son, was an established scientific inventor. He blamed himself with bitterness. After his discovery of dynamite, when he focused his attention on manufacturing methods of nitro-glycerine and the creation of conditions for its safe handling, he was able substantially to render harmless the fearful chemical product. He mourned that he had not been able to accomplish this sooner, so Emil need not have died. He could never forget the dreadful day of the Heleneborg disaster to the end of his life.

35

His father believed in immortality and his belief somehow blended with curious projects that now occupied his mind. He became fascinated in the construction of special types of graves.

Even in days past, Immanuel had conceived strange ideas, but now their weird character became more pronounced. He planned the construction of special pipes in big cities, through which the bodies of dead persons could be conveyed directly from their homes to the cemeteries. He pondered the building of graves of a unique kind. People, he contended, had sometimes been buried alive in error.

Years later, in a half-jocular reply of Alfreds to his brother's request that he write a biography, he said he had only one wish: "Not to be buried alive." Though a jest, it concealed a grain of truth. Alfred must have listened to his father's sick mind in its obsessions with more than a compassionate interest.

The hypothesis of the burial of a live man fascinated Immanuel. He dwelt on its boundless horror: "Suddenly I awake in my grave, I feel that I am alive, and yet there is no escape out of the dreadful abode!"

This thought assumed an acute form in the sick man. He nourished the fancy and, through suggestion, it must have passed on to his son, Alfred. Immanuel proposed the construction of graves with an opening for air to flow into the coffin and the coffin, in turn, was to be equipped with bells to enable the buried person to sound an alarm!

Caroline wrote to her son, Alfred, that the old man had begun to give play to his imagination. She referred to his elaboration of detailed plans for the manufacture of plywood. This play of imagination however, laid the foundation for the extensive plywood industry in America, England, Germany and Sweden.

Until his last days Immanuel continued to work with explosives occupying the forefront of his activities. Sometime before his death he addressed a letter to his son Alfred stat-

36

ing that he had made an invention so that persons possessed of its secret, would have dictatorial powers in matters of war and peace for at least several centuries. No one ever knew what invention he could have had in mind, but his loving sons sorrowed over the deterioration of their father's brilliant powers.

On the other hand, according to Dominique Andre, Immanuel Nobel also deeply concerned himself these years with humanitarian aims and with utopias. He studied the problem of unemployment and wrote a book dealing with this subject. He was still short of money. His sons were supporting him and Alfred made him a partner in his business on a small scale.

Pride must have not permitted the father to enrich himself at the expense of his sons. He left an estate amounting to only 28,000 kroner, while his widow, who died much later, accumulated a substantial fortune, derived from the enterprises of her sons and from Alfred in particular.

On September 3, 1872 Immanuel Nobel died. The date marked the anniversary of the Heleneborg catastrophe. No doubt, that day the thoughts of the old man turned to the most dreadful misfortune of his life. The emotion caused by these reminiscences may have brought on the fatal heart attack.

Immanuel Nobel had inherited from his distant ancestor Rudbeck his versatile talents and passionate temperament, full of vital energy. And if Rudbeck's *Atland,* with its Swedish Eden, was an intellectual vagary of a distinguished man, similar paradoxes could be noted in the life and effervescent work of Immanuel Nobel. Immanuel created comparatively little, perhaps nothing at all of true permanence. He was destined to become a precursor. It was his part to disseminate and not to realize ideas.

He was happy in his family and loved his wife passionately. He was kind and generous, a typical Nobel characteristic. His sons and grandsons were able to give away more

37

than he since they were wealthy men. Immanuel, with the exception of a few years in St. Petersburg, was a man of limited means; however, his life was rich in activity and in colorful changes of scene and episode.

After the Heleneborg explosion, Alfred's career began to evolve in a long series of successes which brought him fame and colossal wealth. They did not, however, change his morose attitude toward life. By nature, he was a man of exalted impulses and marked remorse.

In a letter to Edla, the wife of his brother Robert, ten years after the tragic death of Oscar-Emil, Alfred Nobel gave this hopeless picture of his inner self:

I have no memories to cheer me, no pleasant illusions about the future to comfort me, or about myself—to satisfy my vanity. I have no family to provide the only kind of survival that concerns one; no friends for my affections, nor even enemies for my malice. . . .

And, quite in line with his Schopenhaueresque philosophy, in the days of his declining age, he wrote Baroness Bertha von Suttner: "There is nothing more that I love than to feel myself capable of enthusiasm. But this faculty was considerably diminished by my life experiences and my fellow men."

The enigmas of Nobel's nature are as perplexing as the mystery of his creativeness and inventive drive. His weak spine forced him to walk with a stoop, and migraine headaches plagued him all his days. Often he worked in his laboratory with compresses on his throbbing head and a shade for his tired eyes. Neurasthenia and a lame heart ever troubled him, but perhaps he suffered more from his chronic pessimism and extreme depressions than he did from physical ailments. In his later years, his friends and work associates knew when a black mood seized him, for he would disappear. Sometimes on a journey, sometime into his solitary laboratory, he would vanish for days until the all-consuming mental suffering lifted.

When his brother Robert went into the oil lamp business in Helsinki, he wrote Alfred "to give up the damned inventing business as soon as possible" because "it only brings disappointment." But invention was the real joy of Alfred's life. His hours in his laboratory were his escape from the battles of living.

Alfred gave himself no leisure time, and little recreation. Forever on the move in advising and organizing his worldwide enterprises, newspaper men labeled him, "Europe's richest vagabond." Greedy men tricked him, dragged him into court and stole from him; he fought continuously for what he believed to be right. Beseiged by setbacks, accidents, the hypocrisy of associates, the avarice of nations, he drew more and more into himself. And his bitterness grew with his advancing years.

The Empire Grows

The manufacture of nitro-glycerine could have, in itself, brought Alfred Nobel a considerable fortune. The court judgment on the Heleneborg explosion compelled him to build his factory outside the city of Stockholm, so he transferred the production of the perilous liquid to Lake Malar, not far from the Swedish capital.

Alfred knew well, that by takng exact measures of precaution, the manufacture of nitro-glycerine (the mixture of nitric and sulphuric acids on glycerine) should not cause accidents. He had handled this perilous mixture himself for too many years not to be fully aware of its violent nature. He was also well aware that safeguards depended upon the control of inherent human weaknesses—carelessness, forgetfulness, inattention lack of self-control. Alfred seldom over-estimated the strengths of people. He realized some fatalities in the manufacturing plants of high explosives were inevitable, but he was far from prepared for the horrifying and constant loss of lives that followed the transport and shipping of his nitro-glycerine to its purchasers.

Some disasters caused worldwide indignation, as the explosion at Aspinwall (Panama) did, when a ship transporting a cargo of nitro-glycerine to the Pacific blew up on April 3, 1866. Forty-seven men lost their lives. Almost simultaneously an equally frightful incident occurred at Sydney, Australia. Reports of the accident, loss of property and violent deaths flocked in from all parts of the world to Nobel. They clouded his life, wounded his soul, and caused serious injury to his business.

The very thought of nitro-glycerine began to terrorize people. In several countries its production, in others its transportation and storage, were prohibited. Theoretically, Nobel could have disclaimed all responsibility for such incidents. He had advised people thoroughly on how to manufacture nitro-glycerine and how to handle it in order to insure safety. Was he to blame if people took no heed of his advice? Nevertheless, his despondency grew and his morale was undermined by the tragic accidents.

He centered his creative abilities upon the problem of how to make nitro-glycerine safe to handle without diminishing its explosive properties. Nobel's enemies often asserted that the idea of dynamite was the accidental and lucky find of a man upon whom fate conferred her smile. The famous Russian General Suvorov, whose victories were attributed by his antagonists to "mere luck" once retorted: "Luck today! Luck tomorrow!—For Heaven's sake, can't you conceive a bit of ability?" There was no luck in Alfred Nobel's scientific victories.

In a chemical sense, the path Nobel followed suggested itself of its own accord: he must add to nitro-glycerine other substances, seek to determine if any of these would make the liquid solid and safe for purposes of transportation and storage. His experiments were too numerous to count.

The medicine used for decades in combatting venereal disease, as conceived by Professor Ehrlich, was known as "606." Its name implied the enormous number of experiments conducted by the scientist before he was able to find the right remedy. In Alfred's case, he spoke of "mixing with black gunpowder, guncotton or paper powder," and "of letting nitro-glycerine be absorbed in the pores of porous, non-explosive substances . . . e.g. porous silica, paper, paper pulp, woodwaste, brick dust, coal, dry clay, gypsum bars, clay bars, etc." Originally Nobel had placed his hopes on nitro-glycerine mixed with wood alcohol.

He eventually found what he needed. This was "kiesel-guhr," the porous, non-active substance which absorbed nitro-glycerine. The mixture of 75% nitro-glycerine and 25% kieselguhr was solid, entailed no danger in the process of transportation, yet, with the aid of Alfred's detonator, it would explode with terrific force and "kieselguhr," an earthy sediment, was not difficult to obtain.

He had discovered his easily-handled solid explosive. There remained only the problem of finding a name for it. Nobel found it, a good sound from an accoustic standpoint. "Dynamite" sounds at once sonorous and frightening.

Now the road to fame and millions lay open and inviting for Alfred Nobel to follow. It was not an easy road. It held rough places and seemingly insurmountable obstacles. The first steps were to apply for patents, to raise money, to build plants and to convince prospective customers of the useful-ness of the product.

The patents proved to be the most difficult task. Every scientific discovery, even in those fields of science which have been devoid of any practical applications, entailed controversies over the question of priority. These disputes became a thousand times more acute for Nobel since the question of money was involved. Nobel was obliged to wage a two-fold fight: on the one hand, with those who claimed they had discovered the mixture of nitro-glycerine with kieselguhr before he had; and on the other hand, with those who took advantage of his invention by introducing into it minor changes and representing their results as original inventions.

Litigations swamped him in European countries as well as in America. He dealt continuously with courts and law-yers. "Courts of honor," or arbitration proceedings absorbed much of his money and weakened his health. His mis-anthropy must have developed apace during the consider-able portion of his life spent in the atmosphere of lawsuits, claims and counterclaims, litigations and counter-litigations.

His genuine idealism did not prevent him from being a practical man—a quality he did not gain from his father. The example of Immanuel had, beyond a doubt, taught Alfred how business should be conducted—or rather how it should not be conducted. He proved to be expert at organizing his enterprises and ran them on an exacting plan.

Alfred Nobel very seldom sold his patents for a fixed lump sum; he refused to do this even during his early career when he needed cash badly. He realized that many inventors had died in poverty, owing to the fact that, tempted by a large cash payment, they renounced forever to some sly financier their rights to their invention. Nobel insisted on a share in the enterprise, whether in the form of stock or royalties on the sale price of the manufactured product. Usually his participation in the company that manufactured dynamite was even more substantial. He sometimes took part in the construction of the plant by investing money and time; on other occasions he served as director or president of the board; while in certain other instances, he merely acted as technical advisor.

All this left him little time for his laboratory. No doubt Alfred would have made much greater contributions to science if, after having made his first million, he had severed all connection with industry and finance.

From year to year, the number of his various business ventures became greater and greater. From 1865 to 1873 he and his collaborators built at least fifteen plants for the manufacture of explosives: in Sweden, Norway, the United States (one in San Francisco and one in New York), Finland, England, France, Germany (one in Hamburg and one in Köln), Spain, Switzerland, Italy, Portugal, Austria-Hungary (one in Prague and one in Pressburg). The scale of his enterprises fluctuated considerably, sometimes reaching fabulous proportions. In England the first Nobel enterprise was founded with a modest subscription capital of 24,000 pounds. In 1918, the joint stock capital of the Nobel plants in England, which preserved the firm name even after the death of Alfred Nobel, amounted to 16,000,000 pounds. The largest of Great Britain's industrial complexes, Imperial Chemical Industries, Ltd., originated from the Alfred B. Nobel Company. It was worth $400,000,000 in 1930 and represented the amalgamation of all the principal munitions companies.

In most countries, the factories yielded high dividends. The stockholders of the Nobel enterprises became rich and he, himself, accumulated a vast fortune.

Oil at Baku

Travel was both a wearisome duty and a helpful escape for Alfred Nobel. Since the age of seventeen, he seemed to have spent half his life in travel; the other half, in law entanglements, he thought grimly, as he headed east from Paris to cross the Rhine and edge the mountains for Bucharest. He was bound for the Black Sea and the small steamship that would land him at Baku in the Caucasus. His brothers, Robert and Ludwig awaited him there. Their oil development enterprise had grown rapidly in these three years, and in spite of his glum mood in beginning this journey, Alfred knew he longed to see the two men he was proud to call his kin. And he was anxious to see what they had done.

When Immanuel Nobel left Russia a few years after the Crimean War in 1859, his two older sons remained in that country for the active years of their lifetimes. Before departing for Sweden, Immanuel entered into an agreement with his creditors and conveyed his factory to his sons. The old inventor had no money to give his boys, but he had exerted every endeavor to see that they received excellent training. Robert was a good chemist and Ludwig an able mechanical engineer. By that time both were mature men. Robert was thirty years old; Ludwig was twenty-eight. Ludwig had married his cousin, Mina Ahlsell, and during the year when his father left Russia, their first child was born to the young couple. This was Emmanuel, the third one in the Nobel dynasty to bear this name.

Ludwig did not inherit his father's brilliant inventive talent but he had what had been denied to Immanuel I, a clear, practical mind, free of any illusions. In 1859, his financial situation was not an easy one. He was the son of a man who had lost two fortunes—one in Sweden and another in Russia —and although Immanuel enjoyed the reputation of a scrupulously honest man, nevertheless he had failed twice in business. Ludwig Nobel could scarcely depend on large credit but his practical ability revealed itself at once.

He entered into a stipulation with the creditors, by virtue of which the new owners of his father's factory agreed to continue this business under the name of "Nobel and Son." He succeeded in securing with the firm a position for himself with an annual salary of 5,000 rubles, or $2,500.00. In the Russia of that time this was considered a large salary, exceeding that of an army general or of a professor. Living in Russia was inexpensive and a man with such an income could easily have two or three servants and a coach with a pair of horses.

Ludwig Nobel lived in modest fashion, putting away every kopek, so that in three years he managed to save from his salary a sum sufficient to establish a small concern of his own. This was a mechanical shop which manufactured principally small arms. Business developed. Substantial orders came in, mostly from the government. The Crimean War revealed the backwardness of Russian rifle-manufacturing technique, so the Russian army was being re-equipped. From time to time, Ludwig submitted proposals to the War Department which were received favorably and considered respectfully. He was an excellent mechanic and thoroughly familiar with all matters relating to small arms.

Up to the first quarter of the Nineteenth Century all armies were equipped with pyrite rifles, usually of the 17.5 mm. calibre, which were sighted for about 200 yards. The Napoleonic and revolutionary wars were fought with this primitive weapon. In those days even rifles were considered a great improvement over the old musket with its sharp repercussion that made it usable only by exceptionally robust soldiers.

Real improvements in the design and construction of small arms were introduced only in the Nineteenth Century. The Civil War in America clearly demonstrated the advantage of magazine-rifles and metallic cartridges over muzzle-loading arms and paper cartridges. The American Colonel Berdan suggested further innovations, including the important mechanism locking the chamber.

In the Sixties, the Russian Ministry of War commissioned two of its experts, Colonel Gorlov and Captain Hunius, to proceed to America where, in collaboration with Colonel Berdan, they produced a type of gun which, in 1868, was adopted in Russia—first for the equipment of the chasseur battalions and, subsequently, of the whole army. It became known as the "Berdanka" while the new metallic cartridges were called "Berdan Cartridges."

After the adoption of the new firearms, Ludwig Nobel received an order for 200,000 rifles, subsequently increased to 450,000. In partnership with the Russian Captain Bilderling, he rented for a term of eight years a big plant near the city of Perm, in the Ural Mountains. It was decided to employ, for the gunstock, walnut of high quality, which was said to be plentiful in the Caucasus. Accordingly, Ludwig made up his mind to have someone investigate the matter on the spot. This task was entrusted to his brother, Robert, who by that time had joined Ludwig's partnership.

Robert Nobel had been less successful than Ludwig. After his father's departure for Sweden, he had tried differing business ventures, without marked success. In 1860, he married a Finnish woman, Pauline Lengren. His wife disliked Russia and refused to live in St. Petersburg. Under her influence, Robert Nobel moved to Finland and organized a lamp manufacturing concern that had close connection with combustible oils. His enterprise did not prosper because of

47

lack of funds. More intense than his wife's dislike of Russia was his dislike for Finland. In his letters to his brother, Alfred, he wrote about the Finns, if not with animosity, certainly with irony.

Robert's relations with his youngest brother Alfred, who already trod the road to wealth, were very close. Alfred had a high opinion of him as a chemist and endeavored to enlist his interest in scientific and experimental work. But, Robert had little faith in an inventor's career, and even urged his brother "to drop inventions as soon as possible." Undoubtedly he had no confidence in his own creative ability; however, he accepted Alfred's offer to begin manufacture of nitroglycerine in Finland. He built a small plant, but soon after the corporation had been organized, he ceased to be its owner, and became its paid director, with a good salary. He took charge of the commercial, not the scientific or technical, part of the business.

He had wasted some fifteen years of his life, on enterprises which had been of no help to his future career. This did not dishearten him. Like the Fromans in Zola's novel *Paris*, the Nobels exhibited the same unquenchable energy, the same readiness to be content with little, and the same perseverance in hard work.

In 1870, Robert Nobel was forty-one. It was not easy to start life anew, especially after his previous reversals. But Robert did it. Since he did not succeed in selling lamps or making nitro-glycerine, he might as well try something else. He returned to St. Petersburg and entered into partnership with Ludwig.

His position in the business is not certain; probably he merely contributed his labor, but he never refused any kind of work. The manufacture of rifles was not the specialty of a chemist exploring illuminants and nitro-glycerine, nor did high quality walnut come within the range of his scientific interests. Nevertheless, complying with Ludwig's request, he proceeded to the Caucasus. But he found there no wood suitable for the manufacture of gunstocks. Instead he stumbled on something infinitely more important.

Robert Nobel discovered in the Caucasus that earth-made invaluable product—oil—which was destined to make him and his brother, Ludwig, multi-millionaires.

The year was 1873, fourteen years after the conquest of the Caucasus by the Russians, when Robert Nobel went there to search for walnut to make Ludwig's Berdan rifles. Sailing down the Volga, Robert met a man, Debours. He had served in the Volga fleet and he owned a parcel of oil land near Baku. He discussed the oil business with Robert and after arriving in the Caucasus, Robert Nobel visited the Debours lot and purchased it.

All human affairs, whether big or small, largely depend upon His Majesty, Chance, and so in the case of the Nobel brothers, Chance introduced them to oil, the black gold. In the early seventies, Ludwig had never given thought to oil. Almost no one in Russia even knew about the values of oil. Thus, Robert Nobel pioneered that important industry in the Caucasus. He "fell in love with oil." He became obsessed with the idea of it. He refused to listen to anything else.

For this career he was well trained scientifically; he knew chemistry thoroughly. He had commercial knowledge from selling lamps and combustible oils in Finland, although the Finnish experiment could not have made him optimistic. The people distrusted the new lamps, preferred the old lighting devices. Nor could the earlier experiences of others in Caucasian oil be encouraging to Robert. Nothing had come of Dubinin's efforts to refine oil some fifty years prior to Nobel's time. When Kokorev erected a plant and even retained the famous chemist Mendeleyev as consultant, he escaped bankruptcy only because he was very rich. The business itself proved a losing proposition.

49

Still Robert knew it was not sufficient "to fall in love" with the oil scheme. First, he must enlist the interest of wealthy people in developing an industrial organization. Brother Ludwig would help him, but at that time he was merely a well-to-do man, by no means immensely rich. Also he had a fine rifle manufacturing plant which was going well. He had large government orders and building up his business absorbed much of his time.

However, there was Alfred to call upon. Alfred had the wealth if he could be interested. After Robert's return to St. Petersburg, he convinced Ludwig that they must urge Alfred to finance the oil refining company he would establish. This document is quoted in the Sohlman and Schuck biography. It reads:

Robert returned to Baku from a trip to the eastern shore (the Caspian Sea), where he found excellent oil on the Tchelekensky Island, at a depth of ten fathoms. Thus, he has the needed raw material. It remains to be seen to what extent he is capable of organizing mass production and sales. Upon this, his future success and fortune are dependent. On my own part, I did everything I could to help him out with money and technical advice. Robert claims that he made new discoveries in the field of refining and processing oil. I cannot judge their value because of my unfamiliarity with this business. The main thing is to ascertain how an enterprise of this kind may be rationally conducted on a big scale. I feel that we—that is, you and I—should go there and find out if we can be of any assistance to him. We have successfully achieved independence and, therefore, we must help Robert to attain the same goal. So, I would like you to ponder over the question of a trip to Baku.

This letter indicated that with all his love for Robert and his full consciousness of his brotherly duty toward him, Ludwig held a rather patronizing attitude toward his plan. "It remains to be seen to what extent he is capable. . . . Robert claims that he made new discoveries. . . . I did everything I could to help him out." The whole problem of the Baku oil was treated in the light of mere assistance to Robert. Obviously, Ludwig Nobel at that time entertained no hope that Robert's scheme would immensely increase his own fortune.

The letter just quoted was written in 1875 at the time of Robert's second trip to the Caucasus. When he failed to enlist the wholehearted financial backing of his plans by his brothers, he returned to Baku where he organized the first company for the exploitation of oil. In another letter, written by Ludwig to Alfred, one year later, it shows that Ludwig's attitude toward Robert had changed, completely changed.

As regards quality (of oil), Robert indeed has achieved excellent results. Even though the Baku oil usually yields only thirty percent of a heavy and inferior product, he is extracting forty percent of a good, light photogen, which easily compares with American specimens of the highest standards. Therefore, we can appear in the market with a product which will give the firm a brilliant reputation.

The inventor of dynamite joined the business of his brothers about two years after the enterprise had been founded in an almost exclusively financial participation. Alfred had become very rich, much richer than Ludwig—not to speak of Robert. The partnership consisted of the three brothers and Ludwig Nobel's collaborator in the rifle manufacturing plant—the Russian Captain, Peter Bilderling. The capital increased from 800,000 rubles to 3,000,000 rubles (approximately $1,500,000). Alfred supplied 2,200,000 rubles of the amount.

The brothers worked together: Robert supervised the technical end of the business, and took up residence in Baku; the commercial end, including the organization of transportation and sales, was entrusted to Ludwig, who became the President of the Board of Directors with headquarters in St. Petersburg. Alfred provided backing and also advised. Because he resided in France, he could not actively participate in the management of the Baku enterprise. His financial share was generous and on more than one occasion during a time of difficulty, he came to the firm's rescue. His participation in the Nobel oil firm, while it varied from time to time, always amounted to at least several million rubles: a by no means charitable contribution. It proved an excellent investment of capital and the business grew with fabulous speed.

Robert Nobel did not long remain technical director of the company. Shortly after Alfred joined it, Robert became ill. Physicians forbade him to remain in the island city, with its north winds and a climate that treated him badly. He left the Caucasus and Russia, went to Sweden where he bought an estate on the seashore, and lived there—away from all business—for another sixteen years. He died in 1896.

An accurate description of Robert Nobel's personality is difficult for virtually no written records remain. He was an extremely kind and clever, but melancholic, man—a man of sad moods. No doubt he possessed unusual ability, even though he really never had opportunity to devote himself to serious scientific work. Still, he made useful technical improvements in those enterprises with which he was connected, and, in any event, he rendered a great service to the Nobel enterprises.

He was among the first in Russia, and the first in the Nobel dynasty, to grasp the significance of Caucasian oil. He did not work long in this field: not more than four years—since he became an invalid in 1879, so that his part in the development of the Nobel Company necessarily was less conspicuous than that of Ludwig and Ludwig's son, Emmanuel. But if Robert had not journeyed to the Caucasus, in search of walnut for rifles, the Nobel oil firm would not have been founded. He had not only remarkable foresight, but unbounded faith in the momentous future of the oil industry.

After Robert's withdrawal from the business and his departure from Russia, Ludwig Nobel remained the sole manager of the firm. He took charge of both the technical and commercial ends of the enterprise. Although he was not a chemist, but a mechanical engineer, this fact, proved beneficial to the business.

In those days, the chemical aspect of the production and refinement of oil was not yet complicated, and Robert organized the process efficiently. He shifted to machine-steamship-pipeline construction, as well as to the organization of transportation. For these his mechanical knowledge had more value than chemistry, and his commercial experience grew to be even more important. The great task was that he made kerosene popular, accustomed the Russians to this product and, by creating a steady demand for it, assured a constant influx of orders.

Ludwig was attractive and vital. He took extraordinary interest in all phases of cultural life. Much as Alfred his famous brother, he was a free thinker, and he preferred Voltaire to all other philosophers and writers. To a lesser degree than Alfred, he was also "a bit of a socialist;" at least, he often repeated the ancient maxim: "He who does not work shall not eat." Ludwig kept great interest and concern in the welfare of his workers and employees, and he devoted much of his time and attention to this task. His elder son, Emmanuel, became his assistant when still a very young man, and its was Emmanuel who, beginning in the eighties and up to the time of the Bolshevik Revolution, held the principal responsibilities for conducting the Nobel oil enterprises.

Intensive work undermined Ludwig's health. He might have prolonged his life by retiring earlier as did his brother, Robert. But Ludwig resented the idea of deserting the business and the thought of its sale was, to him, inconceivable. A group of foreign capitalists made him a very profitable offer, which he rejected, saying: "You want me to convert my money into stock certificates and to buy shears for clipping coupons. But what I need is not only money—I need work!"

PART II

HIS LOVES

Nobel in the City of Light

As Alfred Nobel passed his fortieth birthday, he could rate himself as one of the wealthiest men of his time, and a man known throughout the civilized world as an inventive genius. Scientists admired his brillance and devotion to experiment. Financiers sought him for investment in every type of enterprise. Intellectuals courted him for his encyclopaedic mind and cultural wisdom. High society, the *beau monde* of the European continent, tried to draw him into its gay whirl of festivity.

But Nobel was a private man. He had allowed few people to enter his life any farther than to touch the outer edges of his existence. Those few had been of his immediate family, though it was questionable as to how close his brothers were in companionship during the first two-thirds of his life. They become the dear companions of his late years. His mother, on the other hand, was always his confidante, his friendly ally, his ideal of womanhood.

Friends surrounded Nobel, an abundance of friends, but they remained detached entities which he allocated into set groups: those friends of scientific abilities commensurate with his, so they joined him in discussions and projections; those friends who met him on a business or commercial level; and those friends whose political or philosophic ideas arrested his interest and promoted thoughtful conversation. He abhorred the trivial.

Nobel held faith in reason and believed reason's explicit and complete expression lay in the sciences. He had a genius for business, great ability for organization, but such matters held no lure for him. As soon as he had formulated plans for completing the structure of a new business venture, he wanted only to find men capable of executing his guidelines, and then he left such men alone.

In the case of Paul Barbe—about whom he held no illusions—he gave Barbe free rein to take initiative in expansion of the Nobel interests. Over the years, he often expressed his awareness of Barbe's greed and personal avarice to his brothers, or friends, but still he recognized Barbe's organizational ability, and left him free to exercise it. This meant more time for Nobel to follow his real devotion—his laboratory experiments.

In his political leanings, he declared himself a socialist-democrat, but he kept an open mind to all types of political thinking and pondered them throughout his life. His own philosophies seemed an impossible mixture too divergent for combination in one man's mind—but he did somehow encompass them all. He was a romantic in his struggle for the advancement of knowledge, in his idealism about man's goal on this earth, and in his worship for nature. He expressed himself the most freely in poetry; this was purely romantic expression. However, he was rational in his emphasis on reason and intellect, his belief that only the educated and trained minds should rule nations or govern industry, and in his dedication to his own chemical genius. Then too, he was a humanist with complete respect for all human values and the desire to further the knowledge and comfort of the common man.

As with friends and acquaintances, he was able to allocate his beliefs into neat compartments, so that he could open the compartment he needed for a certain matter or the person it involved. Perhaps it was this particular ability to put his ideas and his emotions into these separate segments of his nature that, for years, kept him from learning one of man's greatest fulfillments—the love of woman.

Could not this lack in his life have unconsciously augmented his love of the city, Paris? He had met love there, although he had only fleeting contact with that love.

Certainly of all the cities of the western world, it was Paris he loved. The "city of light" afforded him respite and inspiration, whenever his hurried life gave him a chance to rest from the inspection of his far-flung holdings. Over the years, his schedule was one of enforced and continual travel, over America, England, Scandinavia, Russia, Germany, France, Austria, Italy. He said, "I am a stranger in all countries, for I am citizen of none." At nine he had left Stockholm and he had but entered his teens when his father sent him from Russia to Europe and America. Since that time, travel had consumed his life.

It was Victor Hugo who dubbed Alfred Nobel, "the millionaire vagabond," but rarely does the route of a vagabond lead to love. Yet Paris had given him a taste of passion and the thrill of love, when, at nineteen, he had made Paris his headquarters for travel of the Continent. The only record of this lies within the epic poem he wrote while living those youthful years. The poem relates the distaste and shame he felt over his experience with a prostitute, the woman who sold him his first sexual experiences.

> . . . I came to Paris . . .
> Alas! When youth has lost its faith in love
> When we have known the soul and heart to rot
> In woman long before her charms are gone,
> We pay for that experience a price,
> Which Fortune's brightest gift cannot refund . . .
>
> 'Tis not too nice to feed on common fruits
> And vice has charms which blind us for awhile—
> Thus I drank deeply from its cup, but soon
> I found its nectar poisoned with its dregs.

This experience, revolting to him in retrospect, made him wary of any girl who, even innocently, expressed her admiration and interest in the young Nobel. Instead of adolescent dalliance, he steeped himself in scientific research, buried his natural longings for feminine companship and love in a frenzy of work and wandering.

Paris had never been a place to avoid love. It was a *milieu* of love, a condition of love in itself. Even the busy youth Alfred who considered himself too unattractive for the notice of attractive young women he must have longed to meet, greeted love and became its escort in the most unexpected way.

The recreation of the scene of this meeting, presented a slender, serious-faced youth with a head of thick brown hair and remarkable keen blue eyes. His high forehead and level brows gave him the look of a young intellectual, but his knobby nose and sensitive mouth could not but add boyishness to that look. To be sure he bore little resemblance to the roguish-eyed, red-cheeked young blades of Parisian high-bred families, but Alfred had an appeal of his own. Even then, his resonant elegance of speech and a certain air of distinction gave him the attention of men twice his age and made him appealing to their ladies.

On this particular evening, Alfred's loneliness so choked and tortured him, that he left his habitual reading and study with the decision to attend a ball for which he had received an invitation. He isolated himself in a corner of the grand salon and stood there watching the ladies in ravishing gowns promenade past him on the arms of elegant gentlemen.

After eight years of the "citizen king," Louis Philippe, Paris was caught up in the dazzle of the second Empire: Napoleon III sought to rule through the exotic splendor of his court. His exquisite Spanish Eugenie with her attendant ladies had become models of the extravagant French designers and the luxury craftsmen of the Continent. Paris followed their example with all of the gaiety and glamor inherent in the fabled city.

A parade of beauty and high living passed at the ball. Brussels laces, Maltese fringes, silks from the Orient, velvets from Lyons, Irish linens, Paisley shawls, Italian brocades— all the finery and richness that made some historians label the Second Empire as vulgar, ostentatious, and corrupt. Yet others thought it courageous, merry and idealistic.

Ladies fluttered by in graceful crinolines with ivory shoulders bare, curls cascading down flushed cheeks, the graces of flowing fans and dainty nosegays. Laughing gentlemen followed them in nipped-in tail coats, satin vests and pointed shoes of glove-soft kid leather.

Young Nobel dressed in the most subdued of colors and never wished to push himself forward or to catch attention. He watched the passing show with a distrait and gloomy expression on his face. Suddenly, he was surprised when nearby he heard a charming feminine voice speak. The voice inquired whether Monsieur had lost someone dear to him.

The voice belonged to a fragile girl, more simply dressed and coiffed than others of her age, with a wealth of pale gold hair that fell in ringlets upon her slim shoulders and gave her a natural loveliness that in the eyes of young Nobel was more dazzling than all the sophisticated beauties about her.

Alfred answered her with the melancholy statement that his loss was greater than the loss of one dear to him. He had lost his dreams and illusions.

The girl's delicacy and tender concern entranced him. They found a quiet place where they could talk together, and Alfred, his restraints swept away by her gentle probing into what so distressed him, confided to her the miseries of his young life. He told her of his loneliness, of how he mistrusted the motives of people he met, of his feeling that he would never find the true happiness he yearned for.

The ethereal girl held deep convictions that life could be a good and wonderful experience. She had faith in the gifts life offered to those who would reach out to seize them. On learning of Alfred's inventive mind, of the responsibilities he had taken for the benefit of his family, she showed little patience with his misanthropy, urged him to take full advantage of his brilliant mind, so he would leave his mark upon the world.

At dawn the boy and the girl parted. Alfred had found comfort and renewed idealism in her confident faith. He wrote that he had become a "supremely happy and a better man," that they had sealed their love with a "chaste and hallowed kiss."

In the weeks that followed, he lived for the joy of seeing her, and knew he had found the love he cherished and wanted. He was supremely in love with the noblest of creatures. Then fate dealt him an agonizing blow. The girl died suddenly.

Romance and the pure love of Alfred's youth died with the pale-blonde girl. He wrote:

> ... my love is with the dead
> Nor was I there to soothe her last hours
> But came to gape upon a putrid corpse.
>   ... From that hour
> I have not shared the pleasures of the crowd
> Nor moved in Beauty's eye compassion's tear ...

Only once before had his poetry pictured a girl who attracted him. In Russia he had hoped to find an intelligent, pleasant young woman who would make him a home and be a faithful wife. There was Alexandra. "She had all attractions which would grace a wife, and solid merits of a wife." But when he proposed to her on the coach drive home one night, she refused him. Perhaps she knew, as he did, that no real love existed between them. At any rate Alfred did not suffer over her refusal, but in Paris, the city of love, he suffered with terrible heartbreak over the loss through death of his frail and lovely sweetheart.

Now after the passage of many years in wandering and working day and night, Alfred Nobel determined in his fortieth year to own a home of his own. And he would make his home in Paris. "I wish to live among my dumb friends, the trees and bushes," he had written once, but he found much to enjoy and admire in Paris.

In the late nineteenth century Paris reigned as the intellectual and cultural Queen of the continent. She was a city overflowing with genius, a flower of a metropolis in the full bloom of beauty and artistic gifts.

In 1870, France suffered defeat in the Franco-Prussian War. Paris was prostrated; the citizenry was impoverished and ill-fed during the war. The noble families resided in the spas and fashionable resorts of countries untouched by the ugliness of war. Bismarck exacted an indemnity of 5 billion francs. The indemnity was paid promptly; France's credit grew by leaps and bounds. Economic prosperity was so quickly restored that scarcely two years after the debacle, life was as normal, noisy and brilliant as under Napoleon III.

Nor did France lose any of her attractiveness in the eyes of foreigners who had always regarded her as a promised land. It seems that they never flocked to Paris in such numbers with such curiosity and keen interest as in the years following the Franco-Prussian War. It had been claimed that Napoleon's Second Empire had brought France to her ruin through immorality. But the morality or immorality of the country changed little through war or different political regimes. The Paris of the seventies and eighties in no way differed from the Paris of the time of Napoleon III.

However, greater political freedom encouraged the progress of science and especially of the fine arts. French literature was considered foremost in the whole world. French painting ranked first beyond a doubt, while Paris, from time immemorial, had set the fashions for all of Europe and had enjoyed the reputation of being the most brilliant metropolis of the universe.

Only a year later a revolution broke out in Paris, which was suppressed with great cruelty. Both sides revealed dreadful ferocity and this outburst of bestial instincts also caused universal amazement, so high was the prestige of French culture. The communards burned down historical buildings in Paris, which had contributed much to the glory of the French capital.

All this would have seemed to lessen considerably the fascination France held over Europe. But no such thing happened. The famous theatres, restaurants and places of amusement remained untouched and crowded as always. The charm of the old quarter of the world capital exerted its same magnetic appeal for visitors and citizens alike. The Paris of the left bank housed students and artists from every corner of the globe, some of whom did not have one hundred francs. The Paris of the right bank was invaded by people spending millions.

Not only did they spend millions but they made millions there more easily than in any other European country. England had offered greater business opportunities than France. In the Germany of Bismarck, order was better assured than in a country which had just lived through a revolution. Nevertheless, the French capital soon became again the center of international financiers.

Louis Adolphe Thiers became the first president of the Third Republic, to be supplanted in 1873 by the war hero, Marshal MacMahon.

So, Paris endured the devastation and upheaval of the Franco-Prussian war. Louis Napoleon and his beauteous Eugenie were exiled to England, while Bismarck furthered his own plans of power and Paris starved and shivered. When the fires of the insurrectionist Commune died out, Paris set about rebuilding, replacing, refurbishing the fallen parts of her confines. She accomplished this with such zeal that it was said if a casual visitor came to Paris in the year 1873, he would have wondered whether the place could possibly have been involved in a destructive war. Such was the spirit of Paris.

Damaged buildings were restored to their original condition and, even if to historians like Lenotre a restored historical building lost nine-tenths of its former charm, the average Parisian did not take it so tragically. Newly erected buildings were not always beautiful; certainly, the Grand Palais and the Petit Palais added nothing to the grace of Paris. Yet the architectural style of the Third Republic could not have been judged by such clumsy edifices. The architectural achievements of the Third Republic were by no means inferior to those of the preceding one under Napoleon III.

Why did Alfred Nobel settle in Paris at such a time? He had business interests in France, but he also had extensive investments all over the world, and in several other countries they were on a larger scale than in France. He must have been attracted by the very atmosphere of Paris—by that intangible and elusive aura which, even under political regimes that were neither free nor particularly inviting, always made people dream of that splendid city.

Nobel was a rich man, but he enjoyed his money for what it could buy him and was not motivated by the compulsion of making more. He grew rich quickly but not as quickly as other millionaires. Wealth in itself held no lure for him. He judged it only as the just and honest result of his energy expended and scientific inventions which proved to be practical.

Alfred Nobel's wealth and position had recently been expanded by the organizational efforts of his partner, Paul Barbe. New factories had begun production in Spain, Portugal, Switzerland and Italy. This was a time ripe for such expansion.

The upsurge of change had seized the entire European Continent and America as well. Industry grabbed new outlets; countries welcomed them; the people gasped and accepted. In America, Edison's phonograph was invented in 1877, his first lamp in 1879. The transatlantic cable had been laid for use in 1860, and a patent for the "horseless carriage" was taken out in 1879.

Even more amazing than these material changes were the changes in intellectual interests. In Paris changes came fast in styles, in ideas, in the arts, in politics. She accepted them with little fuss, after the first noisy arguments were over. Perhaps, it was because so much of the old remained.

Paris claimed in this era brilliant and famous chemists, working in fields adjacent to those in which Nobel was working. Though exhausted with patent ligitations and priority claims, he was wary of collaborating with specialists. Then, too, his pride was such that he wished to be indebted to no one but himself—to his own ideas and inventions—without sharing his fame with outsiders.

He chose as assistants in his scientific pursuits, especially in the later period of his life, only young scientists who, although able, merely carried out his orders. They were not collaborators but helpers. To them he was attentive, kind and generous, and they received training that advanced them to high places.

It seemed that the artistic instincts, latent since his youth, awoke in Nobel with the advent of wealth. Paris must have attracted him in this respect too. Not without good reason is the French capital known as *la ville-lumiere*, the city of light. In those years the literary greats like Flaubert, the Goncourts, Zola, Turgenev and Alphonse Daudet, were accustomed to meet in the private rooms of a famous restaurant to converse together. In the Goncourts' diary these rendezvous were called "meeting of talented people who esteem each other," (*des gens de talent qui s'estiment*). Victor Hugo often gave receptions and dinner parties, at which he ate much and talked still more. After these repasts he would light fourteen candles in the drawing room and, standing near the mirrors, he would recite his new verses.

The necessity of maintaining contact with business people, bankers and financiers, centered in Paris, and the prospect of enjoying the free and agreeable life in France and the intellectual fascination of the French capital, must certainly have prompted Alfred Nobel to take up residence in this country.

The Paris of the Third Republic gloried in her artistic sons. Victor Hugo, the great white-haired, white-bearded patriot, had returned from his 18 years of self-imposed exile in the Channel Islands, as his personal denunciation of dictatorship. Hugo was the arbiter of much outside the literary values of the day. A hero to the liberal thinkers, anathema to the imperialists, he was worshiped by the impoverished citizenry, as well as the brilliant circles in which he moved.

Victor Hugo lived on Place des Vosges in the heart of Paris. His home, an imposing dwelling, became a veritable showplace of the great man's versatility. His drawings decorated its walls; he designed his own furniture and had it executed in the fine woods he most admired. His famous Chinese drawing-room displayed his carvings and furniture, done in Hugo's conception of Oriental styles. The doors of his home opened to the great and famous in all fields of the arts. They came from all over France and the Continent to honor and to delight in the warmth and wit and stimulation of the great Victor Hugo.

His plays became the rage of Parisian theater-goers.

The Divine Sarah Bernhardt, in 1871, played Hugo's ravishing Spanish Queen who falls in love with Ruy Blas, valet to her noble, but spurned lover. *Ruy Blas* was then made a top draw of Bernhardt's repertoire and she presented it throughout the entire western world. Hugo's play *Hernani* gained ageless fame as Verdi's grand opera and *Le Roi S'amuse* was set to music by Verdi as *Rigoletto*. Ponchielli chose the play *Angelo* for his book of the haunting *La Gioconda*.

Hugo's plays and his great gift of lyric poetry to France's

literature were considered by many secondary to the drama of his novels that delineated the sufferings and sorrows of the common people. Victor Hugo was a humanitarian who loved liberty and his fellow man. His friendship with Alfred Nobel must have indeed helped to plant the seeds of Nobel's plans to use his vast estate for rewards to those human efforts that brought knowledge and help to all mankind.

France's literary figures in this era were many and superb. Dumas pere, had ended his robust existence, but Dumas fils, having written his *La Dame Aux Camélias*, now reveled in his own popularity. George Sand had reached her late years, but Coppeé, Flaubert, Edmond de Goncourt, de Maupassant, Daudet, Sardou, Paul Bourget, and Emile Zola were at the height of their careers.

This imposing list of brilliant men of literature did much to increase Nobel's devotion to Paris. Of all the fine arts, he most admired literature, as evinced by his choice of the written word as the influential art in his rewards. Gustave Doré and Auguste Rodin were peers in their art along with the Impressionists whose painting was sweeping Europe in a tidal wave of talent. But Nobel expressed little taste in the paintings he selected to hang upon the walls of his own mansion.

Le Beau Monde included Charles Haas, Proust's model for Swann; the Prince of Wales, that roystering royal Francophile; and the Baron Adophe de Rothschild. Nobel however did not seek the companionship of continental society; his respect and admiration were reserved for the cultured and intellectual. On Avenue Malakoff, at that time a spacious avenue that swept out from the Etoile, he found a mansion which pleased him.

The mansion was not pretentious, for Nobel had too much sensitivity to flaunt his wealth in material belongings, but it was a dwelling of charm and character. A coach house and stables guarded its entrance and charming gardens surrounded it.

Undoubtedly an important reason for the appeal of the Malakoff mansion to Alfred was the suite of rooms at the rear of the ground story, overlooking a fine back garden. These rooms became his study and his always most-vital laboratory. Life without constant experimentation would have been purposeless to him. The upper story of the mansion was given over to bedroom suites and a spacious salon. He had an organ built into an upstairs sitting room.

He commissioned a reputable decorator to furnish and adorn the ground floor, whereupon he ignored the man and showed not the slightest interest in any detail of the decor, except in the choice of paintings. Alfred's selection of ethereal mythological scenes could scarcely have pleased the over-wrought decorator, since they had to be hung on walls of rich, red damask, the vogue then in elegant Parisian homes.

Alfred's enthusiasm was boundless in outfitting his study and laboratory. He ordered the finest equipment available on the Continent. For once he would have at hand everything he needed or fancied in his scientific work.

His study held bookcases, built from floor to ceiling. His own massive desk stood before a great window and a smaller desk for his secretary sat next to it. But, he had no secretary. To find a suitable secretary seemed to be a never-ending problem to Alfred. It was not a position for the ordinary secretary, since his correspondence encompassed letters written in six languages.

Alfred Nobel spoke Swedish, Russian, English, German, French and Italian with fluency and grammatical exactness. He wrote most of his poetry in English, the language of his favorite poet, Shelley. Swedish was of course his childhood language; Russian the language of his boyhood. German was a necessary business language, as was Italian. French, in the 18th and 19th centuries, was the language of "civilized mankind."

His elegant use of languages reflected only one facet of the fascination of Alfred Nobel in these years of his early forties. He had an air about him that attracted everyone he met. Not a large man, he dressed in well-tailored black, the usual braid-trimmed cutaway for the distinguished men of the day, snowy white shirts with pleated bosoms, and an ascot tie.

A dark moustache and beard covered the lower part of his face and his hair was dark brown. He kept both hair and beard well-trimmed, for he was meticulous about his person. The feature that most appealed to his friends was the deep blue of his eyes. Set under heavy dark brows, those blue eyes radiated his vigorous intelligence and thoughtful appraisal of all about him. They were eyes of kindness and warm *camaraderie* for his friends, but often they showed deep sadness and uneasy introspection.

Alfred Nobel's bearing held no vanity, no arrogance, yet it befitted a man of power and influence. His whole being gave the impression of considered strength and of distinction in its highest sense.

Although his first months in his new home found him entertaining small groups of friends at well-planned dinners with entrancing conversation and music, he finally agreed to accompany his partner, Paul Barbe, on social forays.

One Friday night he was introduced to the famed salon of Madame Juliette Adam on the Boulevard Poissoniere. He had accepted Barbe's insistent invitation to the salon gathering for the sole purpose of meeting Victor Hugo. The two men were drawn to each other at once. Alfred drove Hugo to his home at the end of the evening, and they became firm friends who met again and again.

Alfred had cherished the hope of knowing Hugo for some time, but what surprised him was the interest and friendliness inspired in him by Juliette Adam. A beautiful and gracious hostess, she attracted Parisian celebrities from all walks of life to her salon dinners. On this evening of their first meeting, her guests included the wild bohemian orator, Leon Gambetta; Paul Deroulede, the simple poet of the people; and Ferdinand de Lesseps, builder of the Suez Canal. With Victor Hugo, the toast of all Paris, this in itself made a varied and exciting group.

The Salon of
Madame Juliette Adam

In the Paris of those days, there existed salons of heterogeneous character and of many conflicting expressions.
There were literary ones, such as those of the editor Char-
pentier, the novelist Alphonse Daudet and the family of
Victor Hugo; there were musical salons, like that of the composer Massenet; and those of scientists, of which the chemist
Berthelot's and the famous doctor Charcot's were perhaps
the most popular. Then again, there were the salons of the
beau monde, the high society leaders.

Alfred Nobel took little interest in these gatherings, ex-
cepting the salon of Juliette Adam. Science and literature
appealed more to him than politics and the orientation of
the particular salon where he became a habitue was hardly
in accord with his own socialistic views. But because the
salon belonged to one of the most beautiful and gracious
hostesses on the continent—a woman of brilliant intellect
and ardent enthusiasms, Madame Juliette Adam, née
Lamber.

Madame Juliette Lamber Adam, born on October 4, 1836,
lived to within five weeks of her one hundredth birthday.
Her father was a modest, hard-working physician who gave
his beautiful and beloved daughter every opportunity that
the era afforded for education and stimulating companionship.

Juliette was born in a small town, Verberie. Quite by
accident, her birth took place in a hotel where her parents

had gone temporarily because of a fire that broke out in their home. Fires in both direct and symbolic senses of the term pursued the future Madame Adam, even from her cradle days. Many social fires and political infernos were the lot of Juliette Lamber. She lived through the great number of political coups, revolutions and wars which characterized her century. She went through all vicissitudes unscathed. Her life was unusually happy and she died a wealthy woman.

At the age of seventeen she married Lamessin, a lawyer by profession, much against the will of her father. The marriage lasted only a short time and Juliette separated from the Lawyer Lamessin in an unfriendly fashion.

Juliette began to write at an early age. Her first article was a sketch on crinolines in answer to the popular journalist, Alphonze Karr, who had declared war on crinolines, no doubt hoping to provoke the ladies of fashion.

Karr's article aroused Juliette's ire. She had no tremendous admiration for crinolines. Her youth and beauty made her a Venus in anything she wore; but, she wrote a sharp rebuke of Karr's article, sent it to the periodical, *Le Siècle*. She signed her work "Juliette," and when it was printed, readers became curious about her. Her debut as a writer had been accomplished.

Next she tested her ability in verse. Béranger, the old poet of those days who was known for his "Chansons" read her poetic experiments at her request and told her frankly that she would never become a poetess. He said, however, that she might become a writer. Juliette then wrote a book, a political discussion directed against the ideas of Proudhon. After futile attempts to find a publisher, she printed it at her own expense.

The book met with some success. In that age there were comparatively few women writers and it was not difficult to attract public attention. That the authoress of the tome that appeared under the dry title of *Anti-Proudhon Ideas* was a young and pretty woman no doubt aroused interest. People began to talk about Juliette Lamessin. The doors of several literary salons were thrown open to her, including that of the Countess d'Agoult, one of the most famous women in those days and a friend of Franz Liszt. Great men from all parts of the globe frequented the Countess' salon.

From that time on until the end of her days, Juliette lived in association with celebrities. The pages of French literature and French history of the Nineteenth Century listed few prominent personages whom Juliette did not know. Most were friends or close acquaintances but a very few were enemies.

In 1867 her husband, Lamessin, died. On the day of his death she became betrothed to Edmond Adam who had been infatuated with her for a long time. A journalist by profession, he was fairly well known. However, his commercial affairs had brought him a large fortune. He became one of the pillars of the bank, *Comptoir d'Escompte,* in existence to the present day. In addition to wealth, he had other attractions that made him an ideal husband for Juliette. A man of the world and a *bon vivant,* he never quarreled with anyone. He dabbled in politics, had an unblemished name and could have looked forward to a successful political career.

At that time the Empire of Napoleon III, notwithstanding its surface glamour, was on the brink of collapse. The misadventures in Mexico and the victory of the Prussians over the Austrians in 1866 had pushed France toward its grim destiny. Politicians of those days had begun to conceive the possibility of a political crash, and some of them were already planning the republican regime. France as a republic would present great opportunities to a man like Edmond Adam.

His large fortune enabled him and his wife to form a salon. Both from a political and a social standpoint this was important to them. They maintained two salons; the winter one in Paris on Boulevard des Poissonieres and the summer one at their country estate.

In 1870, two days after the Sedan catastrophe, the empire of Napoleon fell. The stormy existence of the Third Republic had begun.

Edmond Adam was elected to the National Assembly that in 1871 convened in Versailles. For a long time after the Commune, the government did not wish to return to Paris. There were in that Assembly many capable and eminent men of whom Leon Gambetta was the most famous. He was the son of a small shopkeeper of Italian descent and his enemies, on every [opportune and inopportune] occasion, reminded him that his father was born in Genoa.

In July 1871, Madame Adam saw Gambetta during his first appearance at the Versailles Assembly. She was immediately attracted to him. After the death of Edmond Adam, it was persistently rumored in Paris that Gambetta was going to marry Adam's widow, as she recounted in her memoirs. That it was a sexual infatuation on the part of Madame Adam she did not admit, but she genuinely admired him as a statesman. She declared even in her old age, that Gambetta's eloquence could not be judged by a person who merely read his speeches; he had to hear them. "This is a lion!" she often said to her friends.

Gambetta became a guest in Madame Adam's salon, and at times acted as the host. Edmond Adam had, from earlier years, financed the newspaper *Avenir National*, which supported the policies of Gambetta. In the paper *Republique Francaise*, founded in November, 1871 which became the semi-official mouthpiece of Gambettism, Edmond Adam took a lesser financial interest, but the ideological center of the paper was undeniably located in the salon of Madame Adam.

This newspaper was the organ of the torchbearers of the Third Republic. They all gathered in the salon of the Adams, where Gambetta reigned supreme. The man had risen from the ranks of small shopkeepers; he did not know how to dress, but was taught by the Adams; he possessed an appetite which would have rivaled Louis XIV, for his gluttony. The Adam couple brought about his reconciliation with Thiers, the first president of the Republic who frequently visited them. This accord was a real event in the budding life of the Third Republic.

In his innermost heart, the fascinating Leon Gambetta had been thinking of an agreement with Germany, although he mentioned this to few of his friends. Although he was the main inspirer of the French National Defense in 1870, he disliked the idea of a new war and of war in general. Five or six years after the loss of Alsace-Lorraine, he dared to hope that he might convince Germany to restore voluntarily these provinces to France. He hoped an arrangement of this kind might be made with Bismarck.

There lived in Paris a Count (later Prince) Henckel-Donnersmarck, one of the wealthiest German magnates who had married Paiva, the notorious adventuress. He owned a mansion on the Champs Elysees and entertained with most magnificent receptions, balls and dinner parties. As the impression of events of 1870 became fainter in the public mind, highly-placed and prominent Frenchmen, in ever increasing numbers, began to frequent the home of the German Count. Six years after the Franco-Prussian debacle, Gambetta started visiting him. In a letter to Bismarck, dated October 17, 1877, Henckel-Donnersmarck reported that he was on excellent terms with Gambetta.

These visits to Henckel-Donnersmarck were known to few people. Gambetta must have called privately and never appeared at the formal receptions. Madame Adam, for one, knew nothing about these visits. She disliked both the Count and his wife, regarded them as German agents and enemies of France. The fact they were Germans sufficed to determine her attitude toward them. Gambetta, notwithstanding his close friendship with Madame Adam, never spoke to her about his visits to the Henckels. He knew how she would react to this.

However, she discovered the secret. A French politician, apparently anxious to cause a break between the arrogant Gambetta and Madame Adam, told her one day that Gambetta had dined at the Henckel home. "I felt as though something died in my heart," wrote Madame Adam. Then she heard the report that the Henckel visits were not confined to a dinner. Gambetta was planning a secret meeting with Bismarck!

The report was true. Gambetta had contemplated calling incognito on Bismarck at his estate for a secret conference with the Iron Chancellor.

The news of Gambetta's secret maneuvers was a wounding blow to Madame Adam; she severed political relations with him although there was no personal break between them. During the last years of Gambetta's life, he and Madame Adam met very rarely. He died suddenly in 1882 at the age of forty-four.

Madame Adam had lost her husband in May 1877 at the very height of her friendship with Gambetta. Edmond Adam left his wife a handsome fortune, but on his deathbed he exacted from her the promise that she would not marry for three years after his death. This request and the three year term affixed probably evolved from his feeling that she would marry Gambetta. She was then forty-one years of age and Gambetta was two years her junior. Juliette outlived her husband by almost sixty years and never remarried.

After she had severed relations with Gambetta and after the time when France had become more or less apathetic to the idea of revenge, Madame Adam's interest in politics began to wane. Her salon, closed for only a short while after her husband's death, continued to function, but it changed its appearance! What in days past had been a political salon *par excellence* was now converted primarily into a literary salon.

Juliette Adam had always been interested in literature, in the narrow sense of the term. She considered that she belonged to the literati, inasmuch as she wrote poetry and novels. Her personal connections with writers were excellent and she knew the most famous ones. George Sand was her closest friend. Flaubert, who hated the politicians and the political dames in particular, was very fond of Madame Adam and frequently visited her. Victor Hugo took a benevolent attitude toward her. When conversing with him, she once mentioned that she had kept a diary during the German siege of Paris. The aged poet laureate expressed a desire to read it "that very night." He sent for the diary and praised it highly.

Hugo's sympathy for Madame Adam is the more noteworthy because he differed with her in politics. He was much more radical than she and despised her friend Thiers for his merciless suppression of the Commune. Hugo had no use for Flaubert. He told Madame Adam that after the collapse of the Empire, France, far from rising, would be sinking to even lower levels, "galloping towards the regime of the innkeeper, the municipal councilor and the village schoolmaster."

Juliette conceived the idea, not of a newspaper, but of a magazine which, though not alien to politics would be of a literary character. Both George Sand and Flaubert encouraged her in the project. At that time there were few French magazines. It was somehow taken for granted that no periodical could compete, either from a literary or a financial standpoint, with the antiquated *Revenue de Deux Mondes*. However, Madame Adam's large fortune made financial competition possible. She grew enthusiastic over the venture and, in 1879, founded the *Nouvelle Revue*.

She managed this magazine for twenty years. She wrote articles for it on foreign policy, in which she ably defended her anti-German and anti-Bismarck ideas. The general policy of the *Nouvelle Revue* became the advocacy of glorious and traditional French cultural achievements.

From a literary standpoint, Madame Adam's magazine maintained a high standard. In addition to famous writers of the old school such as Flaubert, she succeeded in enlisting the interest of a large group of young literati who were destined to become famous. Alphonse Daudet, Anatole France, Paul Bourget, Pierre Loti and Maurice Barres were among the contributors to her magazine.

From the very start there was little political cohesion in the group. At the time of the Dreyfus case, Anatole France, who had become a principal leader in the pro-Dreyfus camp, resigned from Madame Adam's journal. Bourget, Barres, and Juliette, herself, were ardent anti-Dreyfussards. But, before that Anatole France's novel *The Crime of Sylvestre Bonnard* was published in the *Nouvelle Revue*. This well known and perhaps his best work brought him great fame. With the publishing of *Nouvelle Revue* the salon of Madam Adam lost its political influence. Both Thiers and Gambetta were dead, and the political weight of the salon had been dependent upon these two statesmen. Through this period, her salon held the prestige of literary and social excellence. Virtually all of the famous French writers and scientists, as well as many foreign celebrities passed through her doors.

Over at least a dozen years of his residence in Paris Alfred Nobel found great attraction in Madame Adam and her entourage. His ideas differed to a large extent from those preached by the *Nouvelle Revue*. As a neutral foreigner, the problem of Alsace-Lorraine had only remote and purely academic interest for him. He was neither a German-baiter, nor a Germanophile. Nobel did not care to indulge in the various "phobias" and "philisms' of his adopted home city.

He resided in Paris and was fond of France, but the nation was not to him a fatherland. Russia was more rightfully his second fatherland.

Irrespective of politics, Madame Adam appealed to him. She was clever, attractive, educated and possessed a great deal of charm. Nobel was fond of cultured women and frequently complained that such women were sadly scarce. In an intellectual sense, Madame Adam's mansion had much to offer. Where, indeed, could he have met such a galaxy of famous writers, poets and scientists? Without doubt Nobel did not take Madame Adam's politics too seriously. In September, 1891 he wrote an old friend, Bertha von Suttner:

I am delighted that your eloquent sermon against war, this horror of horrors, penetrated the French press. However, I am afraid that ninety-nine French readers out of one hundred are affected by the mania of chauvinism. The French government is more or less sound; the people, on the contrary, are intoxicated with success and vain glory. This is a pleasant form of intoxication and—if only it does not lead to war—a less harmful variety than drunkenness caused by wine or morphine.

Then too, Madame Adam's salon made for Nobel a convenient observation post. Nobel was not a man of pure meditation. The character of his work made it inevitable for him to move in the thick of practical life, and he always retained an accentuated, contemplative interest in human nature, in the way men acted and in the things they dreamed about. From the standpoint of the varying human material that entered its doors, Madame Adam's salon must have been most instructive.

Nobel disliked the professional politician, but he took an interest in politics. To this odd socialist, most ideas preached by the European politicians seemed obnoxious. If Nobel did not sympathize with the idea of French retaliation, the Bismarck policy evoked in him still more hostile feelings. Nevertheless, he wished to be well informed on everything occurring in Europe.

From time to time, large receptions, with their usual jostling and bustle, were hosted by the indefatigable Madame Adam. One of these social affairs was described by Bertha von Suttner:

She (Madame Adam) very kindly invited us (the Suttner couple) to a big evening party, which was to take place in a few days. I have a vivid recollection of this entertainment. Her small house was full of guests; they were everywhere from the stairhead to the remotest corners of the drawing room. Madame Adam greeted her friends at the threshold of the parlor. Wearing a dark red velvet gown with a long train, she made an imposing and attractive figure; she had diamonds on her breast and also in the high headdress of her grey hair, in spite of which her face was still young. Of course, the role of hostess required that she speak a few cordial words to each guest.

'Oh, dear Baron,' she said to my husband, with a kind smile, 'I am so charmed. You gave such a vivid picture of that country, that half-barbarian Caucasus; I was really fascinated.'

As we know, everything Russian strongly appealed to Madame Adam's imagination; Aksakov and Skobelov were her favorites. In the meantime I was thinking: 'How can a woman give so much of her time to politics—an occupation which, indeed, draws on one many unpleasant things and even ridicule?'

In the reception room and in other chambers there were many prominent artists, men of letters and politicians, as well as many beautiful women. Madame Napoleon Ney, who was considered one of the belles of Parisian society, was pointed out to us. Unfortunately, it was impossible to meet all the interesting people. The crowd was so dense that one had to stay in his own corner and be satisfied to converse with those few who happened to be standing nearby. Most of the time I remained silent and merely listened. Following the Parisian custom, the guests were entertained with all sorts of artistic divertissements: a pianist played Hungarian melodies, or a writer—with a brilliant future, though not yet prominent—read his stories; Madame Brandes who, at the time, was not yet an actress at the Comédie Française, recited a poem. But, even amidst this artistic and social

81

whirl, the grim word 'war' sounded here and there. Time and again, the names of Bismarck, Moltke and Schnebele were mentioned. Bold prophecies were made to the effect that by the next spring something would occur for certain. Meanwhile, this did not affect the prevailing gay mood. Probably these prognostications evoked in the hostess rosy hopes. She was so transported with the glory of her own country! I was no longer as indifferent to things of this sort as in the days of my youth. I hated war intensely, and I found a lack of consciousness and common sense in this frivolous chitchat about the possibility of war.

Nobel found an intriguing interest in this spectacle of wealth and fashion combined with art and creativity. The politics expressed in Madame Adam's salon repelled him, as they did his guest Bertha von Suttner, who at the time was not yet an active pacifist, yet Nobel attended Madame Adam's receptions quite faithfully. Since in Paris he visited practically no one else, he must have enjoyed the quick wit of repartee, the colorful atmosphere, but more than that, he must have admired the grace and beauty and verve of this famous hostess, Madame Juliette Adam.

Baroness Bertha Kinsky von Suttner

In 1875, after a period of absorption in a long series of experiments, hundreds of them, Alfred completed the development of blasting gelatine, a product 46% more powerful than dynamite. The cutting of St. Gotthard tunnel under the Alps dramatically demonstrated the value of blasting gelatine and again the name of Alfred Nobel was on every tongue of the western world.

He then turned to the completion of his home, hired another designer to furnish and decorate the upper story of the mansion. When the work was finished, Alfred surveyed the luxury and attraction of the rooms, saw that all was in excellent order, his kitchen well-staffed, his household servants and stable men comfortably housed. But the place was empty. It cried out for a woman—a hostess, a housekeeper; the heart and hands of a woman to do the thousand and one things that only a woman can do.

And a secretary—how he needed the help of a proper secretary. His business correspondence burdened him. Even more demanding was the avalanche of mail he received from people asking him to supply funds for business enterprises, for study in artistic pursuits, for charitable plans, and often pathetic pleas for help in escaping the morass of poverty. He had not the strength or time to answer all requests, though from kindness he constantly sent monies and wondered how honest and worthy the recipents were.

If he could find one woman capable of becoming both his secretary and housekeeper, this would be ideal, he decided. To cope with more than one stranger in his household at a time would be not only difficult for his very private temperament, but two strange women might find each other incompatible. He would try first for that superior feminine secretary-housekeeper who might be non-existent for all he knew.

In his life of travel he had often marveled at the cultural background and practical skills blended in Viennese women. Almost as if he dared himself to attempt the impossible, he wrote an advertisement and mailed it to a Viennese newspaper.

The advertisement he wrote did not seem in character for Alfred. Certainly, it was not intended as a droll experiment, for he had nothing of that in his make-up. Its apparent daring could have reflected something of his lifelong interest in the nature and action of human beings. The realist in him had left him no illusions as to how people, men or women, behaved.

At any rate, when he wrote: "A very rich, cultured, aged gentleman, residing in Paris . . ." in reference to himself, it is impossible not to accept these words as bait for the possible applicants of his offered position. In a detached viewpoint of Alfred Nobel, the description was true of him, but there was a feeling of smugness in it that nothing in his nature bore out.

The next phrases: ". . . an equally mature lady knowing foreign languages for the performance of the duties of a secretary and housekeeper." This description was staid and dignified enough to hold off the adventuress types and still the advertisement as a whole, held the door open to all comers.

His letters from ladies of more or less mature age, and of more or less ability in languages, and certainly of more or less experience in rendering house-keeping services must have been startling to Alfred. He received flattering pictures of women and flowery descriptions of feminine charms that had little to do with either secretarial or household duties.

Of the serious applications, he was impressed by an intelligent letter from Bertha-Sophia-Felicitas Kinsky, employed as governess for the daughters of the Baroness von Suttner. Bertha Kinsky wrote forthrightly of her age, thirty-three, and of the fact she was unmarried. She knew languages, but had little experience in housekeeping.

That she was a lady and reared in the manner of Austrian aristocrats was evident from her letter. Alfred's interest was aroused. He answered her in his most charming manner and an amiable correspondence began between the two. They wrote in several languages, discussed philosophical views, until Alfred, perhaps fearful of his increasing desire to know Bertha Kinsky personally, detailed his erratic habits of work, and emphasized his somewhat eccentric personal tastes.

The lady replied with restraint but restated her desire for the position, and made mention of the many rebuffs she had suffered in her life. Alfred responded with a description of his secretarial needs and the salary he would pay, and Bertha Kinsky advised him of her plans to come immediately to Paris.

Alfred made arrangements for rooms for Bertha at the Grand Hotel on Boulevard des Capucines, until the second floor suite of the Nobel mansion had been completed. On the day of her arrival, he met her early morning train, and made an appointment with her for a drive that afternoon.

Bertha recorded her impressions on meeting Alfred in the journal she kept conscientiously throughout her life. To judge from his advertisement, she had expected to see an elderly gentleman, tottering, feeble and hoary-haired. Instead of this, the Alfred Nobel she met struck her as a dynamic man in his mid-years. She described his eyes, as "kindly blue eyes," and his tone, as "melancholy alternating with a satirical tone."

Alfred on the other hand was even more amazed than Bertha, when he saw before him a beautiful and stately woman with an oval face, arched brows and dark hair modishly arranged in coils at the back of her head with a waved fringe over her high forehead.

The style of the time demanded that milady's gown have an overdrape of rich material, gathered into puffs or loops over a beruffled or be-braided skirt that swept into fullness at the back. The bustle was on its way to full acceptance; waists were tiny; bodices fitted over the bosom with graceful sleeves and fancy detail at the throat and wrists. Though Bertha had no money, she must have striven for the fashion ideal, for she was to the "manor born," and had the sophistication of a Viennese noblewoman. One of her outstanding beauties was her stunning figure, finely proportioned and graceful in movement. She was indeed, a picture of delightful femininity, as she descended from the Orient Express to be greeted by Alfred Nobel.

From the moment of this first meeting, their natures harmonized with understanding and stimulation in each other's company. This did not mean they agreed upon their subjects of conversation. In fact they almost always disagreed, but they respected each other's ideas and found a lively interest in comparing their two points of view. Never before had Alfred found a woman's mind so inspiring, so stored with the knowledge that intrigued him. He was charmed by her. As for Bertha, she wrote in her journal:

To talk with him about the world and humanity, about life and art, about the problems of time and eternity, was an intense intellectual enjoyment. He kept aloof from social life; certain forms of shallowness, of falsity, of frivolity, filled him with disgust and wrath ... His studies, his books, his experiments—those were what filled his life. He said he was working on a new invention: "I wish I could produce a substance or machine of such frightful efficacy for wholesale destruction that wars should thereby become altogether impossible."

Bertha spoke freely to Alfred about her past, her parents, her life as a child and young girl. Alfred talked more than she did—an unheard of thing for him, the uncommunicative Alfred Nobel. He told her of his hopes, his ideals, his current project in reading. But the one enigma of this woman, the information he most wanted, remained unspoken. Why this beautiful and desirable creature had never married—and she was thirty-three—was more than a puzzle to him. It was incredible.

A day came when Alfred went to the Grand Hotel for her, and she met him, after a long wait, with a tear-stained face and tragic eyes. He tried to comfort her by confiding the strains and sufferings of his own childhood. Then, he gave her one of his long poems to read.

Poetry was the outpouring of his soul. He created it as the secret expression of the very private thoughts of this very private man. He did not share it easily. As he handed the poem to Bertha, he attempted to belittle his gesture by saying in an offhand way that his poetry was "a lonely man's hobby." To this perceptive woman such a statement must have betrayed his deep feeling.

She praised his poetry as "simply splendid." It was much more. It gave her an intimate look into the affectionate and sorrowful heart of the man. As the poem said:

> You say I am a riddle—it may be,
> For all of us are riddles unexplained,
> Begun in pain, in deeper torture ended.
> Some petty wants to chain us to the earth,
> Some lofty thoughts to lift us to the spheres
> And cheat us with the semblance of a soul
> To dream of immortality.

But Bertha Kinsky could not have known what a riddle Alfred Nobel was. Nor perhaps did Alfred, himself. He was a man of contrasts, of paradoxes too extreme to be believable. Yet they were all there, within him.

He loved challenge, even courted it, but shied away from people who challenged his thinking.

No man could have been more stubborn and uncompromising about his scientific discoveries; he sued relentlessly any person or group who overstepped his patent protections. Scores of trusted associates made off with funds that should have been his and he rarely bothered to pursue them.

He declared himself an agnostic in his youth, an atheist later, but at the same time, bestowed generous sums to the church.

His pessimism, turned to misanthropy, became almost a matter of pride to Alfred, yet his desire to help others out of a slough of despond caused him to give away fortunes in his philanthropies.

He hated publicity, was so averse to self-glory that he erred in belittling himself, yet he strove for the power of wealth and made every effort to extend his holdings to four continents.

Alfred Nobel, the pacifist, invented horror weapons of warfare.

Alfred Nobel called himself the "loneliest of men," and constantly shunned many delightful companions who sought him out.

Alfred Nobel, the genius of chemical science, worshipped culture and literature above all else.

Of such paradoxes was the riddle of Alfred Nobel.

As Bertha Kinsky met Alfred daily, and shared long and deep discussions on each day, did she seek to solve the riddle of this man? Did she feel for him any part of the affectionate regard he gave to her?

She did indeed admire him, respect him, enjoy his company, but she was madly in love with the young Baron von Suttner. Arthur von Suttner was handsome, passionate, and idolatrous of her. She could not look upon any other man as a possible admirer, when she felt such devotion to the youthful Baron. Protectively reared, charming and mannerly, von Suttner did not bear comparison with the brilliance and world distinction of Alfred Nobel. But such is love, young, passionate love. It sweeps away all reason, all judgment. Though Bertha was in her thirty-third year, and had endured many disappointments in ill-fated betrothals she was plainly, for the first time in her life, consumed by a passionate love.

Bertha Kinsky was unique—youthful, remarkable in her elegant loveliness, unusually intelligent, and endowed with a gentle, affectionate disposition—but still unmarried at thirty-three.

Alfred could not understand this baffling situation until he heard the entire story of Bertha's life, and an incredible story it was. Too much misfortune had befallen this well-born young woman since her birth.

Bertha Kinsky's father, Lieutenant Field Marshal Count Kinsky von Chinic und Tettau, belonged to the highest stratum of Austrian aristocracy. The family of the Counts and Princes Kinsky went back to the sixteenth century. Bertha Kinsky's father was a member of the family of Princess Lichtenstein on his mother's side. He stepped outside of the aristocratic circle to marry a modest noble woman, the daughter of Captain von Kerner and his wife, nee Hahn. This was an utter mesalliance which had strong bearing on the fate of his daughter. Young Bertha Kinsky soon became aware of her position. On her paternal side she was related to the most aristocratic families of Austria, yet she could not penetrate the select entourage of the Hapsburgs. She was also handicapped by another circumstance: the Kinskys were not rich and court life required a great deal of money.

Field Marshal von Kinsky died before the birth of his only child, Bertha. His friend and relative, Friedrich, the Landgrave von Furstenberg (one of the oldest, most prominent families dating to the epoch of Charles the Great), became Bertha's guardian. She adored him and to the end of her days preserved a reverent memory of him, even though he was a snobbish man. Nontitled people simply did not exist to him. He remained a bachelor because of his tragic love for a widow of an unrecognizable family. Since he could not face the humiliation of this mad love, he never married at all.

Landgrave von Furstenberg loved his grandniece, Bertha, and taught her his ideas. In her youth, the young countess must have shared his views, insofar as politics interested her at all.

She lived with her mother to whom she was devoted and with her mother's sister. Neither mother nor aunt had an occupation; both led a dream-life and both, especially the aunt, were passionate card players. They visited health resorts where gambling on a large scale was permitted and every day spent long hours at the casino. Naturally, they had a system of their own that assured their eventual winning. The hours away from the casino gave them time to dream of the fabulous things they would do with the money they were about to win.

Not far away from them lay a glorious estate centered by the Castle Eisgrub, which belonged to Prince Lichtenstein. The aunt chattered about buying the estate and the fact that Prince Lichtenstein held no intention of selling his property mattered not at all to her. She was certain the enormous sum she would offer the Prince would tempt him to sell his castle. The aunt promised to arrange for her niece, Bertha, in the castle of Lichtenstein, a special room with china walls and a china ceiling. Bertha was thrilled. The two discussed in detail the layout of the room. Notwithstanding her excellent system, the aunt lost the major part of her fortune. This compelled the three to live modestly in the country, aloof from the fashionable world.

The young countess, too, exercised a romantic imagination. The aunt's passion was gambling; the niece's: young men. From the sweet age of fourteen the girl's ambition was to make a brilliant match. She would marry wealth and win entrance to the charmed Hapsburg court circle.

The first object of her love was Emperor Franz-Joseph himself, at that time not yet married. She had never met him but for months she dreamed of a chance meeting and of how he would fall in love with her and would marry her, ignoring the absence of "sixteen noble generations" on her mother's side. The young Emperor had a sufficient number of generations of his own.

When Franz-Joseph married Queen Elizabeth of Bavaria, the Emperor was replaced in her dreams by an eighteen-year-old cadet. These amorous imaginings were normal for an adolescent girl. Bertha Kinsky then became engaged to one of the wealthiest men in Vienna. He was an aristocrat almost three times as old as she. Tacitly, she accepted his age and thrilled over his expensive gifts. However, when it came to the first kiss between the engaged pair the youthful countess fled in horror. The betrothal was ended and the gifts returned.

The memoires of Bertha von Suttner recount the incidents of her youth without garnishment. She endured one disillusioning romance after another. On an occasion at Homburg, the Kinskys became acquainted with the Princess Mingrelsky. The Russian Emperor had conferred this title upon the Georgian Princess Dadiani, sovereign ruler of one of the many Caucasian states that surrendered their sovereignty in Russia in return for the protection of their lands against the Turks. Bertha depicted with real delight the imagined grandeur and magnificence of the Princess, whom her subjects called *Dedopali*, "The Mother of Mothers," a slight exaggeration since in Russia everybody, especially the aristocracy, treated Caucasian titled nobility with good-natured but somewhat ironical humor. In reality, the Dadianis belonged only to a wealthy, influential family.

The Princess Dadiani took a fancy to the Kinskys and in

particular to Bertha. She conceived a plan of arranging the young woman's marriage to the wealthy Prince Irakly Gruzinsky. Bertha promptly fell in love with the Prince. On his part, however, there was no reciprocal feeling and he ended the matter by suddenly disappearing from the scene. This was a hard blow to Bertha.

Prince Wittgenstein, a prominent and attractive, but very poor man proposed to her and she became his betrothed. It was decided that her fiance would proceed to America to make money there in order to support his future wife. Prince Wittgenstein left for the United States but while aboard ship he suddenly died. Some said by his own hand.

Then, a youth of half English and half Australian descent fell in love with her in Paris. His father, purported to be an immensely wealthy man, made the proposal on behalf of his son, declaring that the lad had reached the age of twenty. At that time Bertha was much older. She accepted the proposal and the Kinskys endeavored to make inquiries through the Bank of Rothschild concerning the property status of Bertha's fiance, or rather of his father, but they did not receive a reply on time.

An elaborate betrothal announcement party was planned at the home of Prince Achille Murat who had married the young Princess Mingrelsky, a daughter of the Kinskys' protectress.

A few days before the ceremony the fiance's father invited Bertha for a promenade on the Champs Elysees where several mansions were for sale. He asked her to select one of the houses for her future residence as a gift. She picked one that a well-known courtesan, Paiva (later the Princess Hendel von Dunnersmarck) had built for herself. Next the gallant gentleman took his future daughter-in-law to the Rue de la Paix to inspect a display of jewelry, and urged Bertha to choose a magnificent riviere priced at 200,000 francs; the necklace was to be delivered to the home of Prince Murat on the day of the betrothal. Finally, they went to Worth's where they ordered a stunning gown. The great day of the betrothal party arrived and Bertha donned her new Worth creation for the festivity.

Relatives and guests assembled and champagne was being poured but the young man and his father did not arrive. The delay became embarrassing, incomprehensible. At last a messenger brought a short, strange letter; the fiance had been taken ill and asked that the wedding ceremony be postponed. The guests departed at a loss to understand what had happened. Bertha and her mother were in tears.

Another message arrived that announced the departure of the Anglo-Australians, father and son, from Paris saying that they realized the whole affair was a sad mistake, since the boy was too young for his fiancee. He was not twenty, as his father had said but only eighteen. With apologies for the misunderstanding they formally declared that they considered the Countess free. Subsequently the Kinskys learned that the Anglo-Australian pair had no money whatsoever. They were either crooks, or mad, or both.

From day to day the financial situation of the Kinskys grew more insecure. Bertha was fond of singing; for a dilettante she had a fairly good voice though its quality was much exaggerated by her mother who said Bertha should try for a brilliant operatic career. Patti at that time was a great star. "You have a better voice than Patti!" was the verdict of both mother and aunt. They went to Pauline Viardot, then considered the outstanding teacher of voice in the world. The famous singer listened to Bertha and judged her voice to be mediocre with little chance of improvement. They applied to other maestros, but Bertha, disillusioned about her talents gave up the thought of a singing career.

Since she had no independent fortune of her own, she determined to earn her own livelihood. She accepted the position of governess with the family of the Baron von Suttner to tutor the young daughters of the Baron.

There, at last, Bertha found happiness, for the son and heir of the family, Baron Arthur Hundaker von Suttner, fell deeply in love with her. He was a polished, worthy and handsome man, but he was only twenty-three while Bertha had passed her thirtieth year.

Arthur's parents refused to consider his marriage to a penniless woman seven years his senior. Bertha Kinsky, with her sensitivity and fine intellect, felt that her status of governess in that home had become untenable. She made up her mind to find other employment. She began to read the "help wanted" columns of local newspapers. One particular notice seemed interesting to her, despite the fact that it gave no name for the employer.

It was not by accident that Bertha happened across this particular ad. For some time the old Baroness von Suttner had observed that a romance was developing between her son and the governess. In an ice-cold manner, though tactfully and politefully, she gave the governess to understand that such affections were entirely out of place. Bertha Kinsky then announced to the Baroness that she intended to leave the estate at once, that she and the young Baron had pledged to each other their undying love, but she had no wish to stay under the disapproval of his mother. Summoning all her courage, Bertha asked the Baroness to help her, through the von Suttner connections, to find a new position, possibly in London since she yearned to go far away. The Baroness calmly handed Bertha the issue of a Viennese paper containing the advertisement:

A very rich, cultured, aged gentleman, residing in Paris, wishes to meet an equally mature lady knowing foreign languages, for the performance of the duties of secretary and housekeeper.

The position offered was not altogether suitable. Only because of her difficult situation could Bertha have reconciled herself to the category of "an equally mature lady." Moreover, she knew nothing about the duties of a secretary or those of a housekeeper. In her whole life she had held only the one position of governess in the home of the Suttners. Prior to that, she had been the fondled child of her mother and aunt.

The entire tone of the notice sounded a bit strange to Bertha. Why did the prospective employer describe himself as "a very rich, cultured, aged gentleman?" Did the gentleman want more than a secretary and household manager? To hired help, his wealth and cultured background could have no significance whatsoever. Usually, only matrimonial ads were framed in such a style.

Perhaps this was exactly what aroused Bertha's curiosity, for she wrote to the "cultured gentleman," and received an immediate answer signed by Alfred Nobel, a name that meant nothing to Bertha Kinsky. Alfred Nobel? Who was he, anyway?

Baroness von Suttner, anxious to be rid of the governess as quickly as possible, started immediate inquiries. It was easily ascertained that Alfred Nobel was a well known and extremely wealthy inventor and industrialist.

There ensued an exchange of letters that, though never found, apparently contained more than a mere discussion of the terms of employment.

Alfred Nobel, a Swede by birth and half-Russian by education, was always very generous with his employees. No doubt he offered Bertha a substantial salary, certainly much larger than what she had received from the von Suttners. Wages in German-speaking countries were traditionally low. In her memoirs Bertha did not mention the terms Nobel offered her, though she described his letters as clever, witty and in a melancholy vein. Their author seemed "unhappy and misanthropically inclined, although he had a vast cultural background and profound philosophical views."

Alfred Nobel perplexed but at the same time intrigued Bertha. She realized her own letters had a stimulating effect

95

upon him. His command of foreign languages and elegance of style amazed her, for their letters changed from French to German to English to Italian. She grew eager to meet this remarkable man, Alfred Nobel.

Alfred Nobel was always lonely. Herta Pauli justly called him "the loneliest millionaire on earth." Unquestionably, he needed a secretary and also a housekeeper, and when he sent his notice to the newspaper he may have been thinking of nothing else. However, the letter from an unexpectedly intellectual applicant must have pleased him greatly. Instead of a lady of "equal maturity" he had found a young lady, a Countess of aristocratic birth, who even had brains.

Bertha Kinsky had naturally exerted efforts to make her first letter an inviting one. She was fond of writing and wrote well.

Over many years Alfred Nobel had longed for a home and marriage. Erik Bergengren quotes Nobel in a letter to a friend: "I, like others, and perhaps more than others, feel the heavy weight of loneliness and for many a long year I have been seeking someone whose heart could find its way to mine."

He could not have found a more suitable fiancee. Bertha was still a young woman, only ten years his junior. He possessed wealth; she had a title and connections with the aristocracy in various European countries. She knew little about housekeeping but for the salon of a man such as Nobel, a better hostess could hardly have been conceived.

Bertha accepted Nobel's terms. She would come to Paris without delay. At the time, she was convinced that she must leave Baron Arthur forever. This would be the sorrowful end of her romance. Pressed by the demands of the old Baron and his mother, young Arthur had consented to give up his love and never see her again.

Bertha's memoirs describe their parting scene, which abounded in German sentiment and high tragedy. They exchanged "kisses salted with tears," and thereupon the Baron knelt before his inamorata and kissed the hem of her dress! He then uttered these words:

Incomparable lady! Lady with a heart as generous as that of a Queen! I do thank thee from the depth of my soul. Thy love revealed to me happiness which will crown my whole life! . . . Adieu!

Such high-flown phrases belonged to their times and both Bertha Kinsky and Baron Arthur probably knew their Schiller by heart.

Bertha departed for Paris. Nobel had arranged for her rooms at the Grand Hotel. The plural rooms suggested that Nobel looked upon the newcomer as no ordinary employee. She would not remain long at the hotel, as her patron had provided for her an apartment in his own house on Avenue Malakoff, that was being completely decorated.

Bertha von Suttner briefly described her impression of the inventor of dynamite at the time of her arrival in Paris: "He was neither handsome nor ugly, rather short, with a dark, full beard and kind, blue eyes." Even on their way from the station to the hotel they began discussion on cultural subjects.

On the first day Bertha lunched alone. Later Nobel called on her and took her for a drive through the Champs Elysees. Nobel also escorted her through his house. All of this indicated a special, accentuated attention on his part that could not be attributed to the title of Countess. Snobbishness was altogether alien to Nobel.

Bertha wrote her mother: "Owing to many letters which we had exchanged we did not feel as though we were strangers to each other." She was charmed by Nobel who could chat, tell stories about everything under the sun and captivate her mind. As for the ever-skeptical Nobel, her unexpected youth and beauty had taken him by surprise and no one could be more charming than he, when he wished. He was very much the man of the world.

Nobel showed Bertha his laboratory, but she failed to understand his explanation of what he was doing. In his library, she was impressed by the volumes on medicine, biology, chemistry and literature, which extended to the ceiling. She could not believe that Nobel read them all, when so many libraries in her own circle of friends and acquaintances had only a decorative function. They made a well-suited pair: on the one hand was a restless, spoiled bachelor who sought a woman to dispel his loneliness; on the other hand, a woman with expensive tastes and no money, at the low point of her life, who met a man, brilliant, cultured and owning giant wealth and power. Certainly Nobel felt the stir of romance within him, but his secretary Bertha could only mourn for her lost love, the young Arthur. She was tortured by the anguish that comes after a shattered love affair.

Alfred called on his secretary daily, though he could spend not more than two hours with her since he was always overburdened with business affairs. Bertha reported that they conversed on metaphysical subjects, considered typically Russian or Slavic.

Nobel had no confidence in people. He felt his neighbors valued him only for his immense wealth, that his real self was of no concern to them. He deemed himself a repulsive man and could not be convinced otherwise. No doubt many of his associates had intense interest in his millions; yet neither in his appearance nor in his mental make-up was there anything repulsive. Bertha Kinsky wrote of the fascinating discussions they had, termed him a brilliant reconteur.

On impulse he showed Bertha one of his poems, some hundred pages long, written in English. Its beauty and melancholy mood impressed her.

The dawn of romance could scarcely be regarded as a normal relationship between employer and employee. Perhaps this lone and unsociable Croesus, for the first time since his youth, felt the awakening of love. If so, it did not last long. Having noticed that his secretary was sad, he suddenly asked her: "Is your heart free?" She told him the story of her romance with the Austrian Baron. He approved of her behavior and advised her to cease correspondence with Arthur von Suttner. "Eventually you will forget him, while he may forget you even sooner." Did his remark hold a hint of his wishful thoughts?

In connection with business matters, Alfred Nobel was obliged to leave for Sweden. Bertha Kinsky remained in Paris. A few days later she received almost simultaneously two telegrams: one was from her employer, advising her of his return in a week; the other was from Austria. Arthur von Suttner wired that he could not live without Bertha. His desperate and yearning message was all she needed. If he could not live without her, she could not live without him, and all obstacles must be disregarded. The difference in age, the lack of money and the opposition of the young man's parents—what did all this matter?

The Nitroglycerine Company of Stockholm was opening a second factory. The invitation to attend had come to Nobel in the name of His Majesty Oscar II. No doubt Bertha knew this but Nobel would not be back for a week and she could not wait that long.

She had kept a diamond cross, the gift of her beloved, long-deceased guardian Landgrave von Furstenberg. She had always treasured this gem but now it was unimportant. She promptly sold the cross, paid her hotel bill, bought a ticket and rushed back to Vienna. "I was acting as in a dream, as though under irresistible compulsion," her memoirs say. Mere politeness required that a secretary await the return of her employer, even though no important business had been entrusted to her. But simple courtesy did not enter her thoughts at the time. However Alfred Nobel must have felt upon his return to Paris, he could not have overlooked her rude treatment of his kindness. Bertha Kinsky was not a girl of seventeen whose erratic behavior might be understood and condoned. Probably the misanthropic Alfred merely sighed and once more confirmed his conviction that there is nothing to be expected from human beings.

In Vienna, Bertha Kinsky stopped at a hotel not far from Canovagasse, where the Suttner mansion was located. Upon arrival she wrote a few lines to Arthur in a changed handscript. The note stated that a certain lady, just come from Paris, had a commission from Countess Bertha Kinsky. There was actually no necessity for alluding to a mysterious lady with a commission. But, this pretense added to the romance and both Bertha and Arthur had been reared in the traditions of sentimental and romantic literature.

Arthur rushed to his beloved and exclaimed: "Thou! Thouself!" (*Du! Du selber!*)

Both of them burst into tears as they embraced each other. They decided quickly, with the finality of enamored hearts, that they would wed secretly, without sanction from the Baron's parents, and depart.

Bertha recalled the Princess Dadiani, that Russo-Mingrelian lady who had shown her so much kindness in days past. Dedopali would surely help them. She would take the lovers under her wing and in Russia she was all-powerful. She would secure Arthur a good position at the Russian Court, or, at the very least, in the Russian Civil Service. After the wedding they would escape to Russia and find the good Dedopali! Arthur consented, undoubtedly knowing nothing about the Princess Dadiani. They wed secretly in a remote little church on June 12, 1876, and dispatched a telegram to Dedopali. From a social standpoint, the marriage of an over thirty-year-old spinster to a penniless young man, very much her junior, might raise the arching brows of sly Russian society gossips. Dedopali ignored that element and in answer to Bertha's plea, sent this laconic telegram: "Do come." Arthur arranged for passports, visas, tickets and they were on their way.

The Princess Dadiani lived in the Caucasus, either in the Mingrelian capital, Zugdidi, or at her summer residence in Gordi. She lived more than comfortably; but she had no palaces at either her winter or summer "residences"; her mode of living was like that of the wealthy aristocrats in Russia who were not descendants of the ruling houses.

The Princess Dadiana in fact exercised no political authority whatsoever. The Mingrelian princes were nothing more than prominent, wealthy people residing within the borders of the vast and mighty Russian Empire.

Bertha also had overestimated the Princess' fortune. In Russia, there were scores of families far wealthier; the Youssoupoffs and Stroganoffs, the Branitzkys and Sheremeteffs, owned immense treasures which would have even amazed Americans. The Dadianis, on the other hand, were merely well-to-do people. Some ten years before, when the daughter of Princess Dadiani married the French Prince Murat she received a large, but by no means extravagant, dowry.

The von Suttners hopes that Dedopali would procure for Arthur a court position, were naive in the extreme. Court titles in Russia carried with them no pecuniary remuneration; they were conferred with discrimination and Princess Mingrelsky had no part whatsoever in their bestowal. In a great and hospitable country, it might have been possible to find some second-rate position in civil service, but to fill this, a man would need a fair knowledge of the Russian language. Even then, it would have been only a minor post with a nominal salary. The von Suttners learned all this very soon.

After their wedding they sailed for Russia. Hundreds and thousands had migrated to that mysterious land on schooners (later by steamer), in carriages, on sledges and in tilt-carts—all people who, for some reason or another, had not met with success in western Europe. Driven by the same impulse, forty years before, Immanuel Nobel, the father of Bertha's week-long employer, Alfred Nobel, departed for

Russia, a country about which he knew next to nothing and without being able to speak one Russian word. He had never regretted his decision.

The Suttners, too, despite the chimerical character of their hopes, never regretted their voyage to the half-fabulous realm. It was their honeymoon, a somewhat prolonged honeymoon, for they remained in Russia nine years. They were happy—happy as Bertha had never been before. What did they care whether or not they succeeded in obtaining a court position? They loved each other passionately and nothing else mattered.

They sailed for the Caucasus via the Black Sea. Now if in some respects Russia is a wonderland, the Caucasus is the most wondrous part of Russia.

As they disembarked on the Caucasion coast, they were met by an emissary of Princess Dadiani, dressed in a national uniform. He could speak a few French words, and asked the guests to wait a while on the coast because Dedopali was just then moving to her summer residence. This made no difference to Bertha; she could wait, no matter how long, since Arthur was with her.

The Princess' respresentative took them to an inn, part of which served also as a wharf. The Suttners' first impression of this strange land was not too favorable, for due to the abundant fauna of the inn, they were obliged to spend the night on chairs. A wash basin, not to speak of a bath tub, was considered a wholly unnecessary luxury.

Fortunately, they were soon able to leave for Kutais, a town which was more or less civilized. The Princess had sent word to her friend, General Tzereteli, about the arrival of the young foreigners. Tzereteli was also a prominent Georgian. Caucasian aristocracy—the Princess Gruzinsky, Mingelsky, Tzerteli, Orbeliani, Chavchavadze, and others—at that time constituted a peculiar and picturesque little circle. Russia has always been famous for her hospitality, but nowhere was it as lavish as in the Caucasus.

Immediately after the Suttner's arrival, Tzerteli gave a dinner in their honor. The young Viennese couple plunged with delight into a world where everything was so gay, so strange, and so captivating. The Kachetinsky wine (unfortunately unknown to the European and American markets) was delicious. The Caucasians once drank it from hunting horns, served by the host himself, and the quantity of wine in the horns seemed far beyond human capacity. The General's cuisine may not have been as delicately flavored as the Parisian or the Viennese, but the gastronomic part of the dinner was not all-important. The charm of the entertainment lay in the incomparable hospitality of the hosts, who only the day before knew nothing about the Suttners. Since the pair was introduced to them by Princess Dadiani, they must be treated as bosom friends; every effort had to be exerted to make their brief sojourn in Kutais as pleasant as possible.

After dinner, Lesginka, a graceful Caucasian dance was performed. Later, when Arthur von Suttner played Viennese waltzes, these met with enormous success. The hosts and guests alike, with enthusiastic expressions, assured the Suttners of their warm friendship.

The musical evening was followed by picnics and other diversions. The German guests wondered when these people worked, since they spent entire days giving parties to entertain their friends.

In Russia there is an old proverb: "Business is no wolf; it will not run away into the woods!" This saying can not be taken literally for in the course of their long and difficult history, the Russian people worked often and hard; in the Caucasus, too, in every field of human endeavor, creative work was in full swing. The Nobel brothers oil development in Baku almost coincided in point of time with the arrival of the Suttners in the Caucasus as guests of the Princess Dadiani.

After a few days in Kutais, the newlyweds continued their journey to Dedopali with the rosiest of expectations. If they were thus received in Kutais by people who had never known them before, what wonderful times must be in store for them at the home of the old Princess who had always shown devotion to the Kinsky family! All they wanted was to reach the Princess Dadiani, for by that time the Suttners were penniless. Their voyage to the Caucasus had been possible only because considerable money was derived from the sale of the old Landgrave's diamond cross.

Arthur, just as Bertha, had no independent fortune. His parents, angered by the secret wedding, had severed all relations with him. Bertha's mother had no funds to spare and she was by no means delighted with this marriage that her friends judged a mesalliance for her daughter.

Bertha waited a long time to hear from Alfred Nobel. When his letter finally came, it was polite and friendly. They exchanged perhaps a dozen letters during her years in the Caucasus.

Arthur corresponded with his sisters, the former charges of Bertha who remained devoted to her. His parents refused even to accept letters from him, so he could never have thought of asking them for financial assistance. All hope lay in the connections and influence of Princess Dadiani.

Sofie, the Flower Girl

Bertha's impulsive departure without even a courteous farewell had been one more of a long series of crushing blows in the life of Nobel. In this forty-third year of living, he must have reached the low point in his morale. His success in amassing a fortune could not balance the frustrations and bitterness he had endured over the past dozen years. Going back to 1863, he could still hear the spiteful laughter of his father and his two brothers, Ludwig and Robert, when the first tests of his nitroglycerin product failed to explode as he had hoped. Their derision hurt sensitive and sentimental Alfred more than even he would admit, and he never forgot it, although he was never ungenerous to them in the time that followed.

A year later, his father challenged Alfred's patent of the perfected product, and attacked his son harshly for cheating him out of credit in its invention. This—after his father had jeered at Alfred's efforts—was too much to take. Alfred refused to budge an inch in his stand of deserving full credit for the successful invention. Only Caroline, loyal wife to Immanuel and gentle mother to Alfred, was able to make an uneasy peace between the two. As always she made excuses to Alfred about his father's temper being due to his poor state of health.

The tragic death of Alfred's talented and lovable younger brother, Oscar-Emil came in the same year, 1864. Alfred accepted blame in this explosion that killed Oscar-Emil and three others, but in actuality the burden of blame should have been placed upon Immanuel, his father, for the lack of responsibility. The needless death increased his father's heart trouble and ever after haunted Alfred.

Then a great epidemic of explosions broke out over Europe and America, due to careless and faulty handling of the violent product of Alfred's genius. Each death-dealing eruption staggered him. His hopes of having created a valuable tool for construction and usefulness to the world were buried in the knowledge that his invention had become a deadly instrument.

In 1867 Alfred obtained patents on his perfection of the new product he named dynamite. He felt deep pride in the gold medal given him by the Swedish Academy of Science for this discovery. The medal came jointly to him and his father, for Alfred gave his father full credit for the foundation work that underlay Alfred's later experimentation for dynamite. However, Immanuel kept the medal for himself, exhibited it in a glass case in his living room. A bitter thing for Alfred, the truly creative man, to see.

Immanuel Nobel died on September 3, 1872, the eighth anniversary of the death of Oscar-Emil. Alfred did not claim the medal in its glass case until the death of his mother twenty-two years later.

The success of his business interests brought out the worst in some of the most brilliant and trusted men he employed. There was the duplicity of Colonel Shaffner in New Jersey, the high-handedness of Julius Bandman in California. Another American, Carl Dittmar, attempted to prove that he, not Alfred Nobel, had invented dynamite. It would not have been strange if Alfred had found it difficult to put trust into any untried person again.

But he had trusted Bertha Kinsky, implicitly. He felt she embodied the finest qualities of womanhood. He even shared his intimate poetical thoughts with this beautiful, charming, and brilliant woman. Surely, Bertha's unceremonious leave-taking came as the greatest disappointment of all to Alfred Nobel.

At this time Alfred's brothers urged him to come to Petersburg to look over their newly acquired oil holdings. Alfred refused to go to Russia, so Ludwig made plans to meet him in Paris. Alfred knew they needed funds for investment in the oil distilling and refining plants they were undertaking. He hoped this business interest would set Robert on his feet financially, for Robert had as yet gained no real security for himself.

Alfred made his way back to Paris after a business meeting in Pressburg, and decided to stop in Baden, the spa just south of Vienna, for the week-end. He enjoyed Baden for its simple, old-fashioned ways, and its pungent sulphur waters had always proved beneficial to him. Also, since it was not considered a stylish watering place, he did not find there the ever-complaining, overfed rich whose aging years were spent in flocking from one smart spa to another.

En route to luncheon with a business acquaintance, Alfred entered a small but pleasant florist shop to buy a bouquet for his hostess. The shop was fragrant, alive with the sparkling colors of fresh blossoms, and a young and pretty girl waited upon him with earnest attention. He could not help but watch the girl's slender body move among roses and carnations and lilies in their water-filled stands. She looked like a graceful child in a garden of flowers.

The girl inquired about the lady for whom Alfred intended the bouquet. Was she married? Her home? Her age? Then he saw the girl-child's brows knit in distracted fashion above her eyes. They were arresting eyes, big and glorious in their gray-blue color, set far apart and shaped as if they wished to match the lines of her arching brows over them. Eyes you could write poetry about, Alfred thought, as the girl hid them under a curving sweep of lashes to shut out the directness of his gaze.

107

Not only her eyes deserved poetry. Something about her glossy black hair, parted in the middle of her child-head and swept down into gleaming ringlets at her neck, and something about her soft red lips that smiled at him reminded Alfred of his mother. The delicacy of the girl, the thoughtful attention she gave him, her walk that bore her in gliding grace about the store without any of that bouncy trot of most women he saw—all these were like his mother when she had been young.

When the girl's tapered fingers selected and prepared a sheaf of fragrant pink roses for his luncheon hostess, he suddenly leaned close to her and asked if he might drop by after his engagement to take her for a ride.

Her cheeks flushed; her blue-gray eyes opened in sweet surprise; the little hands flew to her face; and she stared into Alfred's face. Of course, she would be pleased to go driving with him.

So began the love affair of Sofie Hess and Alfred Nobel, the only serious love affair of Nobel's life.

The fiacre, a shiny new one drawn by a fine white horse, spun out of Baden's flower-decked square into the quiet woods. Alfred hailed the high-hatted driver to slow his speed, as they entered the rich greens of the forest park. Pines, beeches, oaks, an occasional linden tree edged the road, and Alfred settled into the comfortable seat of the carriage. Nature's growing things always soothed his anxieties and rested his nerves.

His slender girl companion had no eyes for the delights of the countryside. Sofie Hess centered her attention upon this well-dressed, soft-spoken gentleman who so unexpectedly had asked her to drive with him.

Sofie made a charming picture, perched on the silken seat of the fiacre. She wore the simple clothes of the usual shop girl, but Alfred thought they became her. Her full skirt of indigo clasped her tiny waist, and the white garibaldi blouse fastened at her throat in a narrow collar. Embroidery work of bright colors adorned the shoulders and cuffs of her blouse.

Then, she had wound a length of white tulle about her glossy black hair. Alfred knew she must have cut it from the florist shop's display materials, but it added a dramatic touch to her attire. The girl had natural style, he realized, even though she had no money to indulge it.

Sofie's conversation amused him. She was bent on discovering her middle-aged escort's position in life and what he did for a living. He did not discourage her questioning; was he a merchant, a hotel owner, a musician? Her voice pleased him. It was young with a vague, dreamy quality. A completely impractical voice, he decided—the voice of an untutored innocent.

Finally, he answered her questioning about his business with the declaration that he was the inventor of materials that killed the greatest number of people in the shortest amount of time with the least amount of exertion.

He said this with some bitterness, but he laughed when she remarked gravely that he must be a wealthy man.

Next she asked him forthrightly if he were married. At his "No," she smiled in satisfaction.

They drove through endless trees and meadows, past silvery streams where birds sang and dipped into the water. Sofie told him of herself in an unaffected way. She had taken the job in the florist's shop to help out the family's scanty income. Her father made a bare living in his confection shop on the Praterstrasse of Vienna. A well-to-do relative of his delivered the confections to the shop to be sold, so there was not much profit in that kind of an arrangement.

Her step-mother did well at stretching the small budget to keep up their cramped home and feed her four daughters. Sofie, the eldest girl, worked so they would have clothes to cover them all.

Alfred questioned her adroitly. Her father? He rarely spoke, even when a customer queried him, unless it was to give his gloomy forecasts of the downfall of the nation, the collapse of business, or the uselessness of women. Her mother? *Mutter* and the four daughters clung together, made ends meet in any way they could. Sofie's suitors? *Mutter* wouldn't permit Sofie to be courted by the common, stupid neighborhood men. Sofie was to learn to be a lady, so she would attract a man who would give her a better life than *Mutter* had.

Her sisters? Three pleasant girls, Sofie said. All good girls and hard working; it was a pity not one of them had looks. As she answered Alfred's questions, she looked up into his face. Her eyes were limpid and the blue-gray of the sky; her face without a trace of guile. The sun shining through the tree tops flecked the ivory paleness of her cheeks with bits of golden light, and her soft lips parted in a smile.

What a lovely child this Sofie was, Alfred thought. So sweet, so unaware of the snares that could entrap her in the cruel and sensual world about her. She wanted to improve herself, she had said. What a perfect creature she would be with education and culture added to her exquisite beauty.

As they drove back into Baden, he found himself conjecturing. Suppose he subsidized her, gave her a chance to get away from the sordidness of her home and surroundings. It didn't take a clever man to piece together what she had said, and to know her mother hoped the girl's unusual attractions of face and figure would lead her into a liaison with a man, any man as long as he was wealthy and generous.

Alfred bade Sofie goodnight at the door of the tumble-down old house where she had taken a room in order to be near her job. Her family lived in Vienna, too far away to visit except sometimes on a Sunday. He told her that he must catch a train back to Paris the next day to attend urgent business.

When her lips drooped and she turned a disappointed face away from him, he lifted her chin with gentle fingers to watch happiness again light up her glorious eyes. However, he said, he would drop into the florist's shop before noon, and he would have time to take her shopping.

True to his promise, he escorted her to his jeweler's the next day and she selected the most beautiful bracelet in the shop. He took a kind of pride in knowing the girl had good taste. When he paid for the fine jeweled bracelet, he smiled to himself. It was also the most expensive bracelet in the shop.

While Alfred relaxed on the train ride to Paris, reading and musing on the passing scenery, he would never have believed the excitement brought into the Hess household by his gift to Sofie.

The girl's delight over the jeweled bracelet was too great for her to consider returning to her salesgirl position that afternoon. Without a thought for her florist employer, she roamed Baden's busy squares until she found a carriage en route to Vienna. Pleading the imminent death of her mother, even managing to shed a few tears along with her sad story, she was granted a lift to Vienna by the wealthy passengers of the carriage. How she kept her doleful manner through-out the drive was proof of her histrionic ability, for Sofie was a born actress. Actually she saw only one thing the entire way to Vienna and that was the fine gold bracelet that clasped her wrist. Frequently she moved her hand so she would catch glints of light on its embellishments of gem stones. It was hers and she had never before owned even a cheap imitation of precious stones. She couldn't believe her luck.

When at last she reached home, she opened the creaking door and aroused the household with cries of greeting that brought her mother and sisters to her in alarm. But her radiant face told them she was not ill, not even upset. She threw herself into her mother's arms holding up the bracelet for all of them to see.

"*Schön, schön,*" they said in unison, but they could not believe the stones were real.

Sofie told her story. Sitting beside her mother on the threadbare loveseat in their parlor with the three sharp-featured, pale-eyed sisters clustered at her feet, she told them about Alfred Nobel; of how he came into the shop yesterday like an ordinary man, though Sofie saw at once that his clothes were of the most expensive materials; of how his voice sounded like the deep elegant voice of a nobleman; of how he asked her to drive with him that afternoon and then to shop at noon today.

Frau Hess's perturbed expression changed to one of pleasure, when Sofie repeated her conversation with the owner of the florist shop. Sofie had asked her employer if he knew anything about a man named Alfred Nobel. The florist replied that Alfred Nobel was a brilliant inventor, worth a fortune. This news was all any designing mother could wish and Frau Hess took charge of the situation at once.

Did Herr Nobel say he would see Sofie again? Oh, yes, Sofie assured her. He would be back in two weeks and he said he would come to the shop to see her. "Lovely child," he had called Sofie.

Frau Hess quickly dispersed the three younger daughters on errands and chores. She closed the parlor door, and proceeded to give Sofie a heart-to-heart talk on the facts of life, as Frau Hess had gleaned them from her fascinated study of the easy morals of rich and noble court figures.

Sofie must keep herself well groomed and delectable at all times. Her lovely hair must be fresh-washed and shining; her body bathed in scented soaps. *Mutter* had a little money put by, unknown to *Vader*, and she would buy Sofie sweet smelling soap, a good hairbrush and new shoes for her pretty little feet. Men always admired small and pretty feet.

So this man of wealth and substance had called Sofie a "lovely child"? That name must be the clue for the manners she would adopt to please the man. She must be ever-admiring, wide-eyed with wonder over whatever he did to please Sofie. But, helpless and soft and too innocent to fight her own way in this harsh world.

She must ask the gentleman's advice on how to improve her lot; seek his advice on the simplest thing, for whenever a man gives advice, he feels in debt to the one he advised.

Sofie must be grateful for all he does. Talk only when he urges her to talk. Listen to everything he says, whether it interests her or not. Ask him often what he means, for when a man is urged to explain his thoughts or ideas, this becomes the subtlest form of flattery.

"But he is old," Sofie objected. "He is older than *Vader*."

"He is rich," her mother rejoined tartly. "What more do you want? It is better to use your head than your heart any day."

No new clothes for Sofie. Far better that she be beautiful and desirable in her simple shopgirl clothes, for then the man sees that she has nothing to spend. If Sofie stands entranced when a lady in a stunning gown passes her, the man will quickly get the idea and want to dress Sofie in the best. A man likes nothing more than to feel his sweetheart's beauty is enhanced by his own selection of her pretty clothes. Except the shoes, Sofie and *Mutter* would walk down the street to the cobbler at once and put soft and well-fitting kidskin shoes upon Sofie's dainty feet.

"Like mother, like daughter," the old saying goes, and in the case of Sofie Hess, its truth may be accepted. From the beginning of her relationship with Alfred Nobel, Sofie was clever beyond her years and experience. At eighteen she had been closely guarded by her mother whose pride in Sofie's beauty was boundless. To be sure she had gone to work in the florist shop in Baden, but Frau Hess knew that Baden attracted the wealthy by its waters and charms. Frau Hess also knew that a bunch of flowers for sale on a street corner might be bought by a poor man, but only the well-to-do entered a florist shop and selected hothouse blossoms. The position of salesgirl for the florist was not a bad one, if the girl was to catch the attention of a wealthy patron.

Sofie had been well trained to become a rich man's mistress, but not even her mother could have hoped for such good fortune as Sofie's winning of the world-known financier, Alfred Nobel, for her protector.

Before developing further this astonishing involvement of the distinguished Alfred Nobel and the little nobody, Sofie Hess, it is well to consider the background of the girl. Frau Hess had coddled and flattered her step-daughter with the lovely face and exquisite body from babyhood. As the three younger daughters were born, homely and awkward, the chores of keeping up the home and garden fell upon them.

Sofie was the lady, the peeress of this lower class family. Constantly reminded of her charming gifts by mother and sisters, it is no wonder that she moved with a presence of grace and confidence. Her hands, spared of all labor, were delicate and fine-skinned; her face alive with happiness and dreams; herself blessed with the kind of magnetism that comes to those who are sure of their own excellence.

Sofie could have looked into the face of anyone, even that of the Emperor Franz Josef, with a clear and self-reliant gaze in her wonderful eyes. She knew with certainty that she made a lovely picture in those eyes viewing her and that they held for her masculine admiration or feminine envy.

There had been no need in these eighteen years of Sofie's life for her to be anything but beautiful in her appearance and charming in her manner. She had no desire to be anything more than that. To spend time in study or in reading anything but the frothiest of romantic novels would have bored her, so Sofie never studied or read for information.

What is more she had no intention of ever doing so. She liked herself exactly as she was.

Could such a creature bring anything of happiness to Alfred Nobel?

He thought so. At first, he saw her whenever business necessitated a trip to Vienna. He found Sofie interested him, not in the trivialities and ignorance of her conversation, but in her pleasure in simple things that were commonplace to him. To dine in a good, quasi-fashionable restaurant delighted her. To enter a shop of elegance and be fitted to a gown of handsome materials and recent style put her into a trance of pleasure.

Alfred's generous heart opened to this lovely child. When he agreed to accompany her on a visit with her family in Vienna, he became convinced that all the commonness in the girl came from the appalling circumstances of her birth and rearing. He determined to give her a chance to raise herself above such vulgarity. He leased an apartment in Vienna for Sofie, bade her give up her job, and established a bank account in her name. At the same time, he made clear to her his hope that she would study and educate herself to appreciation of cultural interests and the arts.

Herr Hess, Sofie's father, had impressed Alfred as a man of good enough looks and considerable dignity, but the man's morose outlook on life depressed all about him and had created his own failures. Alfred considered Sofie's stepmother utterly lacking in taste or quality. Frau Hess fooled him not at all with her silly pretentions and flattery. He disliked the strong influence she had over Sofie and hoped that the girl would rid herself of it.

The three homely younger sisters of Sofie deserved only pity. She had so outshone them in every way and had so deprived them of the mother's affection, that the girls would become even more shy and more colorless year by year. This would be their fate, unless he could help them by removing

115

Sofie from the home nest and the mother's clucking and cooing.

So the lovely Sofie was settled in her own apartment with money at hand to begin a new life. Whether Sofie did or did not begin a tutoring schedule is unknown, but she did become a ward of Alfred Nobel. He regarded her much as a generous man of middle years might regard a very young and very poor and very remote niece.

If a citizen of this opulent period in Vienna had happened to be strolling up the Praterstrasse on one of those fine bright days for which Vienna was famous, he might have been amused at the spectacle of Sofie and her entourage. Sofie cut a stunning figure in her shopping costume of the day. Her bodice and full skirted gown of violet and blue plaid taffeta boasted a redingote of sky-blue flannel with gold-braided designs. This fashionable braiding edged the figure-fitting flow of the redingote and its bell-shaped sleeves. Her glossy black curls fell down over her ears and neck under the curling brim of a ribbon-trimmed hat, and she carried a frivolous parasol of sky-blue silk with a bobbing fringe of violet around it.

No man she passed on the street could resist the impulse to turn and stare after this delicious young lady, and Sofie knew well that the company of one, or two, or even at times all three of her sisters had safeguard value. Also, the thin-faced, beak-nosed, shabbily dressed sisters made her own beauty the more startling by contrast.

But Sofie would often have been lonely without her sisters. One of them, at least, was always ready to attend her for a shopping tour, or an afternoon at the park concert, or a walk past the magnificent palaces of royalty.

Sofie Hess was not satisfied however with her leisure time and her bank allowance and her apartment, a luxurious living to a girl reared with only the simplest necessities. Sofie knew Alfred felt only a detached kind of affection for her.

When he came to the apartment, he inquired about her family, her health, her activities, with the formality of a not too close family friend. He sometimes chided her for not making better use of her time, but excused her by expressing himself willing to allow her a period of rest and recuperation from her duties in the florist shop. Nevertheless, he reminded her that he expected her to work at her studies very soon now.

Ever since her adolescent years, Sofie had dreamed of a rich, good-looking youth who would fall madly in love with her, would fill her ears and woo her heart with words of worshipping love. Instead she sat on a stool at the side of a man older than her father who had so much wealth that it was impossible for her to comprehend its extent. The man talked to her of books, of the arts, of travel, of deep thoughts she didn't even attempt to understand. His voice was musical and he used fine-sounding words she admired, even if she didn't know what they meant.

He would stroke her hair and say that it shown like polished ebony. He would hold her hands in his and praise the grace and delicacy of them. He would touch his lips to her forehead when he left the apartment and call her his "lovely little maiden," or his "charming child."

But none of this meant he loved her, not as man loves woman, and Sofie knew it. She became consumed with fear that she would lose the protection of this generous man. She feared he would weary of her, become bored in her company, for Sofie was not so stupid but that she realized Herr Nobel's energetic mind and limited free time required more than a beautiful face to become close to him. She had no culture and the very thought of study made her squirm.

She had something else to give Alfred, something better than intellectual companionship to her way of thinking. She had the gift that most men would have demanded before considering the establishment of her in an apartment. She had herself and it was a strongly sexual self. Her dreams of sex fantasies, her own easily aroused, but thus far frustrated, sexual longings gave her confidence that she could hold a man for as long as she wished to intrigue him. She had none of the prissy apprehensions and restraints that she saw in so many lower class girls who sought marriage. Sofie was blessed with the grand passions of a born courtesan and she knew it.

She conjectured shrewdly that Alfred knew little of love and women in spite of his 43 years and his world travel. He respected women too much to have experienced many affairs and he told her he had never thought of marriage; that he had lived too busy and too involved a life to think of settling down before his own hearthstone. She showed even more shrewdness in her conjecture that Alfred, an affectionate man by nature, had become more frustrated and more lonely with each year that he forced his emotions into the molds of work and experiment and expansion of his holdings. If once she could release the throttled passion in this man, she knew she could chain him to her by her compelling sexuality.

Aside from her speculations about Alfred and her hope of keeping him enthralled with her, she felt a sincere affection for the man. His expensive and immaculate dress pleased her, the elegance of his bearing and speech intrigued her, and the profundity of his mind impressed her even though she couldn't keep up with it. He could have had her in his arms at any time during these weeks in Vienna. The very fact that he made no move to do so made her the more determined to win him in her own way.

Now, a new business began to absorb Alfred's organizational genius. It was the oil business in Baku that Ludwig had come from Russia to discuss with Alfred. Both brothers, Ludwig and Robert, hoped not only for the investment of Alfred's money, but also for his interest and advice. Their hopes were more than fulfilled. Alfred became a vital part of the organization and for a while he saw Sofie seldom.

He wrote her proper letters of the doting old uncle type:

My dear sweet little child:
It is now past midnight, the third directorial meeting has just ended. It is still the old story you know about that keeps us deliberating. To-morrow I'll go over to Pressburg where my presence is necessary. In fact, I ought to stay here because things are badly neglected, but I won't. It is repugnant to me. And I don't like to be in the company of these gentlemen. I long to be back with you. I'll write or wire as soon as I know when and where we shall meet. Until then I send you a thousand hearty regards and best wishes.

Your very affectionate friend
A.N.

On his next visit with Sofie, she broke into hysterical weeping and refused to be consoled. He begged her to tell him what troubled her and she confided her fear that he did not love her enough to do more than drop in on her for duty calls when business brought him to Vienna.

Alfred took the girl into his arms, kissed away her tears, and assured her that he would try to save more time for her, that he would take her out to dine, to attend concerts and to see some social life of gay Vienna.

But, Sofie sobbed, he could never find time to come to Vienna often. Why not move her to Paris where she would have to learn French in order to get around, and could absorb the gentilities and arts of France? Alfred agreed to this plan and was so overwhelmed by her lingering kisses and her delighted reaction to his promise to find her a Parisian apartment that he left that evening with a far different feeling for Sofie.

At once Nobel commissioned a real estate representative to lease a furnished apartment for his pseudo-niece. Delightful rooms, elegantly furnished, were available on Avenue Hugo only a short distance from the Nobel mansion. Alfred signed for them, and hired a cook and a maid to wait upon the dainty girl who would occupy the rooms. He also checked upon possible companions to teach Sofie French and show her Paris, but left the final choice for her to make.

The day arrived when he filled the rooms with flowers and hastened to meet Sofie's train from Vienna. He could not have avoided the memory of how he met the Orient Express for the arrival of Bertha Kinsky, now Bertha von Suttner.

The train pulled in and the girl came to him, as shy and unsure of herself as Bertha had been poised and gracious in manner.

Alfred put Sofie at her ease. While they drove to the Avenue Hugo, he teased her by avoiding her eager questions as to where he was taking her.

Upon reaching the apartment, she wandered about exulting over the damask furniture, the velvet hangings, the silken puff upon her bed. It was all a dream, too good and too wonderful for belief.

After Sofie came to Paris, a change in the nature of Alfred's correspondence intimates a change in the nature of their relationship. The tone of his letter writing became more affectionate and the use of terms of endearment became more frequent.

The letter Sofie received from Ardair, Scotland, held its ambiguities, but Sofie was pleased with it. She was sure of her power.

Dear little Sofie:
I am sitting in this corner, the wind howls from all directions and my thoughts revive the pleasant time we had in Paris. How are you, dear little child, far away from your Brummbär? Does your imagination spin the thread of the future or does your young soul linger over the treasury of memories? Or perhaps the delight of the present keeps your days in its charm? In vain I try to solve this riddle. But I whisper to you from this distant land my heart felt wish that you be well.
Goodnight,
Alfred.

The von Suttners
and Princess Dadiani

Young Baron Arthur von Suttner and his "passionately beloved angel," Bertha had reached their destination, Mingrelia. There the Princess Dadiani had welcomed them affectionately, but she could not help them to wealth and position. The von Suttners learned a new and extraordinary way of life.

Mingrelia was in the Kutais region of Georgia (Caucasus); a savage, seductive land, it lured all comers to throw cares to the wind, to taste of its voluptuous adventures and join in the plaintive songs of Georgia to the accompaniment of *tar* and *zurna*.

The people had a curious gift: they could spend days and nights drinking and dancing, yet appear fresh and neat. Under countless lighted wax candles, after many slim-shouldered, gold foil covered bottles of champagne lay empty, the cadence of the *Lesghinka* would increase and the tempo would gain speed. The effect it produced on its listeners was astounding. Their dull eyes would sparkle and a kind of intoxication seized them. It acted like hypnotism. They joined in the revelry.

Mingrelians were originally Orientals. Related to the Georgians, they shared their language and physical beauty. They had hair as black as midnight and lustrous dark, large eyes. One evidence of Orientalism was the position of their women who remained, for the most part, secluded.

The nobles and tribesmen in their soft leather boots

moved catlike; young or old wore a tight belt with a gold or silver-encrusted dagger.

Since 1864 Mingrelia had been under Russian Protection. The Dedopali received the von Suttners in her gracious, kindly way. She had no palace, to Bertha's disappointment, but there were several small villas scattered in a beautiful park. This seemed to be a well-settled custom in the East. Such, for instance, was the layout of Ildiz-Kiosk, the famous residence of Sultan Abdul-Hamid in Constantinople. In Ildiz-Kiosk there was no spacious mansion with hundreds of rooms crowned by spires and minarets to term palace, but there, too, was a beautiful park with a number of villas. In one of them lived the sultan himself; another housed his harem; others his stablemen and slaves and all.

Princess Dadiani lived in her finest villa. Another, a tiny, cozy one, she placed at the disposal of the newlyweds. The day of their arrival, on the verandah of the old Princess' villa, a dinner was served to thirty persons. The old Kachetsinky wine flowed in profusion. Again the *Lesghinka* was performed. And once more, to the delight of the audience, Arthur von Suttner played Viennese waltzes. All this was staged against the magnificent setting of the Caucasus, with its beautiful landscapes. The feast was a joyous occasion; the Suttners felt supremely happy. Bertha said she was so happy that she pitied all other people because they were not as content as she.

However, it became at once clear that both Court and civil service positions were out of the question. The Princess Dadiani's eyes must have reflected amazement when she heard of the plan conceived by the Suttners. In days past, she had probably had no idea about their limited finances. She was quite taken with the young couple and sincere in her desire to help them. At first, friendly loans were extended them, but the young Suttners did not belong to that breed of people who are willing to live in a strange home at the expense of their hostess. They asked Dedopali not for money, but for employment.

The Suttners decided finally that they would accept any kind of employment, even though poorly paid and in no sense privileged. They began to give French and German lessons, also piano and singing instruction. This brought in little revenue, but fortunately living in the Caucasus was cheap. The poverty of the Suttners in no way changed the attitude of Dedopali and the Caucasion aristocracy towards them; everywhere they were regarded as equals and, in many homes, as close friends.

In April 1877, war broke out between Russia and Turkey, a war for the liberation of the Slavs. A wave of patriotic enthusiasm swept Russian society.

In the Caucasus there were but few Slavs, since the local population was largely made up of Mohammedans who naturally were supposed to be pro-Turkish. So it seemed Slavophile ideas could not become popular there. Strangely enough, the wave of Moscow patriotism affected also the Caucasus. Not only was there no uprising, as had been feared by the authorities, but even a large portion of Caucasion society took active part in aiding the Russian army in the Balkans.

The Suttners fell under this spell since they had developed into great Russophiles. The newlyweds offered the government their services for work at the front, he as a hospital attendant and she as a nurse. They insisted only on the condition, for separation would have been unbearable to this devoted couple, that they be assigned to the same hospital.

This condition, for practical reasons, could not be accepted by the authorities, and they were not sent to the front. Bertha's subsequent activity as a famous pacifist made her desire to serve in this war seem incongruous, but in 1877, Bertha was still convinced that there was such a thing as a just war, in which the belligerent defending the right cause must be helped.

A day came when the idea occurred to Baron Arthur that he might write a newspaper article on the events and moods prevailing in the Caucasus. He wrote the article and sent it to the Vienna daily, *Neue Freie Presse*. It was accepted and printed. The *Neue Freie Presse*, in those days one of the leading European newspapers, kept close track of events in Russia, but had no correspondent in the Caucasus. That region with its unexpected zeal for helping in the war, obviously held a special interest for the Austrian public. Several more articles written by Arthur on this subject appeared in the paper, then he received only rejections. He concluded that the *Neue Freie Presse* had taken sides with the Turks and no longer sympathized with the ideas of the young von Suttner.

However, the publication of Arthur's articles in one of the most famous European papers created an important new field of activity for the Suttners. The first, and most difficult step in a literary career had been taken by Arthur, and taken successfully. He wondered if it might not be a good thing to devote himself to literary work. At first, this thought amazed not so much Arthur as his wife.

Bertha Suttner was a highly educated woman. She had read extensively. She was familar with German literature and knew Teutonic writers well, besides Goethe and Schiller in particular, since those two literary masters were obligatory reading for every German. With her facility in foreign languages, Bertha knew also most of the works in French and English literature that, though not necessarily classics, had a vogue in those days. She had even read some Russian authors, in the original Russian, for their long sojourn in the Caucasus had given the Suttners command of the language. Bertha often quoted her favorite, Tolstoy.

For a woman of her time, Bertha had extraordinary gifts.

She studied Darwin, Spencer and Haeckel. Though in her later years Bertha gave herself heart and soul to politics, or at least to pacifism, during the first part of her life she took no interest whatsoever in either social or political problems. In these fields she formed no opinions of her own. Among the members of the Kinsky and Furstenberg families, it was traditional to adore the Hapsburg Empire, Franz-Joseph and Radetsky, and accordingly she complied. In the entourage of Princess Dadiani it was modish to applaud the liberation of the Slavs and to hate the Turks. Bertha von Suttner, almost automatically, embraced these views too.

She was endowed with literary talent. She wrote with simple style and knew how to express her thoughts without attempting to dazzle the reader with a display of doubtful wit and dubious wisdom. She refused to borrow Freud's statements that had come into continental writing fashion then, or theories derived from naturalism, or any ideas pilfered from Dostoevsky.

Lay Down Arms, the novel which brought Bertha world fame, was conceived directly from Bertha's own overflowing heart and knowledge.

In her time, Max Nordau reigned supreme in Vienna as the author of *The Conventional Lies of Society, The Paradoxes, The Generation,* and other works; an able pamphleteer, a mordant critic, but a mediocre novelist. For a while he was extensively imitated in Austrian literature and Bertha von Suttner did not escape the Nordau vogue, so much so that one of her works, published anonymously, was ascribed by public opinion to his pen.

Bertha had all of the qualifications for becoming an authoress. Baron Arthur possessed no such gifts; at best he was a capable journalist and he never claimed to be anything else. Before his tenderly-beloved Bertha began her serious writing career, the burden of earning their common livelihood was borne by him.

He refused no kind of work. In addition to giving lessons, he wrote articles and designed cartoons for the German humorous magazines. His varying occupations brought in little money, and though living in the Caucasus was as cheap as ever, the Suttners' requirements became greater, as time went on.

A cottage sufficed for newlyweds who could visit other people's homes without the obligation of giving return receptions of their own. The Suttners however, in the eyes of their Caucasian acquaintances and friends, could no longer be regarded as a bridal pair and they now wished to return the courtesies of hospitality. Social code began to impose upon them its commonly-recognized precepts.

Baron von Suttner looked for other means of earning money. In the circle of the Caucasian aristocrats in which the Suttners moved there were many dreamers, schemers and projectors who kept busily engaged in concocting plans for making millions overnight. They were certain that they could succeed; most of them needed money badly. They had princely titles which, after the annexation of the Caucasus, were recognized by the Russian Government. But no one could live on a title; and the estates of these Caucasian princes were either small or not productive. They understood next to nothing about business. Arthur von Suttner became active in deliberations concerning their chimerical projects. At these conferences he acted as a representative of European business experience, though his experience, coupled with the business ideas of the Caucasian princes, was in no sense a promising combination.

As an exception, one of Arthur's friends succeeded in establishing a modest enterprise by organizing a factory for the manufacture of wallpaper. He offered the Baron a dual position of designer and bookkeeper. The work demanded that Arthur rise every morning at five o'clock, but he earned one hundred and fifty rubles a month, a good salary for the time. The Suttners decided they need no longer undergo the drudgery of giving music and language lessons and, at last, Bertha fulfilled her dream; she started to write.

She wrote first a short sketch *Fans and Aprons*, and sent it to the same *Neue Freie Presse* where her husband had made his literary debut. The article was accepted and she received an honorarium of twenty guldens. Bertha knew the delight of her first printed article and her first honorarium. It seemed like being transported to heaven to see those lines she had copied several times in her precise handwriting now neatly set up in print. She could, however, attain no personal prestige because she signed her sketch "B. Oulot."

She knew she had launched her new career when orders came to her for other articles, and also for books, which to Bertha, appealed more than journalistic items. Other published articles that reflected her diversified interests were: *The Confessions of Dora, Inventory of the Soul* and *Children of the Caucasus*. These met with modest success. Gradually she began to make a literary name for herself in the book market that guaranteed additional income and the Suttners' financial condition improved substantially.

From then on, husband and wife contributed more or less equal shares to the family budget. Baron Arthur worked hard, continually changed his professions since he would try his hand at anything. Though he had had no academic architectural training, he became an architect.

When Prince Achille Murat, the son-in-law of Dedopali, arrived in the Caucasus, the Second Empire in France had ingloriously come to an end. The Murats were descendants of the son of an innkeeper who became one of the best cavalrymen in history, a Marshall under Napoleon, and the King of Naples, so the Murats were closely linked to the Bonapartes by history and fate.

The Murats considered themselves not ordinary princes but princes of royal blood and, in the marriage of Achille Murat to the daughter of Dedopali, significance was attached to the fact that the Princes Mingrelsky were also not ordinary princes, but descendants of the potentates of Mingrelia.

Under the Third Republic there was nothing the Murats could do in France, so Prince Achille settled on the former state of his mother-in-law. In distinction from the Caucasian princes, he had some business sense, and the young Baron Suttner's honesty, diligence and industry impressed him. He offered Arthur the position of superintendent of his estate.

Literature, jounalism, business ventures, architectural pursuits—all of these combined—assured the Suttners of financial independence. They no longer needed to appeal for support to Arthur's parents, but could, without placing themselves in a humiliating position, start overtures for the "restoration of diplomatic relations." The parents gradually grew reconciled to this marriage that had proved to be extremely happy despite the difference in their ages. Bertha had become an authoress with a name; she had made no claim to their money, though her father's family was more prominent than the Suttner family. These things were taken into account. An "amnesty" was declared and a gracious invitation came to the Caucasus from the castle of the von Suttners in Austria.

By this time the young Suttners had experienced misfortunes of their own, which marred their pleasure in this foreign land. In 1882 their protectress Dedopali died. As their chief liaison with the Russo-Caucasian *beau monde* her patronage, coupled with the inherent democratism of the Russo-Caucasian people, had placed Arthur Suttner, in spite of his modest kinds of employment, as a social equal in the high circles of Caucasian society. The death of the old lady was a great loss to the Suttners.

Then Countess Kinsky died. Bertha, always deeply devoted to her improvident mother, had not seen her for eight years and now she was deprived of the opportunity of a last farewell. Both Bertha and Arthur strongly desired to return to their native land. The amnesty granted by Arthur's parents and the literary earnings of Bertha made it possible for them to leave the Caucasus. They had lived in that land nine years and dearly loved it. Nevertheless, it was not their country. They yearned to see again their fatherland.

The Villa at Bad Ischl

Alfred's love affair with Sofie Hess burned hot and flickered cold in turn over the next two years. He would return from an exhausting business trip to be revived by relaxation in Sofie's apartment. The sweetness of her manner, the naivete of her questions and her simple good humor gave no hint of her art in passionate love making. Sofie seemed to be two personalities, the sweet, passive daytime beauty, and the ardent nighttime siren. Alfred deplored her lack of ambition and abhorrence of mental exercise, but longed for the magnetism of her small perfect body in his arms whenever he was away from her.

Still he never knew whether his return would be welcomed by her loving concern and rapt kisses, or whether she would disdain his gifts and his arms with her ever-recurring complaints about his neglect of her. She begged him to allow her to stay near him during his periods of experiment. In vain, he explained that her presence was not conducive either to business or to scientific concentration. She would accept none of it.

When a persistent cough prompted her to call upon a doctor who, much taken by her fragile beauty, became overzealous in his attendance, she discovered that the way to gain Alfred's solicitous attention was to complain of poor health.

Alfred Nobel had suffered all his life with illness. Never had he known the feeling of being entirely well and strong. So he had depths of compassion for those who suffered, that a healthy man could never have. His tender care of Sofie when she kept to her bed was unfailing. He showered her with flowers and gifts, sat by her bedside and stroked her temples, or held her hand.

Within the year Sofie had begun to tire of Paris. She was bored with the teaching and admonitions of her companion, used the lady as interpreter and chaperone on shopping expeditions. Sofie had a good eye for details of costumes worn by the elegant ladies of high society, and she dressed herself with taste. She selected the finest of materials and trimmings, and, since she wore clothes with a flair, her appearance was enchanting on every occasion.

Alfred must have felt a keen distress by Sofie's failure to improve her knowledge and appreciation in any way. If he brought books to her, they lay unopened on a table in her living room. If he tried to speak French with her, she exploded with anger. When he tired of her chatter, limited to personalities and gossip, and left her abruptly, she reminded him of his actions for weeks after. The usual complaints of the bored mistress were hers: Alfred had too little time for her; the selfish man never took her anywhere; he wanted only one thing from her—sexual pleasure.

In late August of 1878, Alfred had decided he had been selfish with little Sofie. He should yield to her entreaties to join him in travel. Though on a hurried trip which had brought him business problems, he took time to mail her a note.

If you are a good girl and soon well, I will try to arrange that you accompany me on my trip to Stockholm. But only if you are in perfect health which I wish for with all my heart. Thus, dear Sofiecherl, don't worry unnecessarily but hurry to recover and make happy
Your old Brummbär.

Sofie's delight at the opportunity of travel was combined with her triumphant satisfaction at having gotten her way at last. She also was well aware that her serious-minded Alfred did not mean this invitation lightly. Alfred would not be taking her to Stockholm unless he intended to show her off to his relatives there. A man took only his intended wife into the company of his family. That was the mannerly way of the times. Sofie had a month in which to prepare herself for this auspicious journey, so she took her companion for company to Schwabach for an indefinite stay. This delightful German resort town, close to bustling Nürnberg would be the ideal spot for strengthening her physical self and adding enough courage to her mental self so that she would not dread the ordeal of impressing Alfred's family. She had heard enough about his relatives from Alfred to know that he placed great value on his mother's and brothers' judgments.

With Sofie in Schwabach, Alfred found her at a distance not easily reachable for the first time in the two years of their close relationship. He missed knowing she was safely ensconced in her apartment in Paris. Also, since she had chosen to go to a country where her native tongue was spoken, he sensed she was trying to escape, however unconsciously, the bonds of France and her complete dependence upon Alfred even for conversation. When a day passed without a letter from Sofie—sometimes they had exchanged two or three letters in one day—Alfred became disturbed. When the second day passed without word from her, he knew the bitterness of jealousy.

He could imagine how easily Sofie had found companions in the beautiful resort of Schwabach, and undoubtedly companions who were younger, more attractive than Alfred. So of course, Sofie could not take time from her round of festivities to scribble a line to poor old Brummbär, the "old gruff," she pretended to love. All she wanted from him were the always increasing amounts of money she seemed able to spend without even a thought of gratitude. His jealous fantasies kept him awake throughout the night.

If Alfred seemed to have been enduring all the thrills of passionate love, and all the exaggerated sufferings of jealousy and despair associated with adolescence, his right to them could not be denied. He was a man who had missed being a boy or an adolescent. Too early in life he had been thrust into positions of great responsibility. He had even been denied the years of schooling his older brothers had received, since he had joined the older boys in leaving school at that time to become helpers in their father's Russian factory. Only Alfred's brilliance and industry secured for him the liberal education that was his. He never felt his education was sufficient, but studied always until the last years of his life.

His youthful years were starved for love and the companions of his own age and he had sublimated his adolescent longings and desires into work. He withdrew into himself, held a morose and melancholy view of the world that surrounded him. His loneliness in youth made him a lonely man throughout his life.

But, now he had Sofie. With her away he realized that all of Sofie's shortcomings—her selfishness, pettiness, ignorance, greed—were as nothing compared to the delight she gave him. His heart ached with the thoughts of her little hands that soothed the ache in his brow, her kisses on his lips and eyes, the gift of her lovely and ever-desirous body.

Sofie had wrought chains to bind Alfred to her more closely than she had ever dreamed in those days when she was his pseudo-niece companion. Although Alfred soon realized that he had been too impulsive in offering to take Sofie to Stockholm, and although he was certain that his mother would be appalled at his considering marriage to a girl of such inferior mentality and common instincts, he could not bring himself to ask Sofie to change the plan for fear she would be cruelly hurt by the request.

If Alfred could have known Sofie's growing agitation over the prospective journey, he need not have worried. She was never so stupid as to misjudge Alfred. She had filled in any gaps in his reports of his family to her, and she was fully aware that his mother had remarkable qualities of intellect and charm and sensitivity, that Ludwig's wife was a woman of culture and warm-hearted civic activity, and that Robert's wife held an enviable position in social circles. Sofie was terrified of women, especially of women like these.

Her inherent good sense told her that she would not fit into this family group. The men worried her not at all. She could depend upon her beauty and simple charm to win men to her side, but she could not make good impressions upon women. They would look down on her for her lack of education. They could even destroy her in Alfred's eyes. Her terror made her ill.

She wrote to her mother. "Advise me," she begged. "What shall I do? How shall I conduct myself? Those Swedes won't even understand my language. They won't even care that I have made their precious Alfred happy."

Frau Hess wrote a long, detailed letter in reply. Sofie must cater to the wishes of Alfred's mother. She must wait upon Alfred, show obvious concern for his health and needs. She must speak little, only when spoken to. She must listen. She must make herself a helpful little body in the housekeeping and preparation of the food.

Sofie hated the whole idea. That she, the spoiled and pampered love of Alfred Nobel, one of the world's noted men in wealth and prestige, should have to act the part of an ingratiating child repelled her. She wouldn't do it.

Frau Hess grew wild with anxiety. She knew Sofie's stubborn will and bouts of temper. Sofie was entirely capable of ruining her present desirable situation. She was capable of throwing away all the ease and grandeur of her life, and that would include, of course, the funds she sent her mother from time to time. These monies had made life more palatable to her mother and sisters.

In a frenzy of fear, Frau Hess packed up the eldest daughter Olga, and sent her to Schwabach with instructions to quiet Sofie and put some sense into her. Frau Hess told Olga to ask Sofie if she wanted to return to the florist shop!

The sister found Sofie in bed, pale and exhausted from her emotional outbursts. She wept in Olga's arms like a heartbroken child that would not be comforted. Olga had developed into a sturdy woman of ordinary looks, but she was good-natured and kind. She dearly loved Sofie and gave her their mother's counsel along with her own sympathy and concern.

But their mother's words threw Sofie into a spasm of grief and rage. She walked the floor, looking the part of an avenging angel in her trailing blue nightrobe of sheer silk with her cloud of dark waving hair about her shoulders. She announced to Olga that she intended to escape it all—her own family, Alfred, and his idiotic idea of tucking her under his arm to pull out for display to that pack of grim relatives. Sofie would go to a new country and make a new life for herself.

Since Olga had years of familiarity with Sofie's tirades in their Vienna home, she believed that, the storm passed, her beautiful sister would again become her sweet, lovable self, and do exactly what Alfred wished her to do.

Olga left for Vienna, and Sofie went to bed. All the aches and pains imaginable, she felt sure, must have entered her body to make her so utterly miserable.

As she wept for her tragic state, Alfred's gifts began to arrive. Sofie's favored sweets, the Hungarian champagne she loved, the roses and blue delphinium that Alfred thought befitted her beauty, and the usual velvet-cased piece of jewelry that would delight her. Sofie knew the next arrival would be the man, Alfred, and she made ready for him.

A fragile figure, her great blue-gray eyes more startling than ever in the pallor of her face, Sofie lay in the huge hotel bed. Her nightrobe exposed one satin shoulder and her dark hair made a frame of splendor about her. What could Alfred have thought when he entered the room? What else, but how exquisite was the beauty of this lovely being who was his? And that she was ill made him more gentle and compassionate than ever.

When he spoke of the Stockholm journey, Sofie said she refused to go with him. His mother had insisted that Alfred must take a bride of robust health, but she, poor Sofie, was too delicate to fulfill this requirement. He should look for some strong cow of a woman. This brought Alfred to his knees with renewed assurances of his undying love and his wishes only for her recovery and well-being. The journey would be postponed for her, until such a time as she felt strong enough to undertake it.

In some magical way his assurances and ready agreement with her decision brought such a surge of health to Sofie that she was able to rise from her bed of pain, dress in her exciting new gown of gay-striped taffeta with its silk velvet mauve bodice and overdrape that enhanced her pretty bustled rear. A deep-fringed sash of mauve and a flowered bonnet completed her toilette, and the two lovers rode in fine carriage to dance at tea-time and to enjoy the night life of the resort.

The days at Schwabach were pure heaven. All cares seemed lifted from both Sofie and Alfred. The jaded business traveler found himself able to join Sofie's laughter at everything and nothing; to share her delight in the blueness of the sky, the fragrance of the flowers. The glorious green shade of the woodsy paths they walked, the solicitous service in the good restaurants where they dined, the smiling greetings of the people they met, everything was wonderful.

Never before had Sofie been so precious to him—from the moment when her eyes opened to the new day, through the leisurely pleasures of morning, of afternoon and evening, until the night gave her into Alfred's arms again. Throughout his remaining years Alfred remembered this time at Schwabach with hungering nostalgia, as a perfect time of love.

Resort life pleased Sofie. Health and amusement dominated the schedules of the days. Morals were easy and she escaped the scornful glances of virtuous middle-class conventionals. In other *milieu*, a single girl who spent money lavishly and was not a hideous cripple aroused suspicion and talk. Sofie determined to follow the pleasant and irresponsible resort life and Alfred agreed readily since he considered it of importance to her health problems. Indeed Alfred was too glad to see her vivacious and smiling again to refuse her anything. He dreaded leaving her and the tears he saw in her eyes when they parted touched him deeply.

The Nobel family reunion that year held particular satisfactions. Caroline Nobel had reached the age when each added year of her life seemed a Divine gift to her sons. The three, Robert, Ludwig and Alfred, held their mother in the greatest esteem for her still excellent judgment and impeccable taste, as well as for her loving regard and pride in them. Busy and ever ready for a congenial family gathering, Caroline had lost no part of her alert mind and optimistic philosophies.

Many times in Stockholm, Alfred sighed in relief, when he considered how impossible it would have been for Sofie to fit into his family picture. Sofie would have been made miserable within the first ten minutes of their arrival in Stockholm, and his relatives, particularly his mother, would have been even more miserable than Sofie.

He askd himself, as he had many times before and would many times after, what was it in Sofie that he clung to? Why was he loath to let her go? He determined that he must give her up, but he must do it without hurting the girl's feelings. Sofie had considerable sensitivity in spite of her selfish nature.

He wrote her:
My dear, sweet Sofiechen:
I had no letter from you yesterday and this makes me feel uneasy and anxious at this long distance from you, particularly because the sea-

son is trying on your fragile health. I hope the weather is fine over there, as even here in the North it is sunny and quite warm.

Dear child, you complain that my letters are short and reticent. You cannot understand the reason unless I tell you clearly, and I do it against my will. I have to do it, for people and especially women, are egoists who think only of themselves. But I realized in the beginning and feel and regret increasingly since, that your position in life has been wrong. Therefore, I force myself to be cold and ill-tempered towards you to prevent your affections from settling deeper roots. You may think that you love me, but what you really feel is gratitude or perhaps respect, not enough to fill the need of love in a young soul. Time will come, perhaps fairly soon, when your heart will seriously care for another man. How you would blame me then, had I enclosed you in the ties of deep and intimate love! This prospect compels my reason to restrain my emotions. My heart is not stony as you so often charge. Perhaps more than others I feel the weight of loneliness, and for many years I looked for a way to the heart of someone. But it must not be a twenty-year-old heart whose feeling of life has no connection with my own.

Your star rises on the sky of fate, mine declines. Youth lends to your hopes all colors, while the remaining colors of my hopes is but the afterglow of the evening. We thus do not fit as lovers, but we may yet become very good friends.

What I am troubled about is your future. Should you fall in love with a young man and he with you, the present wrong way of life might stand in the way of your happiness. I know you don't care a bit for what others think, and this is a blessing that spares you many a pinprick, but no one can be indifferent to it. Self-respect, without the respect of our fellowmen, is like a treasure that cannot bear the daylight. Such thoughts worry me and make me irritable in your presence, distressed at a distance. I know you are a nice, kindhearted girl, even if you have brought and still bring me trouble. I am fond of you, and think more of your happiness than of my own. My happiness! I can hardly keep from laughing, as I seem to have been created only for suffering. But life, my little child, smiles upon you as on very few. If you feel at times slightly unhappy it will shortly pass and you will be merry and cheerful again. But to be really happy, your education must be on a level with your position. Therefore you have to go to work diligently. You are still a child who does not worry about the future. Thus it will be good for you to have an old uncle to keep watch over you.

This letter of Alfred Nobel's to Sofie revealed much in the character of this complex and beset man. His strong feeling for Sofie plainly showed through his words, though he endeavored to mask his emotions under the guise of an old uncle. The sincerity of his blessing upon her falling in love with a young man must be doubted, since he could not resist the expression of his own tragic feelings: "I seem to have been created only for suffering." And indeed with the coming of a letter from Sofie the following day, that lacked the expressions of love Alfred longed for, though he would not admit this even to himself, jealousy made him fire off an angry reply:

... I see even if you don't say so, that you are having a good time and that you have other things on your mind when you write me. Sometimes one cannot find a reasonable sentence on half a page. This may be the reason why you cannot get along with Miss B. She probably sees with misgivings your too many new male acquaintances. Don't take this as a reproach. I only want a reasonable explanation for what you write me.

This will take care of the grumbling. Be careful, especially in this season, and don't let your flirting lure you into much walking and being up late at night. Do not force yourself to write me long letters, as you evidently did in your last one.

My sister-in-law has now come in with the children. I have to stop. But not before sending you a tender kiss.

Your old brooder.

P.S. I shall stay here until October 1st. My telegram address is: Grand Hotel, Stockholm. Don't forget to add my first name, for my brothers also live up here. How about your financial situation?

Upon dispatching this letter, he was overcome with the fear of losing Sofie. He couldn't bear to think of the loneliness of his life without her. Hastily he wired her to overlook these last two outpourings of bad temper, for he was sending her the assurance of his enduring love.

This pattern of decision to end his liaison with Sofie, then being struck by jealousy that brought about his abject surrender to any and all circumstances of their relationship, was repeated again and again. The pattern had its pathetic aspect for Alfred's position, since each time his surrender involved him the more deeply in Sofie's demands. He could not resist playing the benevolent genii who could grant her wishes without turning a hair.

Such was the case when Alfred returned from Stockholm to join Sofie in Schwabach, and she told him of a magnificent villa in Bad Ischl, the most famous spot in the Salzkammergut, Austria's Alpine playground.

Sofie reported that the villa had fifteen spacious rooms, could be leased fully furnished, and stood in extensive gardens. Everyone knew Emperor Franz Josef, himself, kept an estate in Ischl, so the villa must be desirable. Sofie's sister had told her about it and Sofie urged Alfred to consider how all their quarreling and disagreements came when they were apart. Problems vanished as soon as they were united, so if they could lease this fine villa in Ischl in the midst of the Alpine scenery he loved, and if he would liberate himself from the demands of business so he had time for his inventive work, they could live there happily ever after.

That Sofie Hess could undergo metamorphosis in less than three years from the simple salesgirl of a florist shop to the *grande demoiselle* who asked for a villa in Bad Ischl speaks importantly of the life Alfred had given his beautiful mistress.

Since he had first leased an apartment for her in Vienna, and established bank credit for her, she had wanted for nothing. However, her wants increased and enlarged, apace. Extravagance was born in her, for she never had to learn how to spend money. She never lived within her allowance, no matter how large it became. She roamed the shops and intimate salons of the fine *couturiers* and bought whatever caught her fancy. Alfred paid her bills without fuss, but he did not approve of wilful extravagance. It hurt his sensibilities to see his Sofie so self-indulgent and unthinking in her expenditures. He felt that purchases should be made with thought and knowledge of how best to secure the highest quality for the money.

The villa in Bad Ischl did not come under his quality classification. It was in poor repair, needed redecorating and refurnishing. The vast gardens must have been fabulously beautiful in their heyday, for blossoms were more vivid, trees, a richer green, vines, more graceful, and shrubbery, more abundant in the Salzkammergut than in any place in the world. But, now the villa stood in the center of shapeless overgrown grounds.

The forty square miles of the Salzkammergut did hold a wealth of unsurpassed beauty. Austrians had, for centuries, told the legend that God labored six days to create the world, but on the seventh day of rest he created the Salzkammergut to amuse himself. He put into it all the earthly loveliness of white-tipped mountains, wooded slopes, gem-like lakes and frothing rivers. Even the steep gabled houses with their festoons of vines over small balconies, though built by human hands, kept God's holiday mood intact in Salzkammergut.

Its reputation as Royalty's chosen place for vacationing went back a hundred and fifty years when Queen Maria Theresa built her baroque villa in the green hills of Gmunden overlooking the Traunsee. From medieval days, Gmunden had been the gateway to the great salt treasure of the area.

Energetic Maria Theresa, famed for her lavish entertaining and hospitable nature, encouraged her cronies and palace courtiers to build mansions throughout the Traun River valley that cut through the craggy mountains from Hallstatt. The queen, daughter of the last male Hapsburg heir, Emperor Charles VI, gave birth to sixteen children, and there

141

must always have been small ones playing on the shadowed esplanade and throwing pebbles into the great blue lake where swans and water birds glided on its mirrored surface.

The entrancing Marie Antoinette, youngest and favorite of the great brood of children born to Emperor Francis I, and his quite plain Queen Maria Theresa, spent glorious summers at Gmunden. The youthful princess strolled in the famous gardens, outrivalling the flowers with her startling beauty.

The Traunsee faces a chain of lakes—the Altausee, the Grundlsee, the Toplitzee, and the Kammersee—that wind through the layered mountains. Each lake seems tucked into folds of the high ranges.

The Toplitzee made the scenic background for the romantic meeting in the 1840's of the Archduke Johnson and the rose-cheeked, bright-eyed daughter of the village postmaster, Anna Plochl. She was the loveliest maiden for miles around and when the young archduke saw her make her first shy curtsey to him, he lost his heart to her. He threw his inheritance of the throne into the Toplitzee, and married Anna against the threats and pleadings of family and friends.

However the greatest glamor came to Bad Ischl in the person of Emperor Franz Josf when he was a young man. The Emperor loved two things truly throughout his life: hunting and the charming Viennese actress, Katharina Schratt. Katharina had a stately and serene loveliness, and she was a clever, cultured woman. She held the Emperor in a life-long embrace and undoubtedly influenced him more than she was ever credited.

The woods and mountains of the Salzkammergut offered unparalled hunting of chamois, boar, bear, small animals and birds, including the sporting pheasant. Franz Josef bagged more than two thousand of the fleet-footed chamois of the region during his hunting years.

The Emperor built himself an elaborate hunting lodge upon the west bank of the River Traun. Picturesque Ischl

142

became his summer capital with villas for his court, pavilions for concerts, luxury hotels for visiting nobility and wonderfully executed parks encircling it all. The Kurhaus became the most famous in all Austria through the Emperor's presence. He erected a small but exquisite villa for Frau Katharina Schratt, and almost every day he went to her villa, ever so discreetly, it was said. But that any citizen or visitor of Ischl should be left unaware of Franz Josef's trysts with Katharina was unthinkable.

Sofie had heard the court gossip and the remarks of amazement from Austrians that Katharina Schratt should be able to hold the Emperor fascinated all these years. Katharina must, after all, have endured continual competition for the favors of Franz Josef. The appeal of Ischl to Sofie for its distinctive reputation as a resort for royal romance was most understandable. Also it was the most fashionable of all the spas of Austria, Sofie's native land, and in these few years the florist's salesgirl had become a first-rate snob.

Sofie could always get her own way, though sometimes she had to wait for it. She had learned early in her affair with Alfred that the time to beseech Alfred for the thing she wanted most was to wait for the moment when he felt regret for having criticized or scolded her. One tearful look from Sofie's great blue-gray eyes would change Alfred's mood to the adoring giver of great gifts.

Back from Stockholm with Sofie in Schwabach, he agreed to lease the Ischl villa, to hire a staff of servants, and to move Sofie there with one of her sisters for company.

Sofie begged Alfred to retire from an active part in his financial empire, to concentrate on laboratory work so they could settle in Ischl and give up their wandering. When Alfred spoke of Paris and what the city meant to him, she blamed her poor health on Paris, and wept about the barrenness of her life there. She had never mastered enough French to enjoy concerts and theatre in Paris, let alone to make any friends there.

143

She understood nothing of Alfred's financial problems. She didn't want to know that his retirement was not the simple matter she fancied it. To release the network of organizations he had built up over a lifetime was not only unthinkable, but impossible; so he traveled as he always had, and chafed at his burdensome life and ineffectual experimentation.

Brummbar and the Troll

Alfred had hoped Sofie would so revel in the beauties of Bad Ischl and the spacious old villa that her aimless wanderings would cease. She was "The Troll" to him, that wanderer of Scandinavian folklore, the impish little creature that called to you from her earthy cave or rocky peak, and always wanted something. A delightful, but difficult, little imp.

It was his private name for Sofie. Even if she had heard it, she would not have known what it meant. Bergengren showed a page from the precise cashbook he kept all his life:

Hats the Troll	300.00 (francs)
Gloves me	3.75
The new horse	8,000.00 (he loved fine horses)
Flowers Madame R.	40.00 (probably a hostess)
Coat	0.25 (a tip)
Remittance Ludwig	3,000,000.00 (at Baku)
Auguste	52.00 (his valet)
Wine the Troll	600.00

A day's accounts without "The Troll" items was rare indeed.

Alfred's first two or three visits with Sofie in Ischl were glorious. They strolled through the magical glories of the parks and wooded river banks, where they could catch a glimpse of antlered *gembok*, and listen to the songs of the forest birds. They took the waters, then dropped in on Zauner, the famed *Konditor* who sent *Guglhupf* breakfast cake at 5 a.m. every morning to the Emperor's lodge. Sofie chose the *Zauner Torte*, a chocolate concoction, said to be favored by the Prince of Wales on his visits, but Alfred preferred the *Rouladen* with its sugar-encrusted wild strawberries.

Since Alfred's business kept constant demands upon his time, Sofie would not stay in Ischl without him. He should have expected this to be the case, no doubt—the wandering Troll. Again she took up her resort gadding in quest of amusements to while away her time. Alfred would write her at Carlsbad, but the letter would be undelivered, since she was en route to Weisbaden. He would arrive at Weisbaden only to find she had vacated her hotel rooms and left for another spa. Often he had to await word from her to know where she had chosen to seek excitement during the next week or so.

Their misunderstandings became worse and led to angry bickering, but the bond that held them together in spite of any kind of problem was their need for each other. Alfred, the desperately lonely man, depended upon Sofie's sweet welcome for his arrival at whatever place she was stopping for a while. He depended upon her clinging dependence, and on the aimless but good-humored chatter of this always alluring little companion.

Sofie's loneliness held the same desperation as Alfred's and she loved this distinguished and cultured man in as sincere a way as it was given to her to love. He had lifted her from a penny-pinching drab existence into a world of luxury and thrills, to be sure; but she loved him also for his tenderness and affectionate nature, for his courtly manners, for his delight in her looks and his sympathy for her illnesses and disappointments.

Though as far apart as possible in their interests and their appreciations, these two lonely souls shared the same overwhelming need for love. And in each other they had found it.

When she was distressed, Sofie sought Alfred's arms for comfort. Alfred, also, had the urgency to seek her understanding of his troubles. When beseiged by unmerited lawsuits in the early 1880's, he wrote her of his depression:

My dear, sweet darling child:
Sitting here alone, pained with disagreeable affairs, that totally wear

146

down my already tired nerves, I feel how dear you are to me. The noise of the world bothers me more than it does others, and I wish to live in a comfortable corner without great pretense but also without trouble and pain.

When these lawsuits are wound up, I am firmly resolved to retire from business life. It could certainly not be done at once, but I intend to begin with it as soon as it possibly can be done. I have terribly much to do and no time to write you in detail, my dear, sweet child. I can only express in a few words how I wish you to recover soon, and add to it a thousand heartfelt regards from your loving,

Alfred.

Then in a letter, written sometime later, from Glasgow, Scotland, Alfred revealed that he too was a creature of moods. Evidently, an embarrassing situation prompted him to write a depressed letter in which he belittled himself and put blame upon Sofie in an indirect way.

Dear little child,
I was to go to London yesterday evening but the train that brought me here from the factory was so late that I missed the connection. In this God-fearing country no trains run on Sunday, so that I am stuck in this hotel as large as the whole district of a town.
When I have to be in a gathering these days. I cannot fail to notice how my shunning society in the last year has harmed me. I feel so stupid and lost among people that I must avoid them. For my miserable kindness I probably never again in life will be able to regain my intellectual sprightliness. I don't blame you, little child, for, after all, it is my own fault and you cannot help it. Our concepts of life, of its aims, of the indispensability of mental culture, of our duties as people of higher education and position in society are so enormously different that we in vain try to understand one another. But it is painful for me to feel that my mental capacity had declined and that I emerge shamed from the circle of educated people.
Even as I write this today my heart feels sorely that I am intellectually inferior to other people. Don't be angry with me for my wailings over my bitter experience. You don't know what you have done to me when through the years you undermined my mental strength, abused my compassion and my indulgence. Unfortunately, it is true that if one withdraws from educated society and neglects the interchange of ideas with thoughtful men, he finally becomes incapable of

such interchange and loses respect for himself as well as the respect of others, which he had formerly enjoyed.

I end with a sincere wish, dear, good, sensitive Sofie, that your young life may fare better than mine and that you may never experience the feeling of debasement that embitters my life. Live happily and in peace with yourself and think now and then of your miserable and distressed friend.

Alfred.

Sofie bore his complaints without rancor. Always she teased him and tried to ease him out of his grouches. Brummbär, she had named him in the first days of their love, and Brummbär, he was always to her.

In the fall of 1880 Sofie returned to Paris, since Alfred's time became too involved with financial matters to permit visits to Ischl, or to chase her to the resort of her current choice. Isolated in Paris, she began again to pester him for permission to accompany him to his laboratory. He asked her in a note:

Can't you understand what a terrible burden it is for a very busy man to have a girl who does not know anybody and who prevents him from going his way?

Then later in this short letter, Alfred expressed his complete acceptance of Sofie just as she was:

It is all very tiresome, and I am in great need of rest. Both digestion and sleep are totally out of order, and then even other wheels stop.

I'll come very soon. Meanwhile, the little mite might be kind and wise. Wise, my Sofferl, now I have to laugh: what is sweet in you is just the absence of all reason. Vanished into thin air.

Hearty, if belated congratulations on your birthday.

A.N.

Once more Sofie journeyed between spas, Alfred catching up with her when he could. He was annoyed by her persistent restlessness:

My heart bleeds when I think that you have to drift all alone in the world. But for this you can only blame yourself. For several years, I have kept reminding you that you need a companion. Almost everything both you and I have suffered came about because you did not want to listen to me in this respect...

If you had a companion—of course a kind and reliable lady—I would not have to travel about Europe as a nurse and would probably be more with you.

When in 1883, Sofie met friends who urged her to take an apartment in Switzerland's Montreux during winter months, Alfred's letter revealed his final acceptance of her roving nature. Only a mild rebuke:

We can speak later about your intention to spend the winter in Montreux. It isn't cold here in Paris, nor will it be for some time. Isn't it ridiculous that you have an apartment here? You are away in the summer and now you do not want to come here in the winter either. But you are right. You are not for Paris, nor is Paris for you.

Why not choose a place to settle down? Montreux or any other place you like?... Don't you think that I have enough business trips to take without being burdened with roving about the continent with you? With the warmest love and many hearty kisses, your affectionately devoted,

Alfred.

As his health worsened in the middle 1880's, he wrote Sofie of his pathetic aloneness, although he obviously had given up hope of any improvement in their arrangement:

Everyone my age has the need to have someone around him to live for and to love. It was up to you to be that person, but you have done everything imaginable to make it impossible.

At a time when driven by his exasperation at Sofie's childish restlessness and claims on his time, Alfred wrote again his suggestion that she seek a young man's love:

Now, your young, tender, good soul thirsts for love and finds mine rightly too faint.... I repeat: try to win a good, simple man's honest, durable and devoted affection and a genuine family tie. , . . Your illness has probably its cause in the feeling of emptiness, unsatisfied longing of the heart, which, in your case, turns into physical illness...

He had then at least come to the decision that Sofie's illnesses had their basis in her own emotional disturbances.

149

However, his suggestion of her looking for another man to love—this time a "simple", "honest" man of her own mentality, since she spurned further education—changed at once through his burning jealousy, and he quickly contradicted his own words. He followed his accustomed pattern of relinquishing Sofie only to be devoured by jealousy that made him want to make amends to his "dear, sweet child" for his harshness.

This time his amends cost him a fortune and not a small fortune at that. He purchased the run-down Ischl villa and spent enormous sums in rehabilitating it, in replacing the furnishings with new and tasteful articles, and in surrounding it with freshly laid-out gardens. Next he equipped it with a staff of servants, but the effort of the undertaking tired him, and he wrote in desperation to Sofie:

My dear little child:
I see from your telegram that you are not yet recovered from the cure in Carlsbad I have expected. The best cure for you would be, in my opinion, to keep calm. But instead you insist on going to distant countries where I neither can nor want to accompany you. This insanity has been going on for seven years now, useless for you and exacting for me. It has embittered and wasted my life. I wish to devote my time to my work, to science, and I look upon women, all and sundry, young and old, as encroachers who steal my time....

Had you been content with a life in the country I live in, you would be all right now, and I not harrassed senselessly, which makes me a puzzle to all my friends. A past full of bitterness is between us that I could, however, forget, yet the time lost cannot be regained and this torments me day and night. But let us forget the past....

How are we going to arrange the near future? You want a villa in Ischl. Good. We buy it and then? I will be going on a voluntary Pilgrimage to Ischl as little as to hell. Olga will have to go to school next year and will be unable to keep you company. Then Ischl will no longer do for you, instead you will nag me to buy a villa in Reichenau, Villach, Gorz or Murzzuschlag—or God knows where....

As for me, I am tortured with head and stomach aches so you mustn't be astonished if I am not too spirited in this letter. I am busy late into

the night and have hardly time to send you a wire. I write these lines at 2:30 a.m., the conference lasted that long.
Be heartily and a thousand time greeted and embraced by your old friend who is sincerely sorry for you.

Alfred

Hamburg, Thursday night

The villa at Ischl had been completed—renewed, refurbished and beautified. Alfred decided that if he and Sofie were to live there, at least at intervals, he must give Sofie the protection of his name in order to avoid scandalous gossip. When they had been merely visitors to Ischl, that had been quite different from becoming residents. His motive was entirely kind and commendable to judge by his often repeated concern that, because there was a twenty-five year gap between his and Sofie's ages, he did not want his love affair with her to make it impossible for her to live a respectable life after he was gone.

Nevertheless Sofie's use of his name, which she enjoyed doing even on messages to her family, proved not to be a wise action. Alfred suffered embarrassment from the entirely understandable amazement of his friends, his business associates, and his own brothers that he could have burdened himself with an almost illiterate and obviously common woman.

The arrangement pleased Sofie greatly. She considered his permission for her use of his name presupposed marriage. Since the girl had then reached her late twenties, she could not help but acknowledge—to herself at least—that she was no longer a "dear, sweet little child," but a woman rapidly growing too old for a desirable marriage.

Her entreaties for their marriage left Alfred unmoved:

Even if one were over his head in love, your letter would affect him like a dash of icy water. One can't help being ashamed of a person who writes like this, or better, scribbles or scratches, uses another person's name and mails out her dreadful messages to the world. If

151

you have no education, dear child, you must be satisfied with a sub-
ordinate position in society and must find your happiness in it. You
keep telling me that I am not capable of loving anybody. This is
false. I could even fall in love with you if your lack of education did
not hurt me. Let me give you an example: a wife is very much in love
with her husband, but if he has the mad habit of tramping on her
corns every quarter of an hour, do you think love could survive it?
Self-respect is a thousand times more sensitive—at least to me—than
the most susceptible corn. . . .
But it makes no sense to indulge in explanations. You do not even
understand that a man can have a feeling of self-respect and dignity.
Otherwise, I think we would have agreed long ago on this point.

This letter would have perhaps seemed cruel and unfeel-
ing if written to another kind of woman. Sofie, however,
chalked it all up to "grumbling," and continued on her carefree way, utterly oblivious to the real sorrow in Alfred's
heart. She had no desire to change her way or mode of living, and, what was more, she was certain that she did not
need to be concerned about it.

The weight of Alfred's life-time of poor health now fell
upon him, as he approached his middle 50's in age. He found
that he required rest and peace for recuperation from the
stresses of his mammoth financial organization. Demands
upon his time had not lessened with the years, and he was
often ill and depressed. But when he needed Sofie she was
never there.

He tried to diagnose this strange and unsuitable affair that
still had the power to hold him in its thrall in spite of his
constant struggles against it. He was able to rationalize his
position with the memories of his horror at first on seeing
the exquisite little flower-girl in her shabby Vienna home.
That dreadful family of hers: the spiritless father, the fla-
grantly scheming mother, and the pitiful trio of homely sisters. He had felt forced to take the changeling from the
soiled nest, but what had he done to her?

He would admit that he had tied her to him, made her
dependent upon him, and that he had, at last, despaired of

teaching her to help herself by study and the search for knowledge. He knew that his entire life now was tortured by emotional upsets and the time-consuming trips he made to see her. But why couldn't he bring himself to give her up?

The reason was clear, but Alfred would not give it credence. Passionate sensual love still held the two of them together. He had abhorred the idea of sensuality ever since he had experienced it in his boyhood days when first coming to Paris and though, in reality, the glittering unseen chains of passion had bound him to Sofie these many years, he despised the idea.

There is no way to trace this somewhat abnormal and guilty reaction of Alfred's to youthful shock, or to a traumatic event of his childhood years. True, he was reared in the conventions of most of the European continent in the nineteenth century. The heavy grasp of Victorianism was not limited to the United States and England. But, particularly among men of wealth and position, the custom of keeping a mistress was an accepted thing.

Alfred's intellectual attitudes were not the only influences which made him condemn the normal sexual needs of the human male. He must certainly have borne within himself some psychic injury that would make him loathe in himself the most natural of human urges and fulfillments.

His genius must have repudiated the wants of the human body. But science and culture could not serve him completely. There was love, and there was Sofie. For ten years, there was always his "lovely little child," Sofie.

An Old Friend Returns

The Von Suttners returned to Austria. On their way to the Harmansdorf Castle they stopped at Hertz to pray at the grave of Bertha's mother. When the towers of Arthur's home castle rose against the horizon, he stretched his arms toward them and turned to Bertha: *Willkommen zu Hause, mein Weib!* (Welcome to our home, my Wife!)

The couple was enthusiastically received. Arthur's joy moved him close to tears.

The past was forgotten. The best rooms in the Harmansdorf Castle, eventually to be Arthur's inheritance, became theirs for nearly a year with visits to Vienna from time to time. They both wrote, but the so called literary life was as yet unkown to them. Those meetings in the writers' cafes always particularly popular in Austria, calls on editors, long chats, rarely about literature and more often about honoraria, professional gossip; all this held an intriguing charm for them. To live uninterruptedly in this kind of atmosphere could bring on indolence, they agreed. But, to bask in this atmosphere now and then was useful.

On the day when Alfred received a letter from Vienna, addressed in the hand of Bertha von Suttner, he stared at the postmark a moment before opening it. Throughout the ten years, since Bertha had summarily left his employ and hospitality at Paris, he had received a yearly greeting from her, usually at the time of the New Year. Her last message had come from Russia.

This letter told him that the von Suttners had returned to Vienna to stay, and Bertha sent her warm wishes for

Alfred's health and success. He had often wondered why she had chosen to remember him all this time. Had she ever regretted her hasty action? He determined to see her again and judge the answer to his question with his own eyes and ears.

On his next trip to Vienna, he failed to see Bertha. She and Arthur von Suttner had gone to the family's summer place in Harmansdorf. He wrote her cordially:

> If I have not replied sooner to your kind and courteous letter, it is because I was in hope of bringing you my answer *de vive-voix*, my respects *de vif-coeur*. . . .
>
> How glad I am to know that you are happy and contented, back at last in a land you love, and rested from struggles of which my sympathy can measure the extent.
>
> What shall I tell you of myself—a ship-wreck of youth, of joy, of hope? an empty heart, whose inventory is only a white or gray page.

He could not resist closing his letter with the morose judgments of himself, but then Alfred had reached low ebb in his physical vitality and emotional resources. His disillusionment with Sofie increased day by day. The trials of his financial matters seemed never-ending. Not only did his poor health burden him, but the years were telling on the strong physiques of his brothers. His beloved mother, now in her eighties, had grown frail.

In 1887, the Suttners made a trip to Paris. Baron Arthur had never been in the City of Light and Bertha, who knew Paris well, was eager to show it to her husband. There, they saw Nobel. He was then, as always, scrupulously kind and attentive.

In her memoirs, Bertha von Suttner clearly implied that she aroused the interest of the famous inventor in the pacifist cause, but her contention was not correct. The idea of universal peace had always occupied Alfred Nobel's mind. It crystallized in him under the sway of humanistic literature on one hand and the poetry of Byron and Schiller on the other. Bertha's novel only augmented these major influences.

Alfred Nobel later extended financial assistance to the peace movement, headed by Bertha, but his contributions were negligible, when his enormous wealth is considered. This was because he did not believe in the methods advocated by the Suttners.

Alfred Nobel had no need of pacifist inspiration. He had believed in pacifism since boyhood. His intensity of belief amounted to a religion. That his invention of dynamite had brought him a great fortune greatly embarrassed Alfred. In his writings, he time and again sought to reconcile his invention with the practical problem of assuring universal peace. True, he said, that men utilized for purposes of war, the weapon of destruction he had conceived. But should he be blamed for that? He had aimed dynamite at useful purposes such as tunnel construction. And even as a war weapon, dynamite could play a part which, in the final analysis, would prove constructive. As the weapons were perfected, war becomes so dreadful an affair that mankind would be compelled to renounce it.

Twenty years after the beginning of Bertha's acquaintance with Alfred Nobel, she wrote him of their first meeting:

Then, in the year 1876, you left upon me the impression of a thinker and a poet, a man at the same time embittered and kind, unhappy and joyous, with unusual impulses and with an evil mistrust of man, passionately loving the great horizons of thought and profoundly despising human pettiness and stupidity, understanding everything and hoping for nothing.

This characterization came close to the truth. He must have known his protests only masked his own sorrow over dynamite's successful war career. As a scientist, inventor and industrialist, Alfred Nobel spent most of his time among business men who were not in the least concerned about the moral and ideological aspects of dynamite. Theirs was a world of patents, contracts, orders, prices, joint stock companies and construction projects. Among these associates were some who actually fostered the origin of wars. Nobel despised such men.

In the semi-Bohemian life of the von Suttners an occasional literary convention took place, sometimes an international one. When the Suttners attended one such convention, Bertha conducted herself as though she were celebrating a Mass. This dedication was a touching and precious, but slightly comical facet of her character, one that persisted all her life. She ascribed great importance to whatever activity she was currently pursuing. Soon it would be pacifism, but just then, it was literature.

At this time the Suttners' finances had ceased to concern them. Bertha could choose subjects for her writings without considering whether they would bring large sales. She wrote *The Machine Age,* and the book had a modest success.

Bertha felt that every writer produces one chief work, which constitutes the whole meaning of his existence on earth, and sometimes vindicates it. For her, Bertha von Suttner, the time for such a book was nearing. Perhaps she sensed it only vaguely, but for some time, the idea of a novel dealing with war and its horrors had been brewing in her.

At that time, Leo Tolstoy was already world famous. *War and Peace* was read in numerous translations by every educated man. Now forgotten, but then well-known, the Swiss Jean Henry Dunant and Frederick Passy of France had declared their thoughts on the task of realizing world peace. Bertha realized that peace preachers were not new in politics nor in religion. She put her keen mind and her whole soul into her new novel. She had precursors. Though *War and Peace,* for instance, notwithstanding the gigantic scale of Tolstoy's diapason, cannot be conceived as specifically directed against war, pacifism was one of the many interwoven melodies of Tolstoy's colossal opus. Other novels depicted war in the gloomiest colors their authors could find on the palette of their emotions.

This was the time of Bismarck and the triumph of the military class in Germany; the epoch of nationalism and of General Boulanger's idea of *revanche* in France; and the blossoming in England of the colonial expansion doctrine with Joseph Chamberlain its most prominent political representative and Rudyard Kipling its ablest literary exponent. These conditions furnished a fertile soil for the book Bertha von Suttner conceived. Reaction against the imperialistic doctrines was strong and only awaited its sharp expression.

Bertha von Suttner's novel, entitled *Lay Down Arms,* described the militarism of Nineteenth Century era and the lives of Bertha's contemporaries, against the background of boundless despair. She studied the diaries of people who had participated in the wars of her time; she read old newspapers and the memoirs of army physicians on the diabolical conditions in military hospitals, the sufferings of the wounded and the misery of the families of those who were killed.

With this vast material at hand she wrote a good novel, convincing because of the sincerity of her horror for war. This feeling in Bertha was particularly admirable, since she had been brought up on the cult of military heroes. During the War of 1866, she ardently hoped for Austria's victory and during the Russo-Turkish War of 1877 she longed to see Russia victorious for she believed Russia championed the right cause.

When she completed the book, she offered it to a journal which had printed her writings earlier. Much to her surprise she received a polite refusal. The editor wrote her that the idea of the novel "will insult a large circle of readers." Rejections were received from the other periodicals to which Bertha sent her manuscript. There was no alternative except to have it published in book form, but even that proved difficult. Pierson, Bertha's regular publisher, hesitated to take the work on the same grounds set forth by the editors of the various magazines. Finally he consented to publish it on condition that the title, which he considered particularly objectionable, be changed. Bertha refused to accept this condition and sent him this ultimatum: "Either publish the book under the title *Lay Down Arms,* or else return the manuscript." Pierson at last concurred.

There are many instances on record where editors have rejected manuscripts, whose publication would have made them rich. Marcel Proust was unable to find a publisher for his famous series, *A la Recherche du temps perdu,* and had to print it at his own expense. Fortunately he was a wealthy man. Margaret Mitchell endeavored for a long time to find a publisher for her novel *Gone with the Wind,* which turned out to be an epoch-making sales success. Pierson, however, believed in the ultimate triumph of Bertha's book; otherwise he would not have accepted it. But he was afraid to antagonize military circles and all those who would naturally be opposed to the provocative slogan, *Lay Down Arms.*

In 1889, Bertha's novel was published and its success proved phenomenal. She could have repeated the words of young Lord Byron: "I awoke one morning and found myself famous." Heretofore, she had won a certain degree of recognition in the literary circles of Germany and Austria, but she was not well known. Now the whole world heard about her. Tens of thousands of copies of the book sold in various countries. It was translated into a dozen languages. In Russia alone it was published in five different translations.

The *Neue Freie Presse* printed a review of *Lay Down Arms,* that took up ten columns. The *Bund* carried five articles. Dunaievsky, the Austrian Minister of Finance, speaking before the Reichserat, urged—not without humor—the too combative deputies to take Bertha von Suttner's advice and "lay down arms."

Bertha received a great many letters. One of these she particularly cherished; it was written in French. Here is the English version, minus the concluding paragraph:

Dear Baroness, Dear Friend!
I have just finished reading your magnificent *chef d'oeuvre*. I hear that on earth there are two thousand languages, of which 1,999 are superfluous, but of course, your beautiful work has got to be translated into all of them; it must be read and pondered over in all of them. How long did you work for the achievement of this miracle?—You will answer this question when I shall have the honor and happiness to shake your hand—the hand of the amazon who wages a valiant war against war.

This letter, dated April, 1890, was signed: *Alfred Nobel.*

It was April 1887 and Paris buzzed with rumors of war with Germany. A French customs officer had been lured across the border by German guards on pretense of requiring the Frenchman's consultation on a matter of inter-country traffic. As soon as the Frenchman put his feet on German soil, the guards arrested him and accused him of spying upon them.

Actually a simple letter of protest from the French officials released the man, but through an erroneous report all credit was given to General Boulanger. The case of General Boulanger was one of history's rampant cases of charisma. General Boulanger, a handsome devil, had ridden straight into the hearts of the French people on his snorting black charger. Although his impulsive war orders and petty reactions to international problems brought the Republic into imminent dangers, the citizens adored him. He could do no wrong in their eyes and France trembled on the brink of war for a time.

French patriotism flared high and every street in Paris was a setting for voluble and volatile discussion that focused on the bitterness left by the Franco-Prussian devastation.

But as the Baron and Baroness von Suttner arrived in Paris for a visit with Alfred Nobel, all they saw were the blossoming chestnut trees, the budding flowers in the parks, the tables in front of the sidewalk cafes, for April in Paris is the month of Spring's arrival, and the month of love. Upon reaching the mansion on the Avenue Malakoff and being welcomed by Alfred, Bertha saw the same kindly blue eyes she had remembered, the same dark brown hair with only a patch or two of gray in it now, and she heard the same voice with its deep tone of melancholy. If she had ever feared Alfred would bear a grudge for her discourteous departure from Paris more than ten years before, she misjudged the qualities of understanding and tolerant affection in the man. He was warm, friendly, and interested in them both, and in the recital of their exciting, though difficult adventures during their Russian stay.

Discussion between Alfred and Bertha was the same stimulating exchange of ideas they had known before, though flavored with the added experience of a decade. Both declared their hopes for the future of humanity in optimistic, even glowing terms. Alfred now believed that change would come through the emancipation of the masses, the great horde of common people, by means of stirring technical discoveries and progress. Technology would rid the world of ignorance and put reason and judgment in its place. Bertha, however, had been guided by Herbert Spencer. She insisted on the persistence of a forceful agent that would bring changes and organization to the knowable universe and believed that agent would be the natural sciences. She contended that only the intellectuals, the finely educated minds, must regulate businesses and lead governments. These two, Alfred and Bertha, found stimulation and mental inspiration in their discussions.

The deep love of Bertha and Arthur must have been a wonderful thing for Alfred to behold. As they told him of the Russo-Turkish warfare, of the sickness and hunger that followed it, of the sufferings they had tried to alleviate, and their own trials in making a frugal living for themselves.

This handsome pair, even more in love than ever after their troubled years, could not have helped but add to Alfred's loneliness of spirit. He saw before him the love he had longed to have, love filled with respect and companionship, as well as awareness of the charm and fascination each found in the other. Alfred blessed them with his own satisfaction in their happiness. He studied the writing of each, commented upon it with wisdom and appreciation. He bound them to him through his generous friendship.

Bertha's words: "Unhappy people are prone to become embittered and to want others to suffer too," made him consider himself. Was he embittered? He could not say he was not, for bitterness rode him hard at times. Did he want others to suffer as he did? No, he could not truthfully say he did. Though he did not hesitate to scold Sofie, and often rather unkindly, he felt he did it as an adult would admonish a child.

True, his scolding of "the sweet little child" had no apparent effect, but perhaps she was one of those who took thrice the time to grow up as others did. Eventually, his advice might influence her, and she would try to do more with her life than cultivate her own beauty and fritter her time away. Alfred resolved to be more patient with Sofie. This resolve came naturally to him, but somehow Sofie's lazy ways and endless wandering didn't matter as much. He found himself calm and undisturbed when days passed without a letter or telegram from Sofie.

The fact was that from the time Bertha von Suttner came back into Alfred's life, a distinct change entered his relationship with Sofie. Of his money, Sofie could have any and all she wanted. But of his time, he gave her less and less. And of his love, the glittering unseen chains had begun to slip.

The von Suttners accompanied Alfred to the salon of Madame Juliette Adam where he enjoyed going from time to time. Bertha wrote of the evening in her journal:

> . . . I can remember that on our very first call Mme. Adam, a still-beautiful, captivating figure, steered the conversation into political channels. This was the moment when it was generally believed that the war of revenge, which had been predicted for sixteen years, was coming . . . the dark word "war" was burning through the room. . . . Men prophesied boldly that next spring it would surely come to something, but these prophesies did not detract from the spirit of cheerfulness that prevailed.

War was not a word for cheerful acceptance to Bertha. It was a word that brought her memories of maimed men, of tragic young widows searching for bread to feed their hungry children, of sickness and fear and dying. She'd lived through one war; here another pressed near her. She confided to Alfred that at last she knew why she had been put upon the earth at that very time: to work for peace. From then on, she would devote herself to the fight against War— the destroyer of civilization.

Soon after she returned to Vienna, she wrote Alfred that she had become a member of the International Peace and Arbitration Association, a London group that sponsored the evolvement of an organization to include representatives from all nations. International problems would be referred to the association for discussion and judgment through *wisdom* instead of *war*.

Invention and patenting of ballistite, the smokeless gunpowder, involved Alfred's life for some time, so when Bertha invited him to visit at the von Suttner's summer manion in Harmansdorf, he wrote his regrets:

> The proof that there is no justice in this world is that you take me, I am sure, for an ill-bred man and an ingrate. . . . For a week past, with

my trunk packed, I have not been able to get away; and yet my visit to Manchester is urgent. But at this moment all the dynamiteurs in the world—the dynamiteurs being directors and managers of the dynamite companies—have conspired to come here and bother me with their affairs, conventions, plans, deceptions, etc., and I am ardently wishing that a new Mephisto would come to enrich Hell with these evildoers.

An ironic letter, since Nobel found himself involved with the military heads of nations in quest of better and bigger death-dealing devices. Then, too, a reaction from his kindly concern for Sofie's position and reputation had come to haunt him.

The clique of Viennese society globetrotters spread the news of a Madame Nobel whose gowns were made to order in the smartest shops, and who was included on the guest lists of the most fashionable hotels.

The wife of a business acquaintance first confronted Alfred with the rumor. Soon, he heard it on every hand, always repeated to him with sly secrecy, as if to say, "Since you have not announced such a marriage, what's the real story, old fellow?" Alfred was embarrassed and furious.

When Bertha wrote him in an over-casual way that the report had reached her ears through a Viennese florist, Alfred could sense her feeling of concern. He knew she wondered if her friend, Alfred, had not seen fit to inform of her so important a relationship, or should she consider such secrecy reflected a lack of responsibility in the man she so respected and admired?

He answered her with a lightness that in no way expressed his feelings of disgust at the reckless and never-footfast Sofie.

Dear Baroness and Friend:
What an ingrate this old Nobel is, but in appearance only, for the friendship which he feels for you only increases, and the nearer he approaches the final "nothingness" the more he values the few persons, men or women, who show him a little genuine interest.

164

Could you have really believed that I was married, and married without informing you? That would have been a double crime against friendship and against courtesy. The bear has not yet got so far as that.

In saying I was married, the florist was using flowery language. As for Madame Nobel of Nice, it was, in all probability, my sister-in-law. That is how the secret and mysterious marriage is explained. In the end everything does get explained in this world below, except the magnetism of the heart, to which the same world is indebted for its existence and its living. Now this magnetism is just what I must be lacking in, since there is no Madame Nobel and since in my case the dust that is thrown in the eyes is inadequately replaced by gunpowder.

You see, there is no *jeune femme adorée*—I am quoting word for word—and I shall not find in that direction a remedy for my *nervosité abnormale* (once more a literary quotation)—or for my gloomy ideas. A few delicious days at Harmansdorf might perhaps cure me, and if I have not as yet replied to your arch-amiable and friendly call of hospitality, that comes from a multitude of reasons which I will explain to you by word of mouth.

Whatever happens, it is absolutely necessary that I should soon come to see you, for if not, who knows if I shall ever have this pleasure and consolation?

Fate, alas, is unwilling to be turned into an insurance company, and yet we would offer her very tempting premiums!

On his next visit to Sofie, he spoke of her indiscriminate and indiscreet use of his name in a cold, controlled way. He forbade her to speak of him outside of the village of Bad Ischl, since his permission to shield herself from gossip by the use of his name had applied only to their life in Ischl. For the first time since Sofie had met Alfred, she completely misjudged him. Relieved that the Brummbär's grumbling had been quiet and restrained, she did not recognize that his coldness was a symptom of his real disgust and repulsion.

Adieu, Sofie

Angina pectoris attacked Alfred. In October of 1887, he was bedded nine days with the pain and horror of it. The awareness of death, silently and stealthily approaching, terrified him. Not the terror of death itself, for death comes to everyone, but the terror of dying alone. "When at the age of fifty-four," he wrote a friend, "one is left alone in the world, and a paid servant is the only person who has so far showed one the most kindness, then come heavy thoughts, heavier than most people can imagine."

The tragedy of Alfred's alone-ness reached its climax at this time. That a man who had expended fortunes in helping others throughout the long stretch of years, did not have a soul to put a kind hand upon his tortured brow was crushing to his heart and spirit.

His family were taken up with their own affairs.

His friends? His most loved ones in Paris were gone. The grand old man, Victor Hugo, had been gone now two years. Alfred often thought of the great void Hugo left when he died. The leonine head and massive shoulders of the man had been symbolic of his great gestures in life and the vast scope of his works of art. Victor Hugo died, an emblem of his life-long battle for the liberation of humanity from the shackles of evil. Alfred mused on what he, himself, could do for the uplift of humankind. His inventive genius had played him false; for instead of being the means of developing better communication, of removing barriers, between nations, as he had hoped, his creations had been turned into the cruel tools of war. What power did he have left? He had money, a vast amount of money. What could money do? His plans for his estate began. But they could not ease his loneliness.

He thought of Sofie. He had been sure for some time that Sofie must again be following the advice of her scheming mother, for Sofie's exhorbitant requests for funds—in addition to her usual stack of unpaid bills—could only mean that she was storing funds away for security in her future years. He didn't mind. Let her stash away whatever she liked. Let her do what she wished and go where she wanted to. He had loved Sofie. Whether she had gained his love because of his idealistic hope of educating a young innocent, or whether her fleeting resemblance to his mother had won him to her, or whether the appeal of her femininity made him want to take care of her, did not matter. She held him no longer. And his loneliness meant nothing at all to Sofie.

At times Alfred's feelings of emptiness seemed to drain him of power to reason or to plan. He feared he could not bear to go on living. But the thought of his mother, now in her 86th year, brought him quickly out of this mood. He would never add a burden of sorrow to her aging shoulders.

The death of his brother, Ludwig, in April of 1888 further diminished Alfred's courage and decisiveness. Of the three brothers, Ludwig, had been the most vital physically, had attacked everything in life with tremendous drive and enthusiasm that was his outstanding quality. It seemed impossible that this energetic, virile man could have joined the throng of the dead—"the passing from light to darkness, from life into the enternal unknown, or, as Spencer calls it, the unknowable," as Alfred wrote to a friend.

Ludwig had come to the French Riviera for his last months of life in the hope that the climate might benefit the throat affliction that was killing him. Alfred visited Ludwig there, shortly before his death. Thus, the error of a French journalist in the obituary notice of a dead Nobel financier is understandable. The man wrote an obituary of Alfred instead of Ludwig, and Alfred stared at the dreadful phrase that crammed his own long years of tremendous effort and labor into four words: "The Merchant of Death."

These words struck at Alfred with cruelty; but if they drove him into actual and specific planning for the way to leave his fortune so it would bring true value to the world's people, they served a useful purpose. He determined that when he died all nations of the earth would realize his deeply felt philosophy and his hope for human inspiration. He also decided to return to Stockholm where his mother lived, where his brother Robert and his family were constant visitors, and where he could better keep in touch with Ludwig's splendid sons: Emmanuel, in charge of the Baku enterprises, and Carl, overseeing the factory in Petersburg.

A message came from Sofie, who still filled her days with the aimless amusements in pleasant resorts of German-speaking Europe, in response to a note from him that had spoken of his loneliness. Sofie accused him of making his own loneliness, of spoiling their lover's relationship so they could no longer live together. She said haughtily that she was sure Alfred could not live in happiness with anyone.

Even a year before, this accusation of Sofie's would have hurt Alfred. Now he answered her in a rather bored manner:

. . . you are wrong. Weariness and illness gnaw at me, and often before I fall asleep I think how sad my end one day will be with only an old servant near my bed who keeps wondering, perhaps, whether I have remembered him in my will. He does not know that I have no will at all (the one I once made I tore asunder), and that my fortune is undermined more and more. Any man who throws away money the way I do, has not much left. Also I have suffered gigantic losses. But I don't care at all.

Whether Alfred intended his complaints about throwing away money and having no will to permeate the addled mind of Sofie, who refused to believe anything she didn't want to believe, can only be conjectured. Certainly he did

168

not write her as he did for no reason at all. Alfred's mind did not permit small talk.

On December 7, 1889, Caroline Nobel died. Her life had been a long, dutiful one, but filled with satisfaction in watching the fabulous careers of her three sons. Alfred wrote from Copenhagen to Bertha von Suttner about his mother's death.

> . . . I am just here from Stockholm, where I have been to conduct to her last home my poor dear mother, who loved me as people do not love nowadays, when feverish life serves as a check on sentiment. (Then followed a brief outline of his plan for the Nobel Prizes. He ended:) I press your two hands—the little hands of a dear, kind sister who wishes me well just as I wish her and hers well.
>
> A. Nobel

His addition of the affectionate message to Bertha speaks clearly of the loving regard in which he held her, and gives insight of the thoughts Alfred must have had many times: if Arthur von Suttner had not sent his plaintive telegram to Bertha in Paris those ten years ago, life would have been very different for Alfred and for Bertha. They would have planned the prizes together.

The perfidy of Paul Barbe, Alfred's partner, became evident, and when his greed dragged Alfred's holdings and reputation into the melee, Alfred Nobel seemed to regain for a time the indomitable strength and judgment that had always been his in business emergencies. Then came the theft of funds by Marie-Emile Arton which again involved Alfred in the lawsuits he despised, as he said, "The other members of the board and their lawyers are, it is true, of the opinion that there has been no laxity (on Nobel's part) but when it comes to a lawsuit, Wisdom herself is blind."

Upon the settlement of these complex problems, Alfred did, at last, begin to shake off the tremendous responsibilities he had borne over the years from before the time he had yet come of age.

An amazing piece of news reached him, early in 1891:

Sofie Hess would soon give birth to a child, sired by a young Hungarian cavalry officer. Nothing could have so well proved to Alfred the complete lack of feeling he now had for Sofie, as his own reaction to this amazing news. He felt re-life. Sofie's baby daughter was born in July, and Alfred wrote Sofie as if he were an old uncle, mildly sympathetic but coldly diagnosing:

Poor Child, you need now comforting words and no reproaches for what happened in the past. Your upbringing and environment are to be blamed for the wrong you did to yourself. A very small, but not bad, soul is hidden in you.

And thus it becomes not only sensible, but vital, in a portrayal of Alfred Nobel to acknowledge that a man of his brilliance and taste could not once more blame Sofie's upbringing and environment for her flaws of character and spirit, unless he knew she had been basically bright of mind and virtuous of spirit. At this time, he had reached a period of complete revulsion with her actions. He could view her beauty without the desire it had once aroused in him; he could realize her senseless conduct dispassionately. His great disappointment in the girl lay in her stubborn refusal to lift her sights in the slightest way. That he knew she had mental equipment that would have proved more than ordinarily competent in educational and cultural studies made the more keen his disappointment. Sofie was clever enough in accomplishing anything she wanted to do. Sheer laziness and complete satisfaction with her own pretty, stupid self, kept her from amounting to anything more than she had been in the florist's shop.

Indicative of Alfred's generosity, he did not consider cutting off Sofie's allowance. However, he did obtain the services of a Viennese lawyer to place Sofie in guardianship. This meant Alfred refused to be responsible for her debts any longer. He set up an annuity in a Viennese bank that would pay her monthly sums for her support as long as she lived.

Sometime later, Alfred saw Sofie in Vienna, and though she seemed happy enough rolicking with her little girl whom she had dubbed "suckling pig" (Sofie's nicknames seemed to come from the animal kingdom), she complained about her manless state. His letter after this visit said:

Dear Sofie:
. . . I found you in better health than ever and cannot understand why you pity yourself. You lack, of course, a great deal, and your environment is neither good nor pleasant. But all in all, you are not among the unhappiest though you have done everything you could to become so. You had a big opportunity. Everybody would tell you that. In my place, other men would have left you to the misery you were so busy creating. . . .
Your child is quite pretty. She must get a good education. I don't know your relation to the child's father, thus I cannot judge which is right or wrong. For the rest, it is not my business.
Kindest regards from A.N.

His note to Sofie in 1895 comes as the last recorded bit of writing he sent her. Prompted by a rumor, repeated to him, about the Hungarian officer's intention to marry Sofie, he wrote her another old uncle bit of advice:

Dear Sofie:
Is it true that the cavalry captain wants to marry you? If so, he would not only be doing the right thing but acting wisely as well. Then you will have to give up a lot of vain and stupid ideas. But you are an emotional little person and that is worth something, after all. . . .

The rumored marriage did take place but in less than a flattering fashion for Sofie. Her debonair, fly-by-night lover was a captain in the exclusive and austere Austrian Cavalry that accepted only men of noble birth and impeccable reputation for its personnel. He was charged with scandalous behavior, demoted in rank, ordered to marry the mother of his child.

It is not amiss to consider whether the hand that brought

171

the complaint to the young captain's controlling officer was not the sly hand of Frau Hess. That snide female was ever-present when some material benefit would come to Sofie, and hence to herself.

The dashing captain married Sofie in a proper church wedding, and after the ceremony he led her out of the sacred edifice, helped her into the hired fiacre, kissed her hand and called back a merry farewell, as he walked out of her life. And he stayed out of it. Aside from his own foot-free nature, Sofie's charms were evidently not sufficient to give him stomach for her Hess family.

After the captain had joined the sales force of a champagne company, he had the incredible gall to pester Alfred with written requests for money. Alfred ignored them.

However, responsibilities for Sofie continued in the same way as before. In the one year of life left to Alfred, Sofie wrote constant pleas for money to pay off her bills. Debts and more debts attended her, and she pawned jewelry, furs and valuable bric-a-brac; then wrote frantic letters to Alfred. He always bailed her out of the mess.

After Sofie's experience with the captain who obviously had no spark of stability, Sofie regretted sorely her foolish lack of appreciation for the great man who had once loved her. Because of her youth, he had tolerated and overlooked much in her, that he would never have endured in an older, more worldly woman. She longed for those days that were gone. When Alfred thought of her, it was with nostalgia, not for the Sofie that was, but for the Sofie that might have been.

A rumor rose in Viennese circles that Sofie's child had actually been sired by Alfred Nobel, and that he had paid the young captain to marry Sofie in order to save her name. Whether Alfred was hurt by this rumor was never known; there seems to be considerable question about his even being aware of it. Again suspicion must fall on the indefatigable scheming of Frau Hess. Her warped kind of thinking might very well have led her to a desperate effort to involve Alfred in the future of her granddaughter.

Though any compassionate soul would hope that Frau Hess kept her hands off the little girl whom Alfred noticed, even in babyhood, to be quite pretty, that was not the habit of Sofie's mother. She had managed Sofie's life and she began management of the life of the beautiful baby girl.

PART III

HIS DREAMS

Nobel's Last Days

Of the many injustices Alfred Nobel suffered, the "Barbe Scandal," as it was dubbed by journalists, was the worst. Paul Barbe, seemingly unable to keep his nose out of any situation that smelled like money, involved himself in the Panama Canal project around 1890.

The Panama Canal construction had been harassed by incompetence and bad planning ever since its inception; but in 1890 the work progressed quickly with Nobel dynamite used for all the blasting.

When Paul Barbe died suddenly in 1890, the news broke that Barbe had joined in an unethical lottery and bribery system. His position as manager of several Nobel companies involved Alfred in the dishonest affair. Besides this disgraceful indictment, Alfred learned in Hamburg that Barbe's directors of the French Nobel firm had involved it in dishonest dealings over glycerine supplies.

It looked like ruin for the Nobel enterprises, but Alfred's solid judgment and quick action saved the situation with considerable losses as the result. The French government forced him to close his laboratory at Sévran, and Alfred, discouraged and resentful, left his home on Avenue Malakoff and moved to Italy in 1891.

At San Remo on the Italian Riviera, he purchased an attractive villa in a park setting. Orange trees, bright flower beds and palm trees bordered the villa that looked out over the deep blue of the Mediterranean Sea. Alfred moved the equipment left at Sévran, after it had been ransacked by the French police, and refurnished a fine laboratory at his newly decorated and appointed San Remo home. He named the place "Mon Nid" (My Nest), an indication of his pleasure in it, for no home can become a nest, unless it suits and holds a warm security for its owner.

Again, Alfred Nobel was alone. Alfred Nobel's leave-taking of Paris, where he had been at home for twenty years, must have inspired him with an even more intense bitterness at the fateful events of his life. He had once remarked, "I knew when I was ten years old that equity is only a figure of speech—there is something rotten in the state of Justice."

However his move to San Remo seemed to give him a mellowness he had not had before. Years could not have mellowed this man of iron purpose whose life had been lived most importantly in his brain and not his body. Perhaps his chronic restlessness, his driving force, that pushed him on and on in a ceaseless search for the life values that had eluded him, gave him a certain joy in the purchase and out-fitting of his San Remo villa.

Ragnar Sohlman, the gifted young scientist who became Nobel's assistant and close friend (later made one of the executors of the will) described his noted employer at their first meeting in October, 1893: "At that time Nobel was sixty years old. He was rather less than medium height, had strongly marked features, a high forehead, bushy eyebrows, and somewhat deep-set eyes, whose glance was both keen and changeable, as was his whole temperament, for that matter."

The San Remo laboratory was extensive and complete. The long, low building sat in the midst of the glorious garden-park, surrounding the stately villa. It was divided into three sections: a machine-room equipped with generators for voltages and tensions for lighting and electrolysis; a large workroom for chemical experimentation and other work; and a reference library, with scales and various instruments. A narrow steel pier extended out into the sea for firing tests.

The variety of experiments that Nobel conducted in this laboratory evidenced the scope of his interests and ideas: substitutes for rubber, gutta-percha and leather; a glass pressure nozzle that forced a cellulose solution out of a multitude of tiny openings to create silk fibres; the development of varnishes and paints; improved parts for the telephone, electric batteries, the phonograph and incandescent lights; the creation of rubies, sapphires, amethysts and topazes.

Throughout the years of his experimentation, Nobel secured more than 355 patents in different countries on the creations of his logical, but imaginative mind. He wrote a friend: "If I have a thousand ideas a year, and only one turns out to be good, I'm satisfied."

If, as is said, the usual man employs only from 1 per cent to 10 per cent of his mental powers, Nobel must have come close to the use of the full 100 per cent of his uniquely gifted mind. He organized his factories with attention to even the slightest detail, then placed the management in the hands of the ablest men he could find. The story is told of his speech to the Board of Directors of the Ardeer, Scotland, factory, at the finish of his plans and organization of it. He said: "Well, gentlemen, I have given you a company that is bound to succeed, even if there is the grossest mismanagement on the part of the directors."

Nobel's correspondence amounted to as many as fifty letters in one day. These were written in his careful, flowing hand, and in whichever language befitted his correspondent. More of these were answers to "begging letters" than responses to business queries, or his personal correspondence that gave him one of the real satisfactions of his life. Nobel spoke about receiving at least two dozen letters a day, begging for funds, some of them asking for ridiculous amounts in insolent or fawning terms.

He refused many, but helped more—particularly young people who wished to study and to improve themselves. He often said, "I do not enquire where their fathers were born or what Lilliput god they worship. Charity—of the right kind—knows nothing of national frontiers and is confessionless."

Nobel punctiliously tied the stacks of letters he received into bundles. He had his own categories for them. "Letters from Women", "Letters from Men", "Begging Letters". He had no category for love letters. Perhaps he had no wish to reread the messages from Sofie Hess. "Love quenches enthusiasm for anything else," he wrote sadly to a close friend, and again, "Hope is Nature's veil for hiding truth's nakedness."

His humor was pithy, original, sometimes grim and sarcastic. On his distinguished decorations: "My orders have no explosive foundation. For the Swedish Order of the North Star I have my cook to thank, whose culinary art was pleasing to a highborn stomach. My French Order I got on account of my close acquaintance with a minister, the Brazilian Order of the Rose because I chanced to be introduced to Dom Pedro, and finally as regards the famous Bolivar Order, because Max Philipp had seen *Niniche* and wanted to illustrate the lifelike way in which orders are awarded there."

On sin: "Lying is the greatest of all sins," and "The truthful man is usually defeated by the liar," and "The best excuse for the fallen ones is that Madam Justice herself is one of them."

On love: "A heart can no more be forced to love than a stomach can be forced to digest food by persuasion." On the state of mind: "Contentment is the only real wealth," and "Worry is the stomach's worst poison," and "Self-respect without the respect of others is like a jewel which will not stand the daylight."

Erik Bergengren collected a list of Nobel's aphorisms in his 1962 edition of *Alfred Nobel,* from which those above are taken. Perhaps the one that speaks the most directly of Nobel, himself, is: "A recluse without books and ink is a dead man before he dies." The Nobel recluse, at least, was always able to withdraw in the company of his books and ink.

He termed parliament, "a house of braggarts"; he spoke of his illnesses as "kind regards from Satan" and he dismissed the ever besieging newsmen as "these two-legged plague microbes."

In the winter of 1894, Nobel completed the purchase of the AB Bofors-Gullspong ironworks and munitions factory in Bofors, Värmland, Sweden. In nearby Björkborn, he discovered a charming old manor house that he ordered renovated and decorated for his home. A laboratory was built close to it, smaller than the one at San Remo, but well equipped in every detail. Here he put young Swedish engineers to work under the supervision of his new and trusted friend, Ragnar Sohlman. Nobel wished to develop in Sweden at Bofors a great establishment of iron and steel factories to turn out machinery and industrial needs. He seemed happier there than he had been in years. The thought of his return to his native land as a potent industrial force was both inspiring and comforting to this lonely man.

Since his health could not tolerate the harsh winters of Sweden, he spent his winters in San Remo on the sunny Mediterranean shore, his summers in Bofors, and in between he made consistent visits to his home in Paris. He never evinced bitterness of any kind against the French people or his Parisian friends, though he had been unjustly accused of being a saboteur by the French Government, and unfairly used in the destruction of his Sévran laboratory. But his new home and industrial interests in Bofors seemed his most pleasing concern. Undoubtedly, Alfred Nobel felt that he had, at last, gone back home.

There were two things in life that gave Nobel true and unalloyed pleasure. One was his solitary laboratory work and the other was thoroughbred horses. On his few leisure junkets, he could be seen at the race-tracks, never betting amounts of any size, but watching the glorious racing horses for pure pleasure. He had stables at the Malakoff mansion in Paris, at San Remo, and at Bofors, and they housed thoroughbreds, most of them the frisky Orloff stallions he particularly admired.

Nobel disliked mechanical noise intensely, a sad commentary on a man who had invented materials of the most thunderous explosions known at that time, so he invented rubber treads for his carriage wheels, before that, unthought of by wheel-makers. In a light carriage, drawn by his stunning stallions, he would whisk along the drives outside of San Remo or Bofors. A local Swedish paper reported he had "a telephone to the coachman and light inside the coupé and in the lamps was produced by electricity from accumulators. Thus the Lord of Dynamite sped along. . . ."

In his later years he bought an aluminum yacht that he sailed on the Lake of Zurich in Switzerland. One of his visits with Baroness Bertha von Suttner and her husband, the Baron, was spent on this yacht, but otherwise Nobel seemed to have had no great devotion to water sports. Other than walks through country paths, and his drives behind his Orloff steeds, he had no inclination for exercise. His health allowed him little of that.

As death dogged Alfred's footsteps throughout the last years of his life, his greatest concern was the form in which he would leave his estate to benefit the world's peoples. He wished his death to reveal to the world the inmost, private being of Alfred Nobel.

Ever since he was a boy, confined to a bed of illness, he had felt that charity was the only substitute for love. Alfred's life had held a long list of dishonest and greedy recipients of his charitable aid, so he felt that he must be faulty in judging individual character. He wanted to reach all mankind in his plans for leaving his fortune to the forces of good.

Who were the deserving he had known? Those silent heroes of research who worked without acclaim in lonely laboratories—those unsung explorers who gave their lives for the betterment of knowledge to bequeath to their fellow men. Thus, his plans for his will began.

During his last years, his time was divided into serene days at his new home near Bofors, outside of Stockholm, days of charm and fellowship in Paris, and days of rest and study at San Remo. After the death of his oldest brother, Robert, in August 1896, Alfred's health kept him bedridden much of the time. In November of that year, he wrote his benediction to Bertha von Suttner.

I am enchanted to see that the peace movement is gaining ground. That is due to the civilizing of the masses and especially to those who fight prejudice and ignorance, among whom you hold exalted rank. These are your titles of nobility. Heartily yours,

A. Nobel

But penned invisibly between these lines to the brilliant, lovely Bertha, were the expressions of the devoted love he had longed to give her long ago in Paris, when he called upon her at the Grand Hotel. For Bertha was the one woman in Alfred Nobel's life upon whom he could have bestowed the full glory of his great gift for love.

By 1893, when Nobel had reached the age of sixty, his health, never robust, deteriorated rapidly. Rheumatism affected his heart, and, though he mistrusted physicians and scorned them, he resorted to treatment by them. Shortly before his death he wrote: "Two specialists, both idiots—ascribe my pains—one to rheumatic gout and the other to goutish rheumatism; this is nothing but jargon which does not explain to me why my heart beats like a horse."

He returned to Italy from Paris, where he had been under the care of the "idiotic specialists."

On November 21, 1896, he resumed his work in the laboratory, notwithstanding the fact that he had been urged to take great care of himself. On December 7th, two weeks after his return from France to San Remo, he wrote his last letter to Ragnar Sohlman at Bofors, shortly after, he died in his laboratory of heart failure. His body was transported to Sweden and cremated there. It was Nathan Söderblom, a friend of Nobel and one of the best known clergymen in Sweden (later the Archbishop of Upsala and a Nobel laureate of peace) who went to Italy to accompany Nobel's body home. His ashes were interred in the family vault at Stockholm.

His death and especially his will, when it was made public, caused world comment. He had no personal enemies and in his native country he had won the recognition of all. Sweden was genuinely proud of one of her most famous and one of her noblest sons. Almost three-quarters of a century after his death, history vindicates every glowing statement printed about Nobel in his obituaries. This is unusual, even in the case of prominent and remarkable men. Alfred Nobel would have been entitled to two of the prizes he created: the prize for Chemistry and the prize for Peace.

Only his servants could report the loneliness and suffering Alfred Nobel endured during the weeks before he died. Those last weeks in "Mon Nid" he stumbled from his laboratory to his bed, too fatigued and weak to hold up his head any longer, yet driven, by the inner force of his creative faculties, to continue the work that had been his life.

On nights when his pain permitted him no rest, he would stare upward through the large window. The stars would be out and he and they remained awake until dawn.

Again and again the memory of an old Russian gypsy came into his mind. When he was but a boy entering his teens, the broken toothed old woman with eyes as bright and sparkling as his mother's jet buttons had accepted his coin and read his palm. It was all a lark for him and his brothers, but no matter how he tried he had never been able to forget the words she droned out to him.

"You will cross the widest oceans," she said. "You will dwell in many lands. You will have such riches that you cannot count the pieces of gold you will own. But love will break your heart and—" He remembered how the old gypsy paused and stared into his own blue eyes. "—and when you die, poor lad, you will be left alone without a gentle hand to stroke your brow, or a word of love to comfort you."

Again and again he had written in his letters of his fear that he must die alone with no one near to give him a loving word—only his servants to tend him. At the last, he was able to utter broken phrases in Swedish that his servants could not understand. A terrific force seemed to possess him and he struggled to rise from his bed until his valet, Auguste, had to hold him quiet.

But in these hallucinations that possessed him, there was perhaps one picture that returned to comfort him. He could have fancied himself back in Copenhagen, when the Christmas season filled the city with gaiety. He could have seen again the great bronze statue of that spinner of tales, Hans Christian Andersen, and the small boy who sat by the statue's huge foot with his yellow ball tucked under his arm.

And he could have seen himself salute the honored man of the statue. But then strangely enough, the bronze man doffed his hat and bowed deeply in salute to Alfred Nobel. The honored Dane, Andersen, knew this man, Nobel, had —in a much greater way than any man who lived before him—shown his deep love for his fellow man and that each life is a fairy tale written by God's hand.

Merchant of Death, Man of Peace

Le vraie Dieu, le Dieu fort est le Dieu des idées.
(The true God, the mighty God is the God of ideas.)

This line from Alfred de Vigny could be used as an appropriate epigraph for Alfred Nobel's life. It expresses the fundamental meaning of his existence—his relentless struggles for the cause of "the God of ideas."

His life appeared to be a paradox. During its first half he invented and manufactured explosives of terrific force; in his later years he served the cause of world peace. Yet the import of this seeming inconsistency should not be exaggerated, for the invention of dynamite was neither the only nor the ultimate accomplishment of Alfred Nobel.

In 1875 he discovered another new explosive substance —the colloid solution of nitro-cellulose. This did not receive as catching and high-sounding a name as dynamite and for this reason it was less known to the general public whose knowledge of scientific discoveries is acquired from the press. The term, dynamite, is easily remembered and appeals to the imagination.

The name of Nobel's other explosive, the blasting gelatine, is not impressive, even though the substance holds enormous importance in the technique of explosives.

One day, as Nobel worked in his laboratory, he cut his finger deeply and applied collodium to the wound. During the night the cut gave him so sharp a pain that he was unable to sleep. The thought suddenly occurred to him that the colloid solutions of nitro-cellulose might be utilized in the manufacture of explosive compounds. He got up at four o'clock in the morning, went to his laboratory and began the experiments which brought him more millions. Subsequently, he added to blasting gelatine, a third substance which he had invented, ballistite, consisting of equal parts of nitro-glycerine and nitro-cellulose with an admixture of camphor.

The invention of the blasting gelatine entailed a long series of patent claims, litigations, arbitration proceedings, all the legal intricacies that Nobel despised and was forced to endure for so much of his life.

In 1894 an arbitration in connection with ballistite took place that became known as a friendly suit between Nobel's company and the British War Department. Nobel lost the action he brought against the Crown and was ordered to pay £28,000 for the litigation expenses. He wrote bitterly to a friend on April, 1895: "Think only a poor inventor is compelled to pay £28,000 for 'a friendly suit', by means of which he had sought to protect his rights." The text of the letter does not appear to rate inclusion as one of Nobel's jests or ironical flights, though a man of those days with a more than eight-million-dollar fortune could not seriously have called himself a "a poor inventor".

The suit rose out of a dispute between Nobel, as the inventor of ballistite, and the scientists, Sir James Dewar and Sir Frederick Abel, who claimed the invention of cordite. The two chemists had worked for some time with Nobel and subsequently offered their explosive, together with the patent, to the British Government. It was purchased by the British for the needs of the Ministry of War. After Nobel lost the suit he gave vent to his irritation in a dramatic parody, *The Patent Bacillus,* in which he ridiculed English patent proceedings.

The "poor inventor" gained his wealth from two sources, since the Caucasus oil industry also gave rich profits. Rarely does one family inscribe into its history the creation of two colossal industries that today have become increasingly important in technological advances and have made wars costly, more horrendous, more deadly. Wars could not be fought in these times without oil and dynamite.

The origin of Nobel's fortune differed in no way from that of the Krupps and the Schneiders. Yet, from the standpoint of its disposition, there is a striking difference between Nobels' wealth and the enormous possessions of the Krupps. Nobel designated his estate to be used in the advancement of cultural and humanitarian pursuits and merely retained it during his lifetime. No better purpose could have been chosen by any philanthropic organization.

The second part of the Nobel wealth had no connection with war. Prior to the invention of airplanes and tanks, the use of oil for war purposes was limited. The Russian market and exports abroad required enormous quantities of kerosene for any number of peaceful purposes. In this respect the wealth of Robert, Ludwig and Emmanuel was untarnished. As for the disposition of the money they earned, none of the accusations made in the press against other men of wealth is in any way applicable to the Nobels. They did not create trusts to purchase the blandishments of the press; they did not propagandize wars; they did not finance dubious party savings banks and they did not bribe voters at the polls. No member of the Nobel family engaged in any form of politics and in any speculations.

After his departure from France, Nobel spent part of his time in Sweden and part on the Italian Riviera. His villa at San Remo, where he maintained an excellently equipped laboratory, inspired that superstitious awe in the local populace that the people of the Middle Ages experienced when they approached the abodes of alchemists. Rumors about fatal accidents in connection with nitro-glycerine never actually subsided. For a while they would lie dormant, but on the slightest pretext they would burst forth with new impetus.

Sometimes the business of spreading rumors even proved profitable. One of Nobel's neighbors caused a real commotion by whispering into everybody's ear that should an explosion occur in Nobel's villa, not only the villa but the whole neighborhood would be blown up into the air. In order to be rid of this alarmist, Nobel purchased the man's house and assigned it as a guest cottage. According to Sohlman and Schück, he was expecting a visit just at that time from the Swedish King Oscar with whom he was quite friendly.

At his villa, "Mon Nid", Nobel pursued his usual intensely industrious way of life. He worked all day long, not only on explosives, but also on a variation of other chemical problems which occupied his attention. The pure theory of this science held little appeal to his imagination, but his interest in its industrial ramifications was many-sided, ranging from his specialty of explosives to rubber and synthetic leather.

In addition to his laboratory work, he kept a watchful eye upon potential investments in various new enterprises. For instance he invested two hundred thousands dollars in a firm which sought to exploit a bicycle patent. It was reported that he lost this investment. He also subsidized many experiments conducted by other scientists and inventors.

Today, large industrial firms of most civilized countries spend huge sums on scientific research that may or may not produce items of use. Appropriations for this kind of experimental work constitute a substantial part of the regular budget of some enterprises. But in Nobel's time, this was a rare phenomenon, so in this field, he may be considered a real pioneer.

Throughout the years since Alfred Nobel's death, the question periodically arises: Was he "The merchant of death" or a man of peace?

Nobel stoutly contended for many years, though today this may strike us as a naive judgment, that his explosives would stop warfare because their terrifying destruction would force nations to repudiate warfare. The tragic day came when he admitted he had lost faith in his contention.

The wars he witnessed during his lifetime had grown increasingly more horrible, though they were only child's play compared with the two world wars of this century. In his time wars were being conducted in a comparatively gentlemanly fashion. During the Crimean campaign, for instance, the adversaries are said to have exchanged courtesies and even gifts.

Nobel could not foresee the fortune, but his intense interest in history could have left him no delusions about the horrors of past wars. In days long gone, a defeated country saw its entire population enslaved, its cities burned, its women raped, its war prisoners brutally put to death.

Nobel's mind whirled with these facts during his sleepness nights. To consider his life work in the invention of instruments of destruction, sickened him at times, for he longed always to in some way ease the lot of the human being who must live in a ruthless and oppressive world. Nobel was a logical man. He was well aware of the basic tenet, "The scientist creates, but mere men put his creation to their own uses." However, Nobel was also keenly sensitive and suffering was his lot. He admired and envied the benefactors of mankind.

Nobel was an attractive man, full of fascination. His life held plot and color. His transition from a modest and only half-secure financial existence in his youth to great wealth in his mature years is a success story in itself. The catastrophe that killed his brother, Emil, and the other tragic disasters caused by dynamite, particularly in the first years of its manufacture, could have inspired a Theodore Dreiser or a Charles P. Snow to write a great novel about this remarkable man.

Nobel was a romantic. Romanticism goes back to the 18th century, to Jean Jacques Rousseau but also to such men as Gondorcet, whom Alfred Nobel resembled in many respects. He inherited from that century an unshaken faith in reason which finds its most perfect expression in science in general and particularly in the natural sciences. From that age he also derived his encyclopaedic breadth of intellectual interests and that humanism which was so characteristic of his mental attitudes.

His cosmpolitanism and atheistic leanings must be attributed to the philsophical tenets of Voltaire and Diderot. But unlike many of the minds of that era, he was in no sense an optimist. Here, as in ethics and sociology, Alfred Nobel was distinctly a man of his epoch. He was also a romantic in his striving for the higher things and in his literary endeavors. His early English verses are interesting for their prosodic skill, unusual in a man who writes in a foreign language. This gift was typical of Russian classic writers whose command of the French language was almost as perfect as that of their own. Nobel's verses are noteworthy, too, from an ideological viewpoint. In them the idealism of the French of the early 19th century blends with Byronism. In form, they remind the reader at times of Shelley, at others of Byron.

In his later years his romanticism became tainted with gloomy, almost nihilistic motives, but this element was peculiar to other romantics and writers of the 18th century. For instance, Voltaire who with all his fervent faith in reason and with all his readiness to give aid to any humanitarian cause, at times sank into hopelessly misanthropic ideas. So Nobel, in his later intellectual life, reflected the two great philosophical currents from which he had emerged.

For he was also a realist in the higher sense because he knew all the depths of the human soul. In his stubborn striving for peace, he often met despair. "Give me an idea, write only the facts without describing feelings," he said, hopeless and spent by his seeming failure in finding a way to help the cause of peace.

In 1896, Alfred Nobel died in his villa, "Mon Nid". The day of the individual industrial giant is rapidly disappearing into the archives of history. Today, the great fortunes are made by big business amalgamations or conglomerates. In Nobel's day fortunes usually came from the knowledge, the industry, the foresight of a single man.

A newspaper clipping from a recent Italian newspaper gave this item: The villa at San Remo, where Nobel died, was sold at auction for 88 million lires, about $150,000.

The Nobel Will

On the 27th day of November, 1895, Alfred Nobel signed his will in the Swedish Club of Paris in the presence of four witnesses. The principal portion of the remarkable document stated:

... As to the rest of my estate, it shall be dealt with as follows: The capital shall be invested by the executor in stable securities and shall constitute a fund, the annual income from which shall be designated for the award of prizes to persons who, during the preceding year, shall have rendered the greatest services to mankind. The interest on the fund shall be divided into five equal parts. One part shall be awarded to the person who made the most important discovery or invention in Physics; the second part—to the person who has made the most important Chemical discovery or improvement; the third part—to the person who has made the most important discovery in the field of Physiology and Medicine; the fourth part—to the person who has made the most important contribution to Literature; the fifth part—to the person who has made the greatest contribution to the cause of promoting friendship among nations, disarmament or limitation of armaments, as well as to the establishment and popularization of the Congresses of Peace.

The prizes for Physics and Chemistry shall be awarded by the Swedish Academy of Sciences; the prizes for Physiology and Medicine—by the Royal Institute of Stockholm; the prizes for Literature—by the Stockholm Academy; while the prizes to persons promoting the cause of Peace—by a committee of five members elected by the Norwegian Storthing. It is my express desire that these prizes be awarded to persons regardless of their nationality; they shall be awarded to the most deserving persons, whether or not they be Scandinavians.

I hereby appoint Ragnar Sohlman (Bofors, Värmland) and Rudolph Lilliquist (Stockholm 31, Mälmskilnadgattan) as my executors.

This is my sole testament. It shall cancel and annul all earlier testamentary dispositions which may become known after my death.

In addition, I wish and insist that after my death my blood vessels be dissected, and that after competent physicians shall have ascertained undeniable death symptoms, my body be burned in a creamatory.

This document, "the will of the dynamite king," caused much comment at the time of Nobel's death. As Sohlman and Schück pointed out, from a legal standpoint, the will was framed both "inexplicitly and inexpediently", which could have reflected Alfred Nobel's intense dislike of lawyers, with whom he battled, or wasted time, for so much of his life. Apparently, he did not consult an attorney, though one of the witnesses under his will was seemingly a jurist. The will did not express precisely to whom the money was bequeathed. The purpose it was to be used for was clearly enough stated, but the big question of who was to keep the funds and administer them was left unanswered.

Witnesses testified that in Nobel's industrial affairs he was in the habit of giving general instructions, then leaving their execution to his employees and collaborators. In industrial affairs, the situations were well understood and Alfred Nobel was at hand to be contacted by telegram, or letter, or personal conference. But now he was gone.

One point to clarify was in what particular court should probate of his will be completed. He had frequently changed his place of residence and his capitals and assets were scattered through many countries. This raised the question of what nation's laws should govern the case.

Another complication was that the testator conferred the task of awarding the prizes upon his chosen institutions without having received in advance their consent to assume these complicated, burdensome and sure to be controversial functions. No remuneration was to paid for the performance of these duties. Apparently, Alfred Nobel expected people to give their time gratis to a task that would require endless time, responsibility and judgment.

For instance, under the provisions of Nobel's will, the Peace Prize was to be awarded by the Norwegian Storthing (Parliament). This plan in itself seemed expedient and practical. Norway, by its geographical position and historical status, was generally a neutral country and one that would be able, most probably, to maintain its neutrality. For this reason, in selecting a prize with an international political aspect, the Norwegian Storthing and the Norwegians, as a nation, could be expected to act as unbiased judges. However, the work of the committee of five, from Norway's Parliament, turned out to be far more than a mere matter of making an obvious choice.

During the brief period from 1901 to 1903, the names of three hundred and thirty-two candidates for the peace prize were submitted to it, out of which number two hundred and seventy-four were individuals and fifty-eight were organizations and corporations. They belonged to every conceivable nationality. Among them were thirty-seven Americans, thirty-five Englishmen, twenty-four Germans, thirty Frenchmen, twenty-four Italians, sixteen Swedes, fifteen Swiss, eleven South Americans, ten Belgians, nine Russians, nine Austrians, nine Spaniards, eight Norwegians, six Danes, five Dutchmen, five Poles, four Australians, four Czechs, and so on. The qualifications of each candidate had to be examined and considered. It immediately became necessary to purchase a large library of books and the world's leading periodicals, as well as to organize a staff of competent translators and secretaries. For the expense invloved in all of this work, at least according to the letter of Nobel's will, no provision had even been considered.

In addition to the problems of organizing the essential means for competently carrying out Nobel's plan, there were the offended relatives of the Dynamite King. They felt overlooked, ignored and snubbed without reason by their famous relative, since the Nobel dynasty itself received nothing from the estate. True, the Nobels were all rich people, but one branch of the family contested the will, probably through pique at being apparently forgotten by Uncle Alfred.

My late friend, Emmanuel Nobel, told me explicitly that because of his great esteem for the memory of his uncle, he emphatically renounced all claims to the estate and would contest nothing in Alfred's will. However, other members of the Nobel family started their litigation, although they declared at the outset that in case they were successful, they would dispose of the money in conformity with the spirit of the will.

In order to eliminate the many complications that arose from the differing legal conventions and laws in the nations where Nobel's business and monetary funds were located, the services of the ablest lawyers in France, England, Germany and Sweden were retained. In France, all legal matters were entrusted to Waldeck-Rousseau, who later became head of the French Government.

The Swedish Academy of Sciences chosen by Nobel to select prize winners for Physics and Chemistry at first refrained from participation in this work, perhaps because members of the Nobel family had brought an action contesting the will. Subsequently, however, the Academy agreed to assume the duties conferred upon it by Nobel. As to the relatives, an amicable settlement was reached with them, all due to Emmanuel. 3,840,000 Swedish kronas were paid to the younger children of Ludwig Nobel, in return for the withdrawal of their suit. Six weeks later the family of Robert Nobel acceded to their uncle's will through compromise.

A kind of codicil-note must be added to the executing of Alfred Nobel's will. After his levelheaded and understand-

ing nephew, Emmanuel, had united the battling descend-
ents and business associates into a high-minded group that
backed up Alfred Nobel's desires, a last and most ignoble
demand came to his attention.

An Austrian lawyer who represented Sofie Hess contended
that not only had the girl been Alfred Nobel's common-law
wife, but that she owned letters from Alfred that proved
the discussion of lawful marriage between himself and Sofie
had come up again and again over their eighteen-year
liaison.

The letters were indeed detrimental, for they covered the
entire eighteen years of the affair, and a great number of
them had been addressed to "Madame Sofie Nobel" by Alfred, himself.

Sofie's threat of exposing the scandal was too unbearable
to be considered by the executors. This would have so in-
jured the motives and substance of the Nobel will by label-
ing him a sordid betrayer of a young girl, that the idealism
and spiritual values he had expressed in this world legacy
would have been utterly destroyed. The vengeance of a
woman scorned can be cruel and vulgar. In this case of two
women scorned, for Sofie's conniving Mother Hess was involved, the threats became more cruel by the introduction
of a conscienceless publisher. The publisher would pay an
immense sum, so they reported, for the right to print Alfred
Nobel's letters in all the languages of the civilized world.

Finally the realization that the only power of Sofie's claim
against the will lay in her keeping the affair secret, convinced
her and her lawyer that they had best accept the terms offered by the will's executors. If the secret were made public,
Sofie had no threat at all.

The decision reached gave Sofie maintenance of the life
annuity Alfred had set up for her, and payment of her legal
expenses in the suit. The attorney was given the guardian-

ship of Sofie's funds. She, in exchange, was to transfer to the executors her portrait of Alfred Nobel and the two hundred and sixteen letters from Nobel with their envelopes.

How pathetic the great stack of messages that dated from that springtime of 1876 in Vienna to the announcement of the birth of Sofie's baby. Sofie was bargaining away the love this genius man had given her. Moreover, Sofie could keep her annuity only as long as she did not act or speak in any way detrimental to the memory of Nobel. One word reported of her mention of Alfred Nobel would cancel the annuity. Thus Sofie bargained away even her memories, for there were no silences for Sofie, unless she tossed away all thoughts of those eighteen years. What Sofie thought, Sofie said. She had to throw away the years, cancel them out of her life for money. Sofie did not hesitate; she always wanted money.

Alfred's letters were locked within the Nobel Institute in Stockholm and became the best kept secret of the time. They were released in 1955 to be included with the biographical data of Nobel. But who is there who could see those letters, and read their words of counsel and hope and love to the willful child, Sofie, without feeling a poignant stir of sympathy for the humanness of this genius.

Alfred Nobel had loved an image that had never come to life to give him the love he needed. They were two lonely people who met and touched and remained together a long, long time. But Sofie Hess took his love. Alfred Nobel possessed the great ability to give love.

The testamentary difficulties were surmounted because on every hand reverence for the memory of Nobel had been manifested. An important part in this connection was played by the benevolent attitude of the King of Sweden and the Swedish Government toward Nobel's last will.

Money was arranged for meeting the expenses entailed by execution of the will. The Foundation Nobel was created and at present it possesses all the necessary machinery for awarding the prizes. After the deduction of all expenses, there remained a capital of 31,587,000 kronas. From the proceeds of this capital, monetary awards have been paid, beginning with 1901 until the present day.

The amount of each prize over the years has fluctuated considerably—depending on the rates of state and municipal taxation. The first prizes, awarded in 1901, amounted to 150,782 kronas each (about 30,000 American dollars). The lowest level was reached in 1921, when they decreased to 121,572 kronas. In 1931 each prize amounted to 173,206 kronas. The awards were maintained at approximately that same level up to the outbreak of World War II. The cash awards of 1967 amounted to $61,700 each.

Four years after the death of Nobel, in 1901, the first prizes were presented. Since then cabled dispatches appear every December in the newspapers of the entire world. First, there is speculation concerning the most likely candidates for the literary prize, that arouses particular interest everywhere; later the announcement of the award itself. For each prize there are invariably several candidates, sometimes as many as a dozen. Usually these people know they are being considered. They must experience great concern in those final decisive days, since the prize signifies not only a measure of financial independence, but world recognition as well.

There is an old saying that "he will be saved who has made even one man happy for only one day." During the last sixty-seven years many a Nobel prize winner has left Stockholm a happy man and many have left Sweden with a profound love for that country. In truth, the Swedes are an excellent and noble people. When they set themselves to extending hospitality, they are beyond praise. As a consequence, most Nobel laureates are ardent Swedophiles.

That remarkable Swede who endowed the famous prizes

not only brought happiness to many talented and worthy people in every corner of the world, but he also rendered a great service to his own land by increasing respect for it in the heart of civilized mankind.

Genius Has No Country

To spread enlightenment is to spread prosperity—I mean general prosperity, not individual riches—and with prosperity most of the evil which is a legacy from the dark ages will disappear. The conquests of scientific research and its ever-expanding field wake in us the hope that microbes, the soul's as well as the body's, will gradually be exterminated and that the only war humanity will wage in future will be war against these microbes.—ALFRED NOBEL

The list of the names of great and dedicated scientists in the fields of chemistry, physics and medicine who have been chosen Nobel laureates since 1901 gives the history of world development in technologies, scientific knowledge and the advance of human health.

The scientist's contribution to his field in the light of his lifetime of work constituted his candidacy for the Nobel prize so the laureates included no unworthy or half-time candidates. Physicists, who advanced the comfort and knowledge of everyday human life, included the German Wilhelm K. Roentgen (1901) who discovered x-rays; the French Gabriel Lippman (1908) who developed color photography; Guglielmo Marconi, an Italian, and Karl Ferdinand Braun (1909) who gave the world the wireless telegraph.

Albert Einstein, (1921) started the tremendous surge of mathematical physics that led the ways into boundless achievements through his relativity theory. Some of the vital foundations for putting to use atoms, electrons, ions, and neutrons were evolved by Robert A. Millikan (1923) an American; James Franck and Gustav Hertz, (1925) from

Germany; Jean Baptiste Perrin (1926) of France; the American Arthur H. Compton (1927) and Charles T. R. Wilson from England (1927); Britain's Sir James Chadwick (1935). In 1963, Eugene Paul Wigner and Marie Goeppert-Mayer, both Americans, shared honors with J. Hans Jensen of Germany for contributions to knowledges of atomic nuclei.

Alfred Kostler of France was the laureate of 1966, cited for his discovery of the principle that led to the development of the laser beam. Masers, lasers, liquid helium gas, antiprotons, the hydrogen spectrum, mesons, the ionosphere —these are only a few of the creations of knowledge in physics that would have bewildered the experts of 1901 in this field.

The same remarkable progress of achievement in chemical science has been marked by the names of Nobel chemistry prize winners. Again, the layman will find particularly interesting those who have improved daily human life and have given new knowledge that any man is able to understand.

Outstanding examples of such chemists include: Adolph von Baeyer of Germany (1905) who worked on dyes and organic compounds, synthesized indigo and arsenicals; another German, Emil Fischer (1902), synthesized sugars, purine derivatives and peptides; Henri Meissan from France (1960) developed the electric furnace; in 1911 Madame Curie of France discovered radium and polonium and isolated radium; the German, Richard Willstätter (1915) researched chlorophyll and the coloring matter of plants; Heinrich O. Wieland of Germany (1927) studied gall acids; Adolph Windous, another German (1928) worked on sterols and their connections with vitamins; Sir Arthur Harden, an Englishman, shared honors in 1929 with Hans von Euler-Chelpin, a German, for research on sugar fermentation and enzymes; again in 1938 a German, Richard Kuhn, was acknowledged a forerunner of research on carstenoids and vitamins. And so the progress in knowledge of the human body's chemistry and chemical needs advanced through the years to the British Dorothy C. Hodgkins who received her Laureate in 1964 for x-ray studies of Vitamin B-12 and penicillin and Robert Burns Woodward of America's Harvard University whose achievements included his 1944 total synthesis of quinine, his 1947 "protein analogues" research, the total synthesis of a steroid in human metabolism, then later the synthesis of life-giving chlorophyll. Chemistry laureates have also contributed their life-long works in atomic problems, heart reactions, isotopes, high-pressure methods and chemical chain reactions—all vital research activities that have advanced technology in the world. The American Linus Pauling, for instance, was cited in 1954 for his work on the forces that hold matter together—a basis on which have been founded innumerable research projects without doubt.

In the fields of physiology and medicine, fields that have interest for every human being in the care of his own body and his aid to the health of his fellow man, some well-known achievements by Nobel laureates show the extraordinary leaps and bounds of these sciences through the past sixty-six years.

In many of these prize-winning discoveries, Americans can trace their own increased knowledge in their use of valuable medicines, vitamins, surgical aid and physical treatments.

Genius has no particular country and no favored country. It can appear anywhere, through figures of the distribution of the Nobel prizes to different nationalities could give an unfair picture of genius' development places, unless the population totals and opportunities of education and training in different countries are considered. By 1966, Nobel award winners had come from thirty-three countries. The United States led the list with ninety prizes. Great Britain followed with fifty-eight, Germany with fifty-four, and France with thirty-nine. Nobel's native Sweden is next with sixteen and Switzerland and the U.S.S.R. (including Czarist Russia) each have twelve winners.

Even famine-stricken India and tiny Iceland and several countries where education is not a nationally supported peoples' institution have contributed remarkable men to the exclusive club of Nobel winners. When a man is born with drive and inspiration and industry, nothing can stop him. He has a gift for the world and he will fight to prepare himself to perfect that gift in any way possible. The self-made intellects in the list of Nobel laureates have had the same great values as those who acquired their training in the most expensive and socially prominent schools.

However, the era of the self-educated inventor in science is at its end. Today science is so advanced and sophisticated that it will require a lifetime of self-learning to compete with the trained scientist.

Do geniuses have the assistance of Divine Providence? At times they have taken several different routes that have led miraculously into one definite road, directing them to discovery and success.

Sir Alexander Fleming, English bacteriologist and doctor of medicine, discovered the antibacterial powers of the mold from which penicillin was derived in the luckiest of ways. While he was engaged in research on influenza, a mold similar to a bread or cheese mold developed accidentally on a staphylococcus culture plate, thanks to a period of muggy weather in England. Fleming discovered that the mold created a bacteria-free circle around itself. Experimenting further, he found that a liquid mold culture, which he named penicillin, prevented growth of staphylococci, even when diluted eight hundred times.

One of the greatest scientists the world has ever known was Albert Einstein. Einstein was born in 1879 in Ulm, Germany. He had not been one of those child prodigies; in fact, he had been so late in learning how to speak that his parents feared he was a dullard. In school he taught himself calculus and his teachers were a bit afraid of him because he constantly asked questions they could not answer.

At the age of sixteen he wanted to know whether a light wave would seem stationary if one ran abreast of it. From this thought there arose ten years later, his theory of relativity with its famous offshoot, $E = MC^2$ (energy equals mass times the speed of light squared).

The theory of relativity derived from the study of motion and was primarily founded upon the fact that there is no absolute motion in the universe; that, everything in the universe pertaining to rest and motion is relative, because the entire universe is in constant motion. Light is the only thing Einstein considered absolute; everything else is elusive. The velocity of light is the greatest in nature and is a form of matter in its electronic state; therefore subject to properties of matter. Einstein showed that mass and energy are the same and there are no separate laws for the conservation of either one.

The theory of relativity consisted of two parts: the special or restricted, dealing with straight and uniform motion and the general theory dealing with rotating and accelerating motion. "Time," Einstein said, "changes in heavy gravitational fields, so that the time on the sun or on a different star is different from the time on our earth." Space is curved and interwoven with time. There is no absolute space and no absolute time.

Einstein dressed in ill-fitting clothes; his hair was usually flying in every direction, and he smoked a pipe incessantly. His gentle, relaxed voice set his visitors at ease. With his ceaseless search for cosmic simplicity, the intensity and depth of his concentration were most unusual. Long intervals would pass and then unexpectedly his face would break into an easy smile. He had found the answer to the problem. He used to say that imagination was more important than knowledge. He performed his work quietly, unrelated to the excitements of everyday life. However, his revolutionary ideas often created controversy.

Einstein, in his youth, had already won an honored position among the foremost scientists of his time. With ease, he adjusted to new conceptions; he did not cling to classical principles, but saw all conceivable possibilities when he was confronted with a problem.

Incidentally, he was an accomplished violinist and a great admirer of Mozart because of the purity and beauty of the composer's music. Perhaps he interpreted it as part of the inner splendor and majesty of the universe, waiting to be explored.

The selection committee of the Nobel prize awards granted him the Prize for his work on the quantum theory in 1921 and, while he was aboard ship returning from Japan, Einstein was informed of having hit the jackpot for genius. In 1922 he received the 1921 Nobel prize in physics "for the photoelectric law and his work in the domain of theoretical physics."

In 1933 he joined the Institute for Advanced Study in Princeton, New Jersey. The director gave Albert Einstein carte blanche on the determination of his salary, but the director had to plead with him to accept a larger salary. Einstein wanted too little money, not even enough for a most modest living.

Professor Ivan Petrovitch Pavlov (1849-1936), a Russian psychologist, achieved world renown for his research on blood circulation, the action of the digestive glands and the formation of conditional reflexes. He was awarded the Nobel prize in 1904 for his work on the physiology of digestion, but his name is known far beyond scientific circles for his systematic experimental studies of the conditioning of dogs and other animals.

Pavlov was the son of a priest and spent four years at a seminary, expecting to follow in the footsteps of his father.

But his vivid mind took a profound interest in medicine and he was graduated from the University of St. Petersburg as Doctor of Medicine.

He was a pioneer in the study of mental disorders. He studied unbalanced human beings and specific truths concerning them. His style was fresh and quick and mercilessly ironic, but also generous and serious. Professor Pavlov had a strong personality, completely dedicated to mankind. He knew and understood human nature and was able to do much for his patients through his realistic approach method.

The account of experimental work on conditioning was the result of twenty-five years of labor. His consideration of his patients made him famous in the early years of his medical career. His looks and personality inspired many writers and painters to portray him as the prototype of a doctor.

Pavlov resisted the temptation to develop a general theory of behavior based upon his findings. He considered the workings of the brain to be as much a part of all body functions as the digestion, in contrast to other psychologists who believed mind and body were separate realms.

Pavlov put no stock in Freud's ideas on psychoanalysis. To the dialectical materialist, the Freudian concepts as not being subject to experimental confirmation, were idealistic, founded on meaningless dreams, instead of solid materialistic fact.

There emerged a Pavlovian treatment of mental illness that depended upon education, rather than on psychoanalysis. Not only in the East, but also in the West, Pavlov's classic discoveries are regarded as a starting point for mental therapy.

A recently announced discovery in medical science was commended in President Johnson's speech given in Washington on the fourteenth of December, 1967. He said: "It is a spectacular breakthrough in human knowledge. It's going to be one of the most important stories you ever read.

For the first time, man has succeeded in manufacturing a synthetic molecule that displays the full, biological activity of a natural molecule in a living organism. These men have unlocked the fundamental secret of life." Then he added: "It opens a wide door to new discoveries in fighting diseases and building healthier lives for mankind. It could be the first step toward the future control of certain types of cancer."

On December 13, 1967, in Palo Alto, California, Doctor Kornberg announced at a news conference that his group of five research teams had independently discovered the enzyme that acts to join pieces of DNA together, end to end. This discovery seemed incredible for its vast application to the solving of varying problems.

For years scientists had worked night and day to discover the genetic code to which we owe the origin and continuity of life. They learned that from the instant of conception enzymes play the supreme role in all life processes. Without them the fragile male sperm could never gain entrance to the enormously larger and tougher female egg to complete the act of fertilization. As it is, the sperm is equipped with a minute amount of enzyme to dissolve a tiny crevice in the egg membrane, and thereby gain admittance.

Inheritance hinges on the way two chemicals transfer information from one generation to another and how specific molecules are arranged to form sons and daughters with the characteristics of their mothers and fathers. There are two code centers on the behavior of the two chemicals, DNA and RNA. One marks the blueprint of the future child, the other acts as a contractor and tells the cells what to do. Most messages go to the proteins, the basic material of life.

Every cell has a nucleus that looks like a small circle within the cell. The chromosomes and genes are situated within the nucleus; they are paired off, one set coming from the mother and one set from the father. Every cell in the body contains these elements along with a complete copy of the blueprint of the hereditary characteristics, and the fertilized ovum is destined to reproduce trillions of cells, all containing a message that gives them their orders.

The hereditary plan or mold in the cell nucleus is deoxyribonucleic acid (DNA), containing molecules with chains of four protein units or bases. The order in which these bases are arranged determines how the twenty different proteins (amino acids) outside the nucleus will be arranged.

The question is how to relay the genetic message to these proteins. It is here that the second chemical, ribonucleic acid (RNA) comes to the front. Molecules of RNA are sent out by DNA into the cell, where they pick up the amino acids. These form the proteins that control the cell's metabolism.

How does RNA know which amino acid to select? The code is the answer. Highly technical, it centers on the arrangements of the four bases that are strung along the backbones of the RNA and DNA molecules. It is a matching process and whenever three bases out of four fit perfectly, the genes go into action, and the development proceeds.

Scientists have explained that genetics (the study of heredity) deals with the physical and mental traits passed on to successive generations of men or mice or plants. These traits are determined by the genes. Humans carry in their bodies one hundred thousand or more different types of genes, which are bound to every cell. Some genes tell the cells to form into an eye or an ear. Other genes are a defense against diseases, some even cause illness.

How many different enzymes are there in the human body? More than 650 are known and researchers guess that many more will be discovered. There are trillions of cells in the body. But even the smallest is estimated to contain at least 100,000 enzyme particles. If a cell is regarded as a factory, the enzymes are the machinery that makes the factory work.

209

Genes are composed of bits of nucleic acid strung together on strands like beads on a necklace. Recently scientists have been able to break these strands apart to examine some of the beads.

Today scientists hope more than ever that diseases may be prevented before they occur by manipulating the genes. As research in biology comes to grips with life's fundamental processes, it draws closer to the manufacture of life in the test tube. The custom tailoring of life could produce a race of totally healthy and long-lived people.

Dr. Kornberg, magnanimous in victory, was not a novice in this field. He came to wide attention in the field of DNA when he received the Nobel prize for medicine in 1959. The prize was awarded him for turning a mixture of inert chemicals in a test tube into DNA, but this DNA, unlike the newly synthesized DNA, was biologically inactive.

In comparison with other scientific personages, Doctor Kornberg is a relatively young scientist. He was born in Brooklyn on March 3, 1918. He graduated from the Abraham Lincoln High School practically on his sixteenth birthday. He then attended the University of Rochester, became a doctor and ever since has devoted his life to research.

Naturally the question of what is life comes to the thought of many minds. Doctor Kornberg said: "There is no definition of life which would satisfy either laymen or scientists." However, as the twentieth century is known as the atomic age, the twenty-first century will surely be known as the age of DNA.

In this new century, mankind must enter a new stage of development. Mind and Spirit must be the next climate of the human. The race is undergoing its education, the bridge man crosses from the self-enclosed, self-favoring life into a consciousness of entire community of mankind.

A major scientific revolution has been in progress for decades. Man walks every day in the midst of mysteries and miracles. Powers of light and of darkness are "engaged in some mighty conflict behind the screen of appearances."

Through the Nobel awards, the scientific works, discoveries and inventions of the laureates have gained much in popular recognition and appreciation. The unsung heroes of the laboratories in the years past now find themselves sought after and honored. They are recognized by the entire world. A professor who become a Nobel laureate can usually find a chair at his pick of universities or research institutes. The prestige of any hall of learning grows with the addition of a laureate to its faculty.

For example one of our most vital and internationally acclaimed schools of scientific education is the California Institute of Technology, situated in Pasadena, California. This institute has not only been the research home for many Nobel winners, but has sought them for their unrivaled importance in the development of future men of science. Caltech enumerates eleven illustrious Nobel Laureates whose presence there has been of inestimable value to the school:

ROBERT A. MILLIKAN, *physics*, 1923, measuring the charge of the electron and work on the photoelectric effect.

THOMAS HUNT MORGAN, *medicine*, 1933, the relation of chromosomes to heredity.

CARL D. ANDERSON, *physics*, 1936, for his discovery of the positron.

EDWIN D. McMILLAN, *physics*, 1951, for his discovery of transuranic elements.

LINUS PAULING, *chemistry*, 1954, for research into the nature of the chemical bond; 1962, Peace Prize.

WILLIAM SHOCKLEY, *physics*, 1956, work on semiconductors and the transistor effect.

George W. Beadle, *medicine*, 1958, for his analysis of the the chemical activity of genes.

Donald A. Glaser, *physics*, 1960, for his invention of the bubble chamber.

Rudolph Mossbauer, *physics*, 1961, discovery of recoil-free emission of gamma rays.

Charles H. Townes, *physics*, 1964, for development of the maser-laser principle.

Richard Feynman, *physics*, 1965, for fundamental work in quantum electrodynamics.

Thanks chiefly to its educational institutions, California can claim twelve percent of all United States scientists, thirty-six percent of the world's Nobel prize winners in science, and the educated manpower for continued scientific growth.

Alfred Nobel was far ahead of his time. He foresaw the future and wanted to help mankind to make the world a better place in which to live.

The basic function of science and technology is to improve the quality of human life and Alfred Nobel's prizes stimulated world interest in scientists and stressed a greater interest in scientific research by the scientists themselves. Undoubtedly, the next generation will be even more scientifically oriented than this one.

The realist and life-long pacifist, Alfred Nobel, instilled in humanity a wondrous faith in the ability of science to accomplish anything that man believed can be done.

The Prize for Literature

*"There is a philosophy of feeling
as well as thought . . ."*

These words were written on the plain cover of a journal in which Nobel kept laboratory findings. He had paused in the midst of important experimentation to jot down this thought, just come to him.

Next to his consuming interest in science came his vital and creative interest in literature. He read omniverously of scientific techniques and in the same hungry way consumed the writings of men whose thoughts and ideals he admired. While he studied languages, he set himself to the task of translating Voltaire and other admired authors into Swedish. This work gave him such feeling for techniques of written expression that he turned to writing himself.

Poetry gave him joy, so he wrote his own. Professor Schück remarked that the young Nobel "had every prospect of becoming a writer of reflective poetry as he had great sensitivity and imaginative power, which can be noticed in his youthful, Shelley-influenced poetic attempts in English."

But his burdens of business and laboratory experimentation so completely absorbed his time from young manhood on, that he found no chance to write again until he had reached maturity. Then the spontaneous gift was gone. He completed novels: *In Lightest Africa, The Sisters,* a contemplative comedy *The Patent Bacillus,* but these works, filled with sarcastic barbs at life and people and not smoothly written, never received publication.

His interest in literature, however, never faltered. He read and studied it in whatever time he spared from his enormous duties and crowded schedules. His letters reveal knowledge of myth and allegory; Shakespearian references were his delight; and his favorite philosopher was Herbert Spencer, since they shared ideas and conclusions. Nobel's admiration of the talent of Selma Lagerlöf, the Swedish poet and novelist, did much to bring her the recognition of her talent and compassionate regard for her fellow beings. In 1909 she won the Nobel prize for Literature.

It was his fascination in Victor Hugo's writing that first made Nobel agree to attend Madame Juliette Adam's salon. He and the great, out-going Frenchman were drawn to each other and their companionable hours together became a bright spot in Nobel's life. He also made friends with Maupassant, Balzac and Lamartine, out of the French writers who frequented the Adam salon, but he did not like Zola. He considered Zola's harsh naturistic outlook on life disgusting. He admired the Scandinavians Ibsen, Björnstjerne Björnson (Nobel laureate for 1903), Viktor Rydberg, Jonas Lie, though perhaps *Peer Gynt* became his outstandingly favorite work. His command of the Russian language gave him a knowledge and appreciation of Russian writers that came considerably before Europe's or America's appraisal of them. He most enjoyed Turgenieff, though he felt that Gogol, Dostoevsky and Tolstoy had remarkable powers.

After Nobel's death, fragments of poetic outpourings, notes he had made on future writing he hoped to do, and poems he wrote at the most unlikely times and tucked away in anything that was close at hand, were found.

This poetic fragment held intensity and, too, a poignant tenderness:

> If I have loved? Ah, your query wakens
> within my memory many a sweet picture
> of dreamt-of bliss which life has grudged me,
> of cherished love which withered ere it grew.

You know not how reality doth mock
the young heart's idealistic world,
how setbacks, blighted hopes and sombre thoughts
embitter many a life which seems so glad,
and tarnish all the lustre. Your young soul
sees the world pure in imagination's mirror . . .
O, may you never see its naked features.

A list entitled "Philosophic Reflections to be Written,"
holds his remarkable breadth of interest:

The Interacting Atoms
The Functions of the Brain, Thought and Memory
The Ether and Ponderable Matter
Penetration of the Various Religions
Studies of Economy and Taxation
New Abbreviation System for Chemistry
Governmental System Based on New Ideas
Works on Explosive Subjects
Philosophy of Cells and the Cosmos

It is to be greatly regretted that Alfred Nobel could not
have lived long enough to develop these subjects, obviously
thought through and organized mentally. The world would
have benefited from his logic, his originality and his spirited
imagination.

Through Nobel's keen perceptions, he felt the handicap
of those sincerely innovative and fearless writers who dared
to break the rules of the fashionable writing of their day.
Publishers must be in a position to make money and few
have been willing to put out a book they are aware will
invite no readers. The long history of literature has suffered
from the reading taste and demands of the "conglomerate
mediocrity", as John Stuart Mill put it.

Nobel's personal relationship with writers must have increased his understanding and sympathy for these men
contending with the need to sell their work and not able to
write as they wished, since they had to have money for
existence. A few dared. Marcel Proust was wealthy enough
to publish his own first books, but James Joyce who trans-

gressed all the routine conceptions of easily digested writing died a poor, sick man.

Madame Adam's salon did not cater to poor men or neophytes. The famed and wealthy Victor Hugo could have credited the popularity of his works, readable and valid as they are, as much to his adoration by the Parisian people of the streets for his championship of their cause, as to the deft plotting and great characterizations that were his gifts. In the salon Nobel had opportunity to hear the discussion of writing by writers, to know how they yearned to use their originality, as well as their artistic taste. They were forced to keep their work well within the limits of the ordinary man's comprehension and well within the limits of that man's accepted thinking. Else they invited financial failure and poverty.

From his memories and sympathetic feelings of those years for men whose freedom of will was curbed by financial necessities, Nobel hoped his prize money would liberate the souls and gifts of fine writers. He asked that his laureate literary figures be chosen for their works of "an idealistic nature", that they be selected for Nobel award for the "greatest benefit to mankind."

Whether the prize winners through the years have always merited the Nobel distinctions above all other world writers is certainly a personal matter to decide, but they are all figures of great distinction and with honest expression of their own brand of compassionate judgments. Theodor Mommsen (German, 1902) wrote historical narratives; his greatest work perhaps, the history of Rome. Rudolf Eucken (German, 1908), Henri Bergson (French, 1927) and Bertrand Russell (British, 1950) were writers of philosophy. Dramatists ranged from the imaginative Belgian, Maurice Maeterlinck, in 1911, to the satirist, George Bernard Shaw (British, 1925), to the robust, bitter Eugene O'Neill of America in 1936. The poets came from great variation of national heritage: the Frenchman, Rene Sully-Prudhomme in 1901, the first year of the prize awards; the Indian Sir Rabindranath Tagore in 1913; Eric A. Karlfeldt of Sweden in 1931; T. S. Eliot, the Briton in 1948; Juan Ramon Jiminez from Spain, 1956; George Seferis of Greece, 1963; and Miguel Angel Asturias from tiny Guatemala in 1967.

Since 1930, America's great novelists have won awards. Sinclair Lewis was cited in 1920, Pearl S. Buck in 1938, William Faulkner in 1949. Ernest Hemingway triumphed in 1954 and John Steinbeck in 1962. The common man on Main Street, China's Good Earth, the little town of Oxford in Mississippi, the mid-westerner of conventional low middle-class, the cruel livelihood of sharecropper bands of Oklahoma, figured in books by these powerful writers.

The world watched in sympathy when the eminent Russian novelist, Boris Pasternak, was forced to decline the award in 1958. He died a sad, disillusioned man on his native soil, his only crime the intense quest for freedom of spirit in his country.

Literary laureates, people of inherent dramatic qualities and vital use of languages, often receive immense coverage in the communication systems. Many of them gain prestige and critical attention they never had before winning the Prize. Though the Nobel cash awards are not today the fortune they were in days when money had greater values, they are still a considerable amount that could set any writer free from the curbs of best-seller tastes. More importantly, the author receives the highest literary honor, the Nobel prize for literature for his great benefits to mankind. His work becomes immortal.

The Peace Prize

(I have a) more and more earnest wish to see a rose-red peace sprout in this explosive world.–ALFRED NOBEL, 1886

Peace was born in Alfred Nobel. His early years, as a child-invalid had given him hours and days to think, to brood, to conjecture. Freedom of choice became a corner-stone of his character and with it his necessity for peaceful relations with his fellow man. "I avoid disputes like the plague, even with people who give me every reason," Nobel wrote in a youthful letter.

His study of literature in original languages was one of his joys in education. He discovered the poems of Percy Bysshe Shelley and became devoted to them. Not only did Nobel read and absorb them, fragment by fragment, but his poetic writing showed an imitative form and feeling. In Shelley's passionate freedom of spirit and idealistic peace, Nobel agreed implicitly, and from that time on, he spoke of war as the "horror of horrors and the greatest of all crimes."

When his inventions became the fearsome tools of war, he sorrowed. Men put science to their own use but he had not intended such use to be made of his dynamite. At the time of its invention, he had dreamed of man's use of it to excavate tunnels and mines, to remove nature's barriers for free access between nations, and to ease the slave work of men in construction projects.

When dynamite was put to war destruction, he evolved another hope for its aid to peace; "My factories will perhaps end wars sooner than your congresses," he said to Bertha von Suttner in later years, though it must have been evident to him that his words contained some wishful thinking.

He made this remark out of his studious regard of human nature that had been his habit since childhood. He held no illusions about mankind and felt that war could eventually lead man into spiritual numbness and total self-destruction. War must be stopped before it was too late, but how? His logic and vision had almost made it possible for him to penetrate the future. He knew, at least, that his dynamite would lead to bigger and better explosions, and that the day would come when the holocaust of entire nations was possible and probable. Perhaps he could foresee the times today, when a timid peace through mutual terror is kept between powerful nations, though smaller ones scuffle and scrap at each other like recalcitrant children.

Nobel admitted the error of his "peace through fear" more than ten years before his death. He returned to his original thinking that only knowledge could change the nature of man from a warlike creature into the mind that would work for the brotherhood of nations. In 1896, he wrote of his financial backing of a daring balloonist, S. A. Andrée: "In this too I want to serve the idea of peace, for each new discovery leaves traces behind it in the human brain which makes it possible to hand to future generations more brains which will be capable of arousing new thoughts of culture."

Nobel was baptized and confirmed a Lutheran in childhood, but in maturity he claimed atheistic beliefs. This could have been only a pose he used in his obviously enjoyed ability to shock people out of their placid acceptance of the conformities of life. An example of such a remark was his expressed annoyance that "the Old Man up there is indeed no friend of peace, at all events He acts with systematic cruelty and always shows His claws. One has certainly been made to feel that."

Professor Schück insisted that Nobel's far-reaching and consistent charity expressed his religious attitude. "A religion was of value to him only if it expressed itself in love for mankind. By reason of certain hastily spoken remarks he is considered by many to be an out and out atheist, an enemy of all religious belief. But his so-called atheism was of a special kind . . . the sustaining idea was its high idealism. It was opposed to the divine faith of the dominant religions because their God was a cruel, unjust ruler of the world who was to blame for all religious wars and all persecutions of other faiths. But behind the denial is a glimpse of a Being who is free of the other one's faults, a God of peace and all-embracing love for mankind. . . ."

Nathan Söderblom, in later years the Archbishop of Sweden, who was pastor of the Lutheran Church of Paris during Nobel's residence in that city, held his friendship with Nobel in deep affection and esteem. Nobel contributed important sums to the parish work of the Reverend Söderblom and the pastor treasured a letter from Nobel that gave frankly his religious conceptions:

The difference in our religious views is perhaps formal rather than real, for we both agree that we should do to our neighbour what we want him to do to us. Admittedly I go a step farther, for I have a loathing for myself which I by no means have for my neighbour. . . . In the way of religion, to know what one should believe is just as impossible as to square the circle. But to distinguish what one can *not* believe is well within the bounds of possibility. These bounds I do not cross. Anyone who has thought at all must realize that we are surrounded by an eternal riddle, and all true religion is founded on that. What one sees through the All-Father's veil is nothing. . . .

Erik Bergengren adds to this quotation: ". . . few had a stronger sense of life's spiritual values than he. It was the dogmas and trappings around them which he could not accept."

It would have been a happy event for Alfred Nobel had he been able to witness the awarding of the peace prize to the Reverend Nathan Söderblom in 1930 for his writing and working for peace. The influence of Nobel upon the pastor had exerted him to great dedication to the cause of peace, though it could not be said he had won Nobel to any greater acceptance of church rituals.

At the time of Nobel's death on the 10th of December, 1897, his long-time valet, Auguste, thought he had detected the word "telegram" in Nobel's feeble mutterings. He wired Emmanuel Nobel whom he knew had been Alfred Nobel's favorite and most trusted relative. When Emmanuel arrived, he asked Pastor Nathan Söderblom to come from Paris to conduct a simple ceremony in the San Remo villa, before Alfred Nobel's body was taken to Stockholm for a public funeral and burial. Söderblom's distress at the loss of his valued friend in premature death did not allow him to collect his thoughts until the train from Paris had reached the French-Italian border. There he left the train and walked the high road, *La Corniche,* as far as Menton, in order to prepare the magnificent memorial speech he gave as he stood by the casket that held the emaciated body of Nobel.

Bertha von Suttner's return to Vienna from the Russian Caucasus brought also her return into the life of Alfred Nobel. More than ten years had elapsed since she abruptly left Paris to fly to her beloved, Baron Arthur, and she had endured the Russo-Turkish War terrors and misery at close hand. Not only had she lost the typically Austrian complacence, concerning the omnipotence of the Crown and its army, but she had turned to the development of the International Peace Congress through the influence of Wilhelm Loewenthal.

Bertha and Alfred Nobel corresponded regularly and at length, but they did not see each from the time of their reunion in Paris in 1887 until 1891, after she had gained her European prestige as a novelist through her book, *Lay Down Arms.* She had succeeded in organizing her peace congress with the well-known French pacifist, Frédéric Passy. The young Alfred Fried had become Bertha's assistant.

Frédéric Passy was made a Nobel laureate the first year the prizes were awarded, 1901. His citation came to him for his founding of the French peace society. Bertha von Suttner received the peace prize in 1905 for promoting pacifism and founding the Austrian peace society. Alfred Fried, an inspired journalist, had made his publication into a vital sponsor of world peace, and was awarded the peace prize in 1911. Again the heart of Nobel would have rejoiced to know his close friend and respected acquaintances had earned what was, to him, the greatest honor of all.

The first Congress of International Peace assembled at Rome in 1891 with the Baroness von Suttner in command.

Annual meetings were held thereafter in European and American cities with the support of government officials of the nation that entertained the delegates. Time and again, Bertha urged Nobel to give moral and financial support to the pacifist movement. He did contribute negligible sums out of respect for her efforts, but he felt no approval for the methods adopted by the congresses for their proposed advancements of world peace.

He wrote to Bertha, accordingly:

I am afraid that what you need is not money but a program. Mere resolutions will not secure peace. It is necessary to submit acceptable proposals to governments revealing good intentions. To insist on disarmament is practically to subject oneself to ridicule without benefit to anyone. To seek the immediate establishment of arbitration courts is to create innumerable prejudices and to invite obstruction on the part of ambitious people.

In order that there may be any hope for success, the initial work should be planned on a more modest scale. . . . I believe that few governments would refuse to entertain favorably a moderate proposal, providing it had the support of prominent statesmen. For example, would it be asking too much if it were to be suggested to the European governments that they agree for a period of one year to submit all differences arising between them to a tribunal or, if this should not meet with their approval, at least to refrain from engaging in hostilities during the same term? This may seem but a modest undertaking, yet only if one is prepared to be content with little, are great things likely to be achieved. One year is a short stretch of time in the life of any country, and even the most aggressive statesman will realize that it is not worthwhile breaching an agreement which will soon lose its effect anyway. And upon the expiration of the fixed term, all states will wish to extend the peace pact for another year.

This was Nobel's suggestion for a minimum program. It followed his life habit of beginning small, not only because he felt all great things have grown from small beginnings, but also because he considered this the only way of gaining human cooperation. He conceived an idea, rather a peculiar one perhaps for a business man, but founded upon his belief that the masses of all nations are swayed by the printed word, man's only mass communication at that time. In 1892 he employed for one year a Turkish diplomat, Gregoire Aristarkhi Bei, whose duties were to confer with national officials and to gain the confidence of the press so that pacifistic articles and doctrines would gain entrance into the public's reading.

The experiment proved ineffectual and left both Nobel and Aristarkhi in frustration. During the year none of the results Nobel sought had been attained and he terminated the contract with Aristarkhi, although the man did not accept the loss of employment pleasantly.

Nobel attended Bertha's peace congress of 1892 in Bern, Switzerland, but he could not honestly commend the actions and commendations of the congress. This disappointed Bertha who had hoped to enlist him as a noted and wealthy adjunct to her work, though she had full appreciation of his plans—not fully developed as yet—for his estate.

Bertha von Suttner's congresses of peace gained in prestige and in the world's awareness, as least, if not in actual results. The sixth congress, held in Antwerp, was presided over by Guzo de Lehay, the Belgian Minister. At the fifth congress in Chicago, Josiah Quincy, Assistant Secretary of State, held the presiding chair. At another, Leopold, King of the Belgians, received the delegation. The twenty-first meeting of the congress was to be held in Vienna on September 15th of 1914. Bertha informed all delegates that this would be "the most brilliant of all our Congresses." The Austrian Government offered free tickets on Austrian railroads to the delegates. Count Leopold Berchtold, Austria's Minister of Foreign Affairs, promised to preside at the opening session. Emperor Franz-Joseph graciously consented to receive the delegation.

On June 28, 1914 the Archduke Franz-Ferdinand met his murder at Sarajevo at the hands of a Serbian nationalist. By the end of the summer England, France, Belgium, Serbia, Montenegro and Japan had united in a death struggle against Germany, Austria-Hungary and the Ottoman Empire.

Exactly one week before the Austrian Archduke was killed, the Baroness Bertha von Suttner died. She was old, her heart had weakened, and she was afflicted with cancer, but a witness to Bertha's death reported that her last words were, "Lay down arms! Tell this to many, many people!"

Her congresses of international peace resumed after the World War I, interrupted again by World War II, but resuming after that. She had given to the world its first organized peace effort and a spirit that could never be completely forgotten.

In 1906, America's President Theodore Roosevelt became a Nobel laureate for his negotiation of peace in the Russo-Japanese War. In 1919, President Woodrow Wilson was selected for the prize for his efforts in the League of Nations. America had two women laureates, Jane Addams and Emily G. Balch, both tireless workers for the Women's

International League for Peace and Freedom. Elihu Root, Nicholas M. Butler, Cordell Hull, John R. Mott, Ralph J. Bunche, George C. Marshall for the European recovery plan, and Linus Pauling for his effort to ban nuclear weapons, received Nobel's peace prize. In 1964, Martin Luther King became a laureate for urging his followers to use only non-violent methods in seeking their goals.

All of these laureates were men and women of fine knowledge and educational interests. Alfred Nobel would have delighted in conversation with them, for each one exemplified his paramount belief that with compassion and knowledge comes peace.

PART IV

HIS HERITAGE

Michael Evlanoff's Caucasus

I made several sojourns to the Caucasus, my native land, and I recall the first one in particular; it has never effaced itself from my memory.

The pursuit of happiness becomes more than just hows, whens, and whys. One of the rewards of being a young man is the consciousness that a future lies ahead of him. My desire to move, to travel, to see and learn was insatiable. On the day I left for the Caucasus, I took a train from St. Petersburg to Moscow. It was only a twelve-hour run, but in those twelve hours the traveller was transported into a different world.

The beauty of the semi-Oriental, ancient capitol came to me as a perfect revelation. Moscow, glowing with color, with over three hundred churches, formed a picture of wonder, unlike anything else in the world.

To understand the Russian mentality, the extravagant Slav temperament, it must be remembered that they are Orientals. Russia is not the most Eastern outpost of Western civilization; it is the most Western outpost of the East. The Russian has many traits of the Oriental and one, is being stoic, fatalistic. This fatalism has made him accept his destiny blindly. After 1238 the Russian people for nearly three centuries had been kept under the Tartar yoke. It became proverbial: "If you scratch the surface of a Russian, underneath you find a Tartar!"

On the tedious train ride I thought of many things. I planned to buy a pure bred Kabarda steed and a Tsherkes' jeweled dagger, kindjal. And I was eager to see the fabulous women. Ever since the Tsar, Ivan the Terrible had married the daughter of the Tsherkess prince, the beauty of Circassian women had become world famous.

I noticed how little by little the forests disappeared, how the hills became smaller and the grass seemed harder. In the distance, toward the South, lay the well known and boundless steppe.

The steppe was the prehistoric seat of nomad hoards. They lived on horseback and in tents, used mare's milk as their food.

The next day I came upon a few scattered tents of the Kalmouk people. They are the friendliest people on earth.

Walking slowly, I stopped at one tent where hideous hairy goats were passing by. I walked in and sat on the floor. A boiling kettle hung over a fire in the center of the tent and smoke wound slowly up through a hole in the ceiling.

When my eyes grew accustomed to the dim interior I saw a young Kalmouk girl, quite pretty, who sat near the fire, sewing as she smoked. She had black jet eyes and sparkling white teeth. She was lovely to watch.

Struggling to my feet, I came closer to her, "What on earth are you making?" "A caftan." (a long tunic with a waist band), she replied with a coquettish smile. Then she looked at me again and all the radiance of youth and beauty shone on her face.

I gave her a necklace of colored beads. Her eyes could not conceal her surprise and the joy; they sparkled. Immediately she offered me her pipe. As tea was boiling in the kettle in addition to lamb's fat and salt, she handed me her cup. But these Kalmouk offerings discouraged me and I hastily bid good-bye to my new friend and reclaimed my horse to continue my way.

The sternness and desolation of the prodigious steppe was impressive and crept into my heart. Its barren landscape sketched out in tones of uncomprising color. Herds of horses and buffalos ran alongside us, accompanied by Nagai guides in bourkas and carrying lassoes.

This vast land was spectacular, bursting with a promise not yet fulfilled. The next day I travelled, accompanied by a guide, who kept his eye on me. Since I had purchased a Tsherkes costume, a magnificent poniard forged with silver incrustations, and several good horses, my guide held me in high esteem.

"You must keep close," warned the guide as we plunged into undergrowth. "It is very easy to get lost here," he added sternly. I did not answer him for a new experience came to me. It seemed the whole forest was alive with sounds of murmuring water. A myriad of raindrops fell tinkling from branch to branch, from leaf to leaf, each with a different note. When I paused to listen, it was as though the trees themselves were on the move escorting the horsemen. And yet the place was interwoven with profound and windless silence.

When we left the forest, the afternoon was coming close to its end and the gray light of early evening softly covered the valley. We were surrounded by the peaceful expanse of endless fruit gardens and the famed vineyards that flanked the road. Approaching the village, it grew dark as night. My horse reared suddenly. Something in the path terrified her and no amount of coaxing would induce her to go ahead. I guided her around it.

My guide found shelter for us and for the horses. I was very tired and had lost all sense of time. I lay on my back listening to the braying of distant donkeys. The heat had become insufferable nature; the night irritating and sleepless, for the continual grating of the indigenous two wheeled *arabas* was nerve-wracking.

The next day we rode into gently rising foreland. And there in the far, far distance rose the resplendent Caucasus. Throughout its history the Caucasus has been the cradle and the tomb of many races. Its geographical location made it a meeting place of a dozen nations. In an age dominated by so-called strategic concepts, the Caucasus possessed all the mystique of a highly strategic area.

The long journey on horseback led us always upward through superb, but often hostile land. There was talk about ill disposed Tsherkess mountaineers again. This was nothing unusual, because the nomads had hated the Russians ever since they had been chased from their lands by them. Their surviving tribes had found refuge higher in the mountains and deep in the rocks. Often they wandered from their hill retreats and back to their present abode.

The old timers pointed out that the on-again-off-again action was usual, since the Tsherkess were members of warrior families, vengeance had been their creed, and violence the climate that drove them to constant revolt since the post-Biblical period.

A new mountain panorama faced us constantly. My horse picked her way over the stones as sure-footedly as any mountain goat. In gaining the pass, there were many spots where a false step could have been fatal, a hazard of no concern to an experienced mountaineer, but for me a special thrill as we climbed.

In the far off horizon, the summit of the Caucasus mountains appeared to grow more and more majestically every minute, its crest breathtakingly completed by the snowy summit of the Elbrus, 18,481 feet and the highest point in Europe. As I became one with Nature's fearful handiwork, I reflected on the immensity of God and the smallness of man!

In the valley, the occasional rumblings from the glacier sounded, and its slow release of crystal clear water bubbled cheerfully below. When a rockslide broke loose, the thundering reminded me that man was not alone in being mortal. Not even the greatest mountain lives forever; the signs of a recent ice retreat and the reverbations of falling rock testified that only change is eternal.

Little had changed here since prehistoric times. The wilderness was alive. The air, diamond clear, and the mauve-violet mountains etched sharp against the deep blue sky. The crust of the pass, tortured by heat and cold, was strewn with misshapen volcanic rocks. How many adventurous and foolhardy men had vanished into oblivion there?

In this time of my youth, three sounds echoed through the mountains: In the morning, the sound of a flute played by a shepherd; in the evening, *saccade* rhythm of drum beats, the insistent ritual wild steps danced by men; and in the night, the sound of the wind blowing down the passes.

Meanwhile, the sound of the wind from whining and moaning changed many times in the hell of noise and made me think that there must be an evil spirit outside and I thought of the dismal procession of the doomed and damned.

It takes a kind of heroism to live through such a stormy night. For me, that night was the longest and the most helpless of my life.

It was with relief that I hailed the morning and the rising sun. As we came through the foothills, we took a road bordered by nondescript rows of houses with white plaster walls. My Kabarda steed trotted fast down the dusty roadway that led to a colorful bazaar with bric-a-brac shops displaying the wide variety of silver jewelry items made by tribesmen or the gunsmith's wares. Over all hung the strong odor of cooking and flies descended in swarms.

The light hearted crowd was composed of Tartars, Caucasians, Georgians, Persians, Armenians, Ossetes, Russians, Germans and French, a human mosaic of ethnic groups. The people strolled, talked gaily, or in hurried confusion. They either bought or sold and the harder and longer they bargained the more pleased they were. The rug sellers, displaying their merchandise, sang loudly, in extolling their rugs, and comparing them to the beauty of women.

Above the crowd a row of filamentous camels balanced their hieratic heads and an *araba* transported oxen skins swollen with Cahetian wine to more distant areas where the *araba* would be unloaded to make the marketing more accessible to the people. This chaos was drowned from time to time in the unceasing bleating of sheep, or in the braying of donkeys, who made up in noise what they lacked in size. The sheep ran loose everywhere and I could not figure out how anyone was able to identify his own sheep.

Here I was in this rugged and savage grandeur, virtually untapped, unchartered, untrodden and abounding with clues to the mystery of mankind. I was a carefree, pleasure-loving youth. No one knew where I was going, nor did it matter. I admired the proud women of the Caucasus. Most of them were beautiful. They had very small waistlines and they walked caressingly and gracefully in their baggy Oriental clothes, unhindered by the cobblestone roads. Sometimes they covered their faces with black or colored veils. These women knew how to fight; they were descendants of the Amazons. Beneath their veils they wore a dagger, a gold and ivory inlaid *kindjal*.

Some places in the Caucasus had become popular for their hot springs, distinguished water-cure places to restore health. Since ennui was à la mode, the mineral waters became romantic. What the Russian ladies were really curious about were the Caucasian nobles, or even some untitled, lawless Lesghiens. Every woman's secret dream was to be seized, flung over the saddle of a pure-bred Kabarda steed and forced to submit to the advances of a handsome and dashing mountaineer.

They recounted in a whisper, but bursting with envy and excitement, the case of an aristocratic lady from St. Petersburg, who had been abducted by a Lesghien. With great difficulty she was rescued later, but she fled back to the mountains, so gallant had she found the tribesman.

The swaggering Caucasians, who prowled around cat-like in their soft, stretched out tight leather boots without heels, in their pointed, black lambskin caps and shaggy goat's-hair bourkas, always wore a kindjal (dagger), regardless of whether they were tribesmen from the mountains or nobles. Their *kindjals* were two-foot daggers, double-edged, and used for slashing. To kill with the point lacked artistry. Their *shashkas* were huge sabers, barely curved. Weapons were a cult, as dear as honor itself.

The *lesghinka,* the national dance, was begun by the women in slow steps. The dancers' long flowing sleeves shielded their faces. Gradually the rhythm quickened and then, the men joined and circled round the women. The rhythm became furious, the beat of the drums faster, until they reached the point of ectasy. It was a dance of conquest, of mating.

But before I could join the dance, my guide brought me a telegram informing me that my father had fallen seriously ill and advising my return at once. I tried to think of something to say, but nothing came and everything seemed futile to me.

It was my guide who spoke in his even, soft voice: "I will not thank you because I cannot. I can only pray to Allah that someday, somehow we will be together again!" With a low bow of respect, he left me.

Nobel Brothers Naphtha Company

The Venetian merchant, Marco Polo, in the thirteenth century mentioned that oil, as an illuminant, was exported from Baku on camels to Baghdad, the former fabulous residence of Garun-Al-Rashid.

The Nobel Oil enterprise started in 1873 with Robert Nobel's purchase of the Balakhinsky oil field, three and one-half miles from Baku in the Caucasus. This transaction marked the beginning of the Russian oil industry.

The Nobel Brothers Naphtha Company, called Branabel by its executives was a composite of industrial plants, workers' villages, homes of the men who ran it, and, everywhere, the bore-holes that brought the great deposits of oil to the earth's surface. From Baku to the seashore and through the Balakhinsky area, the company structures spread like the out-stretched fingers of a giant hand.

On this journey to the Caucasus, I had skirted the great ridge of the Caucasian Mountains and crossed the desolate lowlands to the Caspian Sea. I was not prepared for this elaborate and efficient enterprise. It had machine shops that manufactured the company's own machines. The chemicals necessary for the oil refineries were made there. It contained a gas and electric works, engineering shops, laboratories for experiments, as well as research and checking samples. A pipe net work functioned underground, but cistern trains moved stolidly past the refineries to haul the never-ceasing flow of liquid treasure to fill their steam tankers, built for them in Sweden, that plowed through the Caspian Sea, the Black Sea and up the Volga River to Kazan.

It has often been said that next to high explosives, the serviceable oil tanker is the most far-reaching achievement the world owes to the Nobels.

Many times I strolled through the vast mechanical city of the Nobels and talked to the workmen. These sharp-eyed intelligent men had no feeling of subservience to me since they well knew I did not belong to the management. I would chat with them about their natal homes and how they happened to come here to work. Often I heard them say with pride: "We are Nobel's men."

What was the reason for such an attitude on their part? The usual working day at that time in Russia, as in most countries was shocking, judging by present-day standards. It was a twelve-hour day! Even some fifty years ago, the Nobels introduced in their enterprise a ten and one-half hour day, that is, a sixty-three hour week. Today this would arouse the indignation of workers in any civilized country, but in Russia at the turn of the century it was a progressive step. The company built for the Nobel workers comfortable houses and clubs in immediate proximity to the oil wells. Only those of the workers who preferred to live in Baku were obliged to spend time in travelling and, for them, a special steamship was chartered.

The employees had a savings bank of their own, in which, in addition to their own deposits, regular contributions were made to their account by the firm. Finally, two schools were built and maintained at the expense of the Nobels.

Something even more spectacular was arranged by the firm: "The Villa Petrolea," a unique institution for Russia, was organized. Baku had no trees so the Nobels shipped soil, flowers and seedlings from Russia and they laid out a park on the seashore where houses for workers were built, fifteen villas altogether. A special building for bachelors, a library, billiard rooms, other recreational facilities and a club house went up at the "Villa Petrolea." It was like a lovely mirage in the desert of Caucasian lowlands. The Nobels paid high wages and their discharges were rare, so it is no wonder that the workers valued highly their employment and appreciated their employers. The majority of employees participated in the company's profits; this was an inviolable policy in the Nobel enterprise.

In 1883, Alfred Nobel, in a letter to his retired brother, Robert, described the enterprise as "gigantic." It was indeed gigantic compared with a plant for the manufacture of explosives. From a modest partnership of four men, it grew into a colossal joint stock company. At the time when Emmanuel Nobel was managing its business, it produced up to forty percent of the entire Russian oil output.

One of the company's crises occurred in the last period of Ludwig Nobel's life. A serious competitor appeared in Baku in the person of the banking house of Rothschilds, which had just purchased some oil fields in the Caucasus and, naturally, had limitless financial potentialities. The Rothschilds had acquired a majority of stock in the new Baku-Batum Railroad that transported Russian oil abroad.

The dividends of the Nobel firm began to dwindle and caused discontent among the stockholders. Displeased stockholders greatly disturbed the scrupulously correct and ambitious Ludwig Nobel. Then, too, his respected brother, Alfred, resigned from the board. Sohlman and Schuck reported that Alfred disapproved of Ludwig's business policies. He felt Ludwig had developed the business too rapidly and too intensively, had disregarded competition and the condition of the market, and not taken into account the floating funds of the company. Perhaps in this, the more conservative and cautious Alfred Nobel had justification. However, he remained a stockholder in the company and continued to be its creditor. Without his money, the enterprise might never have survived the crises of the eighties.

Ludwig Nobel was not a healthy man. He had tuberculosis of a slowly creeping type. As a rule, this dreadful disease becomes less dangerous during old age than in youth. But in his case, the tubercular process became more acute after he was over fifty. The deterioration of his physical condition was certainly augmented by the complications arising in the conduct of the business. And, perhaps, business lagged because he was unable to work as heretofore.

The firm grew strong again, recovered from the adverse economic conjuncture of that period. Through the insistent advice of his physicians, Ludwig Nobel, in 1887, resigned from the business, just as eight years earlier Robert had retired. He entrusted the management of the firm to his son, Emmanuel, and proceeded to the French Riviera where he died at Cannes on April 12, 1888, at the age of fifty-seven. His two brothers, the elder and the younger, survived him by eight years. They both died in 1896.

Ludwig Nobel was buried at the Volkov cemetery in St. Petersburg.

Here is an astounding paradox: Oil is not necessarily at the disposal of the richest, who possess the black gold for its purchase. Buying it is nothing; it has to be transported. Professor Mendeleyev in his book on oil, after noting the services rendered to the oil industry by Kokorev, who had retained him as consultant, Novossiltzeff, Burmeister and Hadji Tagiev, all of whom had worked for its development, dwelt especially on the activities of the Nobels. "The whole work of the Nobel firm," he said, "has proved a progressive factor in the evolution of the technique and the promotion of trade in Russian petroleum." Such is the judgment of the greatest and most famous among the Russian chemists. But figures are still more convincing. In 1873, before the Nobel enterprise had been founded, the production of oil on the Apsheron peninsula near Baku amounted to only 3,952,000 poods, a Russian weight equal to 36,113 pounds.

In 1886, the last year of Ludwig Nobel's activity, it reached the colossal figure of 123,500,000 poods. This does not mean the entire increase was attributable to, or resulted from the operation of the Nobel firm, but its share in the sum total was enormous, and the balance of the output was largely due to the fact that their example encouraged other Russian industrialists. The work of the Nobel enterprise was far more productive than that of the other concerns. The Brockhaus Encyclopaedia notes that while the Caucasian firms, on the average, received from one dessiatine (a Russian measure equal to approximately 2.70 acres), 860,000 poods of oil, the Nobels received double that amount.

However, transportation became their principal difficulty. The pit-holes for the extraction of oil were dug by hand with shovels; oil was transported in leather containers in tilt carts. The Nobels ordered drilling machinery from an American firm and constructed a pipe line from Balakhan to Baku. This was the first pipe line ever built in Russia; it signified an economic revolution which might have assumed a bloody character. The digging of wells, and especially the hauling of oil in carts, constituted an important source of earnings for the local population and, obviously, it was to disappear with the introduction of drilling machines and the construction of the pipe lines. The workers perceived in these technical miracles something diabolical. However, no riots took place, though discontent rumbled threateningly for a time, then finally disappeared. In many other countries an industrial revolution of this kind had been frequently accompanied by bloodshed.

The smooth work record of the Nobel enterprise, located in a region with a bellicose Tartar population at all times ready to resort to arms, can be explained only by the inherent good sense of the local Mohammedans. They were quick to realize that the loss of earnings in connection with the transportation of oil would be compensated by many other advantages. The owners of the tilt carts found other employment in the Nobel factories, while local peasants found opportunity to sell their produce to the population that invaded Baku from Russia and Caucasian localities. The fabulous growth of the town was accompanied, true, in a slower tempo, by improvement in the welfare of the Azerbaijan peasants. At first, the pipe line had to be guarded by armed men.

The transmission of natural oil through pipes was but one phase of the technical revolution. Three additional features should be noted: the construction of refineries, the construction of tanks for storing petroleum, and the acquisition of oil tankers. From the very first years of the existence of the firm, it put into practice the transportation and distribution devices which were used in Russia for a century.

In Western Europe there was an extreme scarcity of oil. Many of the technical advances achieved by the Nobels existed in the United States, although the geographic conditions were altogether different.

According to Mendeleyev, the Nobels expanded for the construction of the plants, the oil tankers in the Caspian Sea and the barges on the Volga, the railroad tank cars and the kerosene storing facilities, not less than twenty million rubles (approximately ten million dollars). This was a colossal sum in excess of the combined wealth of Alfred and Ludwig Nobel. Either the Russian State Bank extended credits to them or profits for certain years were so large that the Nobels, willing to forget dividends, used them for amortization and the purchase of necessary equipment. Other expenditures also amounted to substantial sums.

Ludwig, and subsequently his son, Emmanuel, devoted close attention to the welfare of their workers. In the official bolshevik literature, harsh statements reviled the Nobel enterprise. As capitalists, the Nobels belonged to the most prominent circles in Russia. Only the Moskow and Yaroslav cotton manufacturers and the Kiev sugar kings could compete with the Nobels from the standpoint of economic prominence.

Emmanuel Nobel
and Michael Evlanoff

In Russia, the end of the past century and the early years of the present one were replete with remarkable men and vital achievements.

The new fortunes of that epoch could not have come into existence without hard work. Not always was it honest labor, but for the most part, great wealth was accumulated by dynamic energy, profound knowledge and unusual ingenuity.

Such was the origin of the oil fortune of the Nobel family. It was created by the combined efforts, industry, perseverance, and bold initiative of three succeeding Nobel generations. Their lineage included illustrious scientists, men who clearly realized the significance of technical inventions and who perceived in the fields of science and technology far greater possibilities than the average business man.

On June 10, 1859, in St. Petersburg, the first child was born to Ludwig Nobel and was named Emmanuel in honor of his grandfather. (The slight change in spelling was for clarity.) At the age of twenty-seven, in the year 1887, Emmanuel was left with the management of the large Nobel Brothers' firm, since his father had departed for Cannes, where he died in the spring of 1888. Emmanuel became the head of the colossal Baku enterprise. He came into power at a difficult period, since the Russian oil industry was then going through the most acute crisis in its history. Prices were down and discontent among the employees almost paralyzed the work in the oil fields and refineries. There was no demand for the product and business had practically come to a standstill. A clever physician was needed to treat the patient and to restore it to health. Emmanuel proved to be such a savior.

Emmanuel Nobel conducted the company's operations in a more conservative manner than had his father. He devoted his main effort to the increase of consumption. The cities were won over to kerosene without great difficulty. In Russia, the urban inhabitants in those days constituted not more than ten percent of the total population, so that the future of the Baku oil industry necessarily depended upon whether or not the villagers would learn to use the new illuminating oil. Emmanuel Nobel reasoned that, with the enormous distances in Russia and the lack of cohesion between city and country, kerosene would never become popular among the peasant masses. Even in the central Russian provinces, farmers who had never in their lives seen a city were by no means exceptions. One old peasant woman had lived all of her life within twenty miles of Moscow but never entered that city.

To solve this problem Emmanuel covered Russia with a network of traveling agents. They visited one village after another, demonstrating the kerosene lamp everywhere. The contrast between this kind of lighting and the wooden torch, the customary means of providing light in peasant huts in old Russia, must have amazed the country folk. It was more impressive than the difference between the kerosene lamp and the electric bulb which came to the succeeding generation. The Nobel agents sold kerosene lamps at low prices, actually at cost. Due to Emmanuel's relentless efforts, petroleum gradually began to be in demand in Russian villages. This restored the firm to solid activity.

Through persistence Emmanuel demolished the Chinese wall of traditional mistrust in Russian peasantry. Setting his aim at the substitution in every hut of the cost-free, but dangerous, wooden torch by the petroleum lamp, Emmanuel eliminated one of the greatest calamities of the Russian people. Fire, called "the red cock" by peasants, had been a common menace because of their straw roofs and wooden buildings. It annihilated entire villages and even spread to adjacent towns. Emmanuel made obsolete the wooden torches in village cottages and the grease burners in wigwams of the Asiatic nomads.

I find it difficult to describe my friend, Emmanuel Nobel. to limit him to words on a page is impossible. His magnetism, his vitality cannot be expressed in descriptive phrases.

Accounts of his grandfather, father and uncles can be accepted from the words of others and by written records. Not so in the case of Emmanuel; not only did I know him companionably, but he was my intimate friend. When talking to each other we used the familiar "thou," instead of the conventional "you" Russian manner of address. Instead of facilitating my task of description, it complicates it. I cannot help but feel that no portrait of the man I knew so well could give an adequate picture of him, like a translation that loses the nuances of the original text. Emmanuel Nobel was a man whose personality was felt as much as seen and heard.

My first association with this remarkable man goes back to the year 1919, when we both risked our lives in the Caucasus. The dramatic horrors and joys of those days make it impossible for me to be objective in my story of him. He was over fifty when I first met him. Of his earlier life I know only those things he told me himself, or which were related to me by others. There is no printed literature on his life.

His appearance commanded spontaneous respect. He was very tall and broad-shouldered and carried himself with dignity. He had wonderful eyes, light blue, sparkling and piercing, and wore glasses only when he was reading. He had a Scandinavian type of face, like the faces seen on the canvasses of Roslin or Lundberg, those portrait painters of the Swedish *beau monde* of the eighteenth century. And yet he often reminded me of one of those old Russian grandees, portrayed so brilliantly by Borovikovsky and Levitsky. Again in *War and Peace,* I could see in Emmanuel, the old Count Cyril Bezoukhov. Perhaps this was a class trait. Whether we like it or not, wealth is power, and the habit of power is reflected in the countenance and bearing of a person.

Emmanuel had the manners of a nobleman, always even-tempered whether dealing with his equals or with those inferior to him. I never saw him in company with those who could be termed socially superior to him. I do not doubt that with them he would have been equally calm and self-assured, without a shadow of subservience. I know his superiors valued and respected him greatly. He was received at the Russian Imperial Court. At the Swedish Royal Court he was entirely at home and the venerable King Gustaf esteemed him greatly.

Because of his self-control, reserve and steadfast character, Emmanuel Nobel gave the impression of a cold man and some men, Rudolph Diesel for one, used to call him *der kalte Swede* "the frigid Swede."

I do not know Sweden well; I know it merely as one who visited the country and associated with the Swedes. Still it is my impression that independence of character and a highly-developed sense of self respect are fundamental Swedish traits.

A man, altogether devoid of envy, Emmanuel had that kind of benevolence toward people which may be described as kingly. True, he was a favorite of fate, but how few of its favorites possess the same characteristic? It seems to me it cannot be artificially developed; it is either there by nature, or it is altogether absent. This trait is not always identical with mere kindness, but Emmanuel was also a kind man, in the generally accepted sense.

He understood human nature, was sharpsighted and could see right through a man. Nevertheless like his uncle, Alfred Nobel, he was often cheated. More accurately, people abused his generosity. Nobel did not overlook their trickeries, he would tolerate them, particularly for the first time. This was his fundamental principal: a gentleman has to consider another a gentleman until the contrary is proved, and if the contrary was proved this was by no means due to Nobel's simplemindedness. That his purse may have suffered slightly, gave him no regret. The gentleman's code was fulfilled, the offender was relegated to his proper niche, and then nothing could compel Nobel to change his opinion of the man.

Kindness has no precise meaning. Every man is kind in his own way. In the case of some, kindness degenerates into mere carelessness or an easy-going tolerance toward everything, and a resulting impotence to react to men's deeds with any degree of discrimination. Of that there was nothing in Emmanuel Nobel. I remember two of his remarks: "Christ taught us to hate the evil in men, but not men themselves," and "to err is human; to forgive, divine."

Emmanuel Nobel possessed superhuman energy, which enabled him to shoulder the Nobel Brothers Naphtha Company. His instinct for divining people and a talent for surrounding himself with competent collaborators helped him but his principal collaborator was science. With its aid he introduced momentous innovations in the oil industry. Americans were his first teachers in the technique of oil production, but it was Emmanuel Nobel who taught them the technique of construction of oil tankers. America built their first ocean-going tankers on designs Emmanuel graciously loaned to them.

The first steamboats appeared on the Volga in 1816. After Röentgen had designed in Holland an engine in which steam was used in cylinders successively, later known as compound engines, a radical change took place in steamship construction. Through this method, engines acquired high steam pressure and, simultaneously, achieved economy in fuel.

Emmanuel conceived the idea of exploiting mazut as a fuel for compound engines. Mazut is the residue of refined oil after benzine, kerosene and lubricants have been produced from it. In earlier days, this substance was thrown away in Baku; it had no use. However, experiments demonstrated that, with the aid of mazut, steam pressure could be increased and only one ton of that product was needed where one and six-tenths tons of coal were formerly required. Thus, mazut proved a less expensive fuel, producing greater pressure, while at the same time it occupied less space in containers.

Emmanuel made an offer to the Russian Ministry of the Navy to deliver mazut for the use of the battle fleet. Further surveys were made and the results proved brilliant; experts' reports were favorable. Nevertheless, Emmanuel's proposal was rejected on the ground that the British fleet up to that time had used nothing but coal, so it was argued, that Russia should not be the nation to introduce an innovation of this sort. Emmanuel continued in his efforts and finally succeeded in winning the Navy and railroad department over to the use of mazut.

The seventies of the past century saw the development of the steam engine; yet, both the physicists and the engineers were fully cognizant of its inherent defects. Its principal drawback was its wastefulness, since it utilized only ten percent of the caloric energy of coal. Moreover, the steam engine was unprofitable in small enterprises because the cost of each horsepower unit of the steam motor becomes higher, but its energy decreases. Big industry was unable to compete successfully with the small enterprises.

The young college student, Rudolph Diesel pondered over a more economical prime mover and devised this scheme: a piston in a cylinder compressed air to a point where it became heated; after that, coal dust in the form of a fine spray was admitted into the cylinder; due to high temperature in the cylinder, it ignited and burned out, while the energy developing from combustion drove the piston forward. The rapid, successive repetitions of this cycle constituted the work of the motor.

The motors of internal combustion, constructed by Diesel were small ones, not exceeding twenty-five horse power. After a while he modified his original designs by substituting heavy oils for coal dust. This invention did not enrich Diesel, whose life was full of disillusionment. Nevertheless, in industrial circles the Diesel motor caused a real sensation, because cheap and heavy oils could be utilized in its operation.

With his usual foresight, Emmanuel Nobel gave careful thought to this invention and made an appointment to meet Diesel at the Hotel Bristol, in Berlin, on February 13, 1898. Early in the morning of that day, Diesel was informed that Nobel had been delayed en route.

On that same day, Friedrich Krupp was giving a luncheon at the Bristol to a group of financiers and industrialists. Diesel, who was in desperate need, sent his card to Krupp, asking for an opportunity to explain to him the principles of his new motor. Krupp thereupon invited Diesel to the luncheon and Diesel outlined the main features of his device. Aside from a few complimentary words, Krupp gave no encouragement to the young engineer and no concrete offer.

On the morning of February 14, Diesel and Nobel met together. At the close of the conference Nobel said that he would think over Diesel's offer and would give him a definite answer within twenty-four hours. On February 16,

Emmanuel signed a contract in which he acquired the exclusive right to exploit throughout Russia the patent for Diesel's internal combustion motor. He paid Diesel 800,000 gold marks at once.

In Diesel's motor the air in the cylinder was compressed to 35 atmospheres. Emmanuel began to admit the liquid combustible material at a slow tempo so that spontaneous ignition was thereby eliminated, and at the same time the combustion, during the backward motion of the piston, was considerably slowed down. Nor did Emmanuel stop at that. He understood the reconstruction of the motor so as to permit it to perform with a backward motion, a feature which had not been anticipated by the inventor. This improvement made it possible to employ the diesels on ships and locomotives. Because of the precision of these motors, their handiness and safety, they soon came into universal usage. Nobel's improvement was so important that Diesel was indebted to him for the popularization of his engine.

Diesel's life ended tragically. On the night of September 30, 1939, while crossing on the mail steamer *Dresden* from Antwerp to Harwich, England, he fell overboard and drowned. He disappeared from the boat without leaving a letter or note. His body was never found and the story of his mysterious death gave birth to many a legend, including the rumor that it was a case of suicide.

Diesel's sudden death caused a panic and the shares of his enterprise lost six times their value. His family was left penniless. Diesel's son, Eugene, stated that, immediately after the crash of his father's business, Emmanuel Nobel sent him a handsome sum of money to enable him to complete his education. Strangely, not one rich German thought it important to assist the family of the man who had contributed so much to the renown of German technique. In passing, it was mentioned that on his last trip on the *Dresden* Diesel had with him Schopenhauer's *Parerga*.

That Emmanuel Nobel, the frigid Swede from distant St. Petersburg, unhesitatingly sent money to the son of the ill-starred inventor, was more than a mere *beau geste;* it was an act of genuine benevolence. I was aware that among his numerous petitioners, no one with the slightest moral justification for seeking assistance, was turned down by Nobel. As the grandson and nephew of inventors, Emmanuel particularly sympathized with scientists and showed them touching kindness.

In this respect Emmanuel reminded one of his Uncle Alfred. He was the favorite nephew of the dynamite king and it was due to Emmanuel's generous stand that the difficulties caused by dissention over Alfred's will were finally overcome. The main difference between the two lay in Alfred Nobel's gloomy, misanthropic moods and his atheist belief, while his nephew Emmanuel was full of cheerful animation and of a pious disposition.

Alfred's life held only a few, not too happy amorous adventures; my friend, Emmanuel, on the contrary, was a passionate admirer of women. Still, both remained bachelors. Kindness, generosity and exquisite refinement were common to both; and, even as Alfred, Emmanuel took an interest in everything. Biology, psychology, chemistry, electro-technics, medicine and literature—all of these attracted his attention and aroused his intellectual investigation.

Even as an older man, he attended university lectures of famous scientists, or took a course in a subject that absorbed him at the time. On several occasions I accompanied him on such pilgrimages to the temples of science. The young college boys would look with amazement at the gray-haired, impressive older man who modestly occupied a seat on the bench next to them. Sometimes the professor would recognize Nobel and say a few appropriate words about him, for in scientific circles he was highly valued and much liked.

On the occasion of his jubilee, a chair in the technology of oil was created at the St. Petersburg Technological Institute and the degree of Honorary Technological Engineer was conferred upon him. Much in the same way as his Uncle Robert, Emmanuel—even though he was not a professional scientist—had introduced into his enterprises technical improvements that indicated he possessed outstanding creative ability.

Emmanuel grew very rich. After he succeeded in organizing the consumption and distribution of kerosene, Russia became an inexhaustible market for fuel and on Nobel's initiative, started exporting oil abroad. Even Soviet writers admit that Nobel, having established hegemony in the Russian market, opened foreign markets to Caucasian oil.

In 1900, Russia produced 10,361,000 tons of oil, or 51 percent of the world output, thus winning first place among oil-producing countries. This was the greatest triumph for Emmanuel Nobel, since, in no other branch of the industry, had Russia ever assumed international supremacy. The success was largely due to Emmanuel's personal efforts, since for fifteen years he had been the sole manager of the Nobel firm.

Russia did not long occupy the leading place in world oil output. Very soon America pushed to the foreground, leaving Russia far behind. Still in the early days of our present century the Nobel firm was second only to the Standard Oil Company.

With the establishment of the Soviet regime in Russia, the Nobel firm there ceased to exist.

I do not know for certain how large Emmanuel's fortune was. It must have been larger than Alfred's, who left over eight million dollars for the prizes bearing his name. It was rumored in St. Petersburg that Emmanuel had about 100,000,000 rubles, something like fifty million dollars. At any rate he was tremendously rich. Emmanuel tolerated nothing glamorous or showy about his wealth. He carefully avoided the noise and drum-beating of the *réclame*.

Emmanuel's father was inclined toward socialism, while Alfred Nobel called himself a socialist. My friend, Emmanuel, had no such leanings. However, he did more for his employees than his father had, or his uncle.

His father, Ludwig Nobel had begun to build houses for the workers, and schools for their children. Emmanuel not only continued this work but expanded its scale. During the thirty years he directed the affairs of the Nobel firm, he inaugurated workers' insurance, bonuses for the employees, hospitals for their families, sanitariums, rest houses, libraries and stipends for the young men who sought to improve their education.

Unlike many other millionaires, Emmanuel Nobel clearly respected the truth that all men must live decently and that, if human living conditions and higher wages be denied them, they will rebel against the economic regime under which they have to live and the men for whom they work. In Russia, unfortunately, this fundamental fact has not always been understood.

To Emmanuel Nobel the mere thought that he might be hated was intolerable. I journeyed with him through Russia during the worst time of the civil war and Red terror and we were compelled to conceal our identities. As ever, he was a calm, well-mannered gentleman, manifesting great personal courage and never complaining even in private conversations with me. But I felt that he was perplexed with the question: "What is it all about? Why should I be hiding?"

Emmanuel led a genuinely industrious life. He would get up at six o'clock in the morning, and go to work. His Uncle Alfred, on the average, wrote fifty letters a day, and Emmanuel's correspondence was no less extensive. The bulk of it did not pertain to industrial affairs but to public and charitable matters. His working day ended late, sometimes two o'clock in the morning. His organism must have required less sleep than that of the average man.

The entire responsibility for the conduct of the Nobel business rested on him alone. The junior members of the dynasty, the children of Ludwig Nobel's second marriage, were much younger than Emmanuel and they regarded him almost as a father. His word settled disagreements and troublesome questions. His father's second wife, who tenderly loved Emmanuel, remarked once that he "was too good for marriage." He himself, half-jestingly, used to say that he "had no time to get married."

He greatly valued his personal freedom. He was passionately in love with life and, in this, he was the direct opposite of Alfred. Though he devoted much time to his work, he was by no means a fanatic in that respect. He spent his leisure hours in the joys of living and treasured them.

He never participated in politics. This seemed to be a tradition in the Nobel family. None of them took an active part in political life, whether in Russia or Sweden or other countries, although it would have been easy for any one of them to have embraced that particular career.

Alfred Nobel was conversant with six languages. In France and England, where a knowledge of foreign languages is a rare phenomenon, because of the wide diffusion of French and English, he was looked upon as a prodigy. In this respect, Emmanuel even surpassed his uncle. He spoke fluently not six, but seven languages.

He was chiefly interested in scientific, social and economic problems. Rarely, and with apparent reluctance, did he discuss with me philosophic and religious subjects, considering these to be matters of one's inner convictions. In any event, he was not a Voltairian, as was his father. He believed that the mystery of religion is concealed from man, but I remember his telling me once that only a creature utterly devoid of reason is capable of attributing the marvelous and perfect order of the universe to mere accident; that its ideal harmony reveals the thought which governs the world. When we see an airplane soaring in the sky, he said, we do not contend that its construction and its motion are accidental and that no rational will directs its flight. Why is this? Simply because, today, we know what an airplane is. Now, then, is it possible to imagine that this majestic universe of ours, where everything is so perfectly balanced, came into existence by mere chance?

Some members of the younger generation are still alive. I know them all, but with none of them am I as intimate as I was with Emmanuel. It is inappropriate to write about the living, even when nothing but favorable things can be said about them. For this reason, it never occurred to me to give an account of Emmanuel during his lifetime.

In what sense was Emmanuel Nobel notable? It might be said there have been many good and energetic men who could have steered an enormous enterprise to the point of brilliant success and assured decent and comfortable living conditions to thousands of its employees. This is so. But the balance sheet of Emmanuel's life contained far greater values than his business achievements and the millions which he managed to make: his unique gift of sympathetic understanding, his inherent generosity, the finesse of his mind, and his exceptional tact in dealing with people. All these precious traits, these intangible assets, gracefully combined in his spiritual self, fully justify my contention that he was indeed a remarkable man.

The service rendered by Emmanuel to the Russian people was, indeed, great; but it was not limited to Russia alone. He feared a repetition of the first World War and the fulfillment of the pessimistic prediction of his eminent uncle who, on January 7, 1893, wrote: "If in thirty years we shall not have succeeded in a reorganization of the world, it will inevitably relapse into barbarism." This is the reason why

255

Emmanuel, with so much enthusiasm, advocated the idea that the peace prizes be awarded to persons of English, French and German extraction.

Emmanuel Nobel clearly understood that the future of mankind was dependent upon the manner in which mutual relations of the peoples of the world and international economics would be organized. He was convinced that the principal task was the establishment of an order based upon the principle of solidarity, according to which, in the interest of common good, each nation must make a concession of some sort.

Emmanuel Nobel died in Stockholm in 1932. The news of his death was one of the greatest shocks in my life. To me, he was not the "oil king." I was never employed by his firm and was in no way connected with his industrial activities. He was my personal friend, one who was sent to me by fate at the turning point of my life and shortly before the expiration of his own. I am happy that I was granted the privilege of rendering him a service at the risk of my own life. I am grateful to God that He gave me the opportunity of meeting Emmanuel Nobel and of becoming a close friend of his.

The Tenth of December

From my window in the Grand Hotel of Stockholm, I could see the panorama of a silver waterway, the unique Stronmen Canal which, despite the freezing temperature, remained unfrozen. On the other side of the canal rose the majestic eighteenth century royal palace.

Restless at waiting, I walked out of the hotel to breathe the fresh crisp air and to feel the pulse of this progressive and interesting city.

This was the big day, the tenth of December of 1967, and the eyes of the world focused on Sweden. The announcement of the Nobel laureates was breathlessly awaited by the press and the people of all nations.

Some of the icicle-covered lamps still flickered in the gloom of this north country. To each side of the main thoroughfare, I could see streets completely covered by the heavy snow. A few people stood at the tramway stop, stamping their feet to keep warm, and in spite of their fur hats and heavy coats, my fellow pedestrians shivered, as they hurried through the swirling snow and cold wind to their destinations. Speeding cars passed one another. Everyone and everything seemed to be hurrying, today.

I walked faster, breathing deeply of the frosty air. When a friendly, smiling Swede bumped into me, he would say, hastily and politely, "Excuse me!" In return I would say in Swedish, "Oh, don't mention it!" until at last I realized I was walking absentmindedly on the right side of the street. Everything in Sweden moves to the left.

I had learned some simple Swedish phrases, so language was no more a problem to me. In this amiable country I felt at ease, I felt like a Swede.

Stockholm, not without merit, is called the "Venice of the North." Sweden, today, is the richest nation in Europe with the highest per capita income and a standard of living, second only to the United States. This was not accomplished overnight. It has taken thirty years to bring this about. Swedish officials have not rested with solving the problems of maintenance of the country, they have constantly planned for the future. Sweden has compromised between socialist and capitalistic methods by using both, rather than concentrating on one ideological allegiance.

The premier of Sweden has called himself a pragmatic Socialist over the last twenty-one years. A man with humor, he advised young couples to marry, if they desired, but since they could not get a place to live in Stockholm for the next ten years, they should try a community where the wait was only eight years. When he was asked if it would not be worthwhile to help the Swedish Laplander to organize the export of reindeer meat, he chided his questioner. Wasn't the man ashamed of the idea of shocking the children of so many nations who think reindeer are part of the Santa Claus image?

I lived with the Nobels in Sweden for many years and I feel a special affinity for this highly civilized country. It has its own feeling and traditions. The Swedish people are friendly, hospitable, modest about their own achievements, great world travellers, and speak three or four languages fluently. They are tolerant of all political ideologies. They have a leading participation in all fields of sport and there is no nation in the world in which all inhabitants are so physically attractive.

However, all is not perfect in the Kingdom of Sweden. There are long delays for entering hospitals, homes for the aged, and new housing is at a premium. The problem of high taxes is always with the Swedes, yet they seem to take it philosophically. With a rising standard of living, more information, more travel, they have acquired an awareness of the world, and the bleeding and starving to death of people of less fortunate nations. The Swedes know well that whatever complaints they may have pale into insignificance in comparison with the tragic lot of others.

Late every autumn, newspapers around the world list the potential candidates for the Nobel prizes. The final selection of laureates is announced in Oslo and Stockholm on the tenth of December, the day of Alfred Bernhard Nobel's death. This is a day of ceremony and national pride. Up to 1967, approximately eight million dollars in prizes had been distributed to men and women and institutions, all of them to become forever distinguished as members of a unique aristocracy in the service of mankind. The peace prize is bestowed in Oslo and the prizes for outstanding achievement in the fields of physics, chemistry, medicine and literature are awarded in Stockholm.

An impressive, memorable ceremony takes place in Norway's capitol city at one o'clock in the afternoon in the Assembly Hall of the University of Oslo. A Norwegian dignitary presents the Nobel peace prize to the laureate of the year in the presence of the King of Norway and the members of the Norwegian Storting.

That evening the King honors the winner at a state banquet, and on the next day the champion of world peace returns to the Assembly Hall to give his lecture. In 1967, for the second consecutive time, the Norwegian Storting announced it would withhold its award for peace for another year.

Stockholm observed the day with great pomp and pageantry. Just before four o'clock, a prestigious international crowd of more than 2,000 persons in formal attire met in the auditorium of the Concert House. At half-past four, a trumpet sounded; the orchestra broke into the Royal March and the King and Queen of Sweden, followed by the princes and princesses entered the auditorium.

The winners of the Nobel prizes for science and medicine followed the royal family. When the King was seated in the front row center with his family and eminent guests, the prize winners ascended the platform. Each of them was introduced to the guests of Sweden who fill the Concert Hall and eulogized by an important Swedish official.

Then, one by one the laureates descended the carnation-decked stage and approached the King. The King rose from his golden chair to shake the hand of each of the winners, presented each with a gold medal and a leather-bound diploma with a memorandum of where and how they would receive the cash awarded as part of the prize. In 1967, the award for each winning category carried about $61,700.00.

The ceremony had solemnity and dignity with the flourish of trumpets at moments of particular significance. Since it was conducted almost entirely in Swedish, the laureates, their families, the diplomatic corps and notables of other nations followed the proceedings with a booklet of translations for the program.

The eight Nobel laureates of 1967 (three Americans, two Britons, a West German, a Swede and a Guatemalan) looked tremulous but proud, as they accepted their awards from King Gustaf VI Adolph, the 85 year old monarch, regal and erect in his white tie and tails. The ceremony was a mixture of formality and the special kind of Swedish simplicity; it held symbolism and sincerity. For the winners, this was their stepping-stone to immortality.

A banquet followed, held in one of Stockholm's most beautiful buildings, the City Hall. It began with a toast to the King; then King Gustaf VI Adolph toasted the memory of Alfred Bernhard Nobel, Sweden's beloved citizen who had dedicated the major part of his fortune to the establishment of the Nobel prizes. Speeches followed by prominent Swedish citizens and by the laureates who spoke in their own languages.

When the banquet was over, the King led the prize winners onto a balcony that overlooked the Blue Hall, where they were serenaded by the students. Dancing began, soon after the student singing, in both the Blue and the Golden Hall. The handsome, distinguished crowd danced until two in the morning.

Over the next few weeks or months critics of all nations would be writing or giving interviews on their agreement or disagreement with the choice of the Nobel laureates, but on the night of the tenth of December, all was accord and celebration.

In 1967, the physics laureate was Hans Albrecht Bethe, Cornell University professor of theoretical physics. He was cited for "his contributions to the theory of nuclear reaction, especially his discoveries concerning the energy production of stars." His research had explained how the sun and stars emitted such quantities of light and heat without quickly burning themselves out, and how energy radiated by stars is produced by the process in which hydrogen fuses to form helium.

Three scientists Manfred Eigen of the Max Planck Institute at Göttingen, West Germany; Ronald G. W. Norrish from Cambridge University, and George Porter of the Royal Institution in London won the chemistry award for "their studies of extremely fast chemical reactions effected by disturbing the equilibrium by means of very short pulses of energy. Eigen had researched on fast chemical reactions and measurements by electronics of the time required for molecules to return to a state of equilibrium. Norrish and Porter had worked together for six years on the development of a research technique they called flash photolysis.

261

The physiology and medicine prize was also shared by three scientists: Ragnar Arthur Granit, Neurophysiology Professor at the Royal Caroline Institute in Stockholm who had been the first to show how differing units of the eye's retina react to colors; Haldan Keffer Hartline of Rockefeller University's Biophysics Department whose work on the electrical impulses, carrying images to the brain, enabled him to explain how the eye, by sharpening contrasts, is able to differentiate form and movement; and George Wald from Harvard University, a Professor of Biology, who was acknowledged to be the world authority on the biochemistry of perception. These three great intellects had succeeded in diagnosing some of the intricacies of the mysterious workings of the human eye.

The last man to approach King Gustaf VI, and be congratulated by him was a heavy set, very bronzed Guatemalan with a face like a pillaging eagle. Miguel Angel Asturias was serving then as the Guatemalan ambassador to France, but his poems and novels were the lifetime attacks of this man against the dictators of his country and their ruthless oppressions of Guatemalan Indians. Asturias was cited "for his highly colored writings rooted in a national individuality and Indian traditions." This fearless and dedicated writer had suffered exile from his country from 1953 until 1967. During those years he lived in Argentina and in France. He seemed impassive as he received the Nobel gold medal, the diploma, and the cash award of $61,700. but his eyes reflected his tremendous satisfaction and emotional feeling at the justification of his literary challange for recognition of a forgotten, abused people.

Asturias' real debut as an author came in 1946 with his novel, *El Señor Presidente,* a caricature of dictators and suppression of the spirited revolutionaries.

These Nobel laureates were on this day dedicated to mankind. They had contributed to the sum total of man, what he is and what he will be. Their selection had demanded the most involved and painstaking research on the part of the members of three Swedish institutions and the Norwegian Storting, or Parliament. Sweden's Royal Academy of Science selects the physics and chemistry winners; The Royal Caroline Institute awards the prize in medicine, and the Swedish Institute chooses the literature winner. Norway's ruling body has the responsibility of determining the man who has contributed most to promoting the world peace. Man or organization, judged on ideal and activity throughout years, is chosen by a five-member committee, named from this Parliament body.

The research on the laureates begins at least a full year before the occasion of the awards. The institutes of selection send invitations to selected universities, government officials of many nations, jurists, previous prize winners, other notables of intellectual circles and world leaders. From these come the nominations of candidates for the year. The deadline for nomination is February first of the current year.

Deliberation continues until the fall of the year, when decisions at last are completed. During these months all people involved in these decisions study, research, read endless works of the candidates, thoroughly diagnose their past and present attainments. When the day of the awards nears, telegrams come to Swedish Embassies in the different nations who contribute the winners. A Swedish ambassador or his representative telephones or contacts the selected laureate.

These selection institutes always receive their share of the usual nomination letters of cranks, venomous critics and personally-believed geniuses. This stack of mail would make a book of unbelievable curiosity and considerable humor.

Alfred Nobel created another form of dynamite when he left his fortune of nine million dollars to establish the world's biggest give-away for merit and learning and inspiration.

The will of the man, Nobel, desired that the man selected for citation be honored since, "Higher knowledge should be the basis for his awards." A Nobel prize is the highest honor possible in the contemporary intellectual spheres.

Over the years of my close friendship with Emmanual Nobel, he often included me in luncheons or more elaborate affairs that honored the Nobel prize winners. I recall in 1926 the luncheon Emmanual gave for the fascinating Aristide Briand who was then France's foreign minister and the chief architect of the Locarno Pact that advocated treaties of mutual guarantee and arbitration between England, France, Germany, Italy, Belgium, Czechoslovakia, and Poland. The world's great sorrow was the failure of this pact.

At Emmanuel's luncheon, Briand was in excellent humor and delighted everyone with his sparkling wit and elegance of speech. Emmanual Nobel included me on his varying activities and I could cite his views on almost any subject, so he considered me a valuable asset in these affairs. An outgoing man with largesse, great charm, tact, and thoughtfulness, Emmanual Nobel's personal attentions were considered most desirable by Nobel laureates.

Aristide Briand particularly delighted me. He had come from poor parents, from a line of Brittany sailors. As a young man, fighting his way up in the world, he could not afford to eat every day. However he had educated himself and his remarkable personal gifts lifted him to the head of the French Government. He had extraordinary eloquence, a beautiful deep voice, the gift of improvisation and dramatic effect. He had the even more enviable gift of captivating individuals by his charm and elegant courtesy.

When the luncheon was coming to an end, I asked courteously and cautiously, as Emmanuel wished me to, what bank Mr. Briand used for his current account. We needed this information in order to facilitate payment to Briand of the peace prize money.

My question obviously embarrassed Mr. Briand. It seemed that he carried no account in any bank. This was a revelation that amazed Emmanuel Nobel and myself. We learned that Briand, reared in the necessity of pathetic frugality and enduring every kind of financial difficulty during his long years struggle for position, had never considered that he had need of a bank account for the few thousand francs he carried in his pocket. His salary did little more than cover his expenses of living and conducting France's affairs.

On receiving the Nobel prize with its attendant money, Briand became a landowner. He purchased a country place, typical of a Brittany peasant. His estate, Cocherelle, had some 500 sheep grazing on its meadows and he had a small cottage of four rooms and bath. He loved Cocherelle and retreated there as often and for as long a time as possible, between his government duties. It is good to think of the many great men, handicapped by lack of financial resource, who have gained some security and personal joy through the Nobel prize money.

Perhaps my most involved and unique assistance to Emmanuel in his concern for the best treatment of Nobel winners in countries, strange to them, was attending the Indian author, Sir Rabindranath Tagore. This occurred after World War I, and since I was passing through Berlin en route to Paris and London, Emmanuel asked me to look after Sir Tagore who would stop in Berlin for ten days before continuing to Stockholm to receive the Literature Prize.

I succeeded in getting lodging for Sir Tagore in the Esplanade Hotel, at that time one of Berlin's best hotels. I, then, arranged meetings for Tagore with foreign diplomats, Berlin officials, professors, and the intellectuals the Indian poet would find interest in knowing.

When Sir Rabindranath Tagore stepped onto the streets of Berlin he actually stopped traffic. He was one of the

Apostles, incarnate, looking as if he had just descended from the skies to our earth below. He wore flowing white robes; his feet shod in sandals; long white hair fell down his back and an equally long white beard fell down his front. But even more curiosity arousing was the baaing she-goat that came along behind this biblical figure. And horror came to me when I learned that he insisted his goat be kept in his hotel on the same floor with Sir Tagore. It seemed that he drank goat's milk each and every day of his life and could not be parted from this smelly, bewhiskered creature

The goat lived for ten days in splendid luxury in the most fashionable hotel in Europe. She would not budge by herself and had to be pulled and pushed and practically carried into her beautifully appointed room. The desperate sounds she made were never ending and caused considerable consternation in this exclusive, ultra-clean German hotel.

Complaints piled on the hotel management from all directions and to one and all explanations had to be made as to why this dirty, smelly, noisy goat resided in the hotel. She had to be fed and attended, like any other paying guest. When it came time to milk and clean her, the racket became worse than ever. Frenzy dominated the management, but somehow I managed to keep Tagore's goat with him. He refused my offer of domiciling several goats for his milk supply near the hotel; he insisted on his own goat close at hand. She stayed there for ten days.

Alfred Nobel was a man of genius. His scientific achievements were notable, but—more notable was the great service he rendered to world culture in connection with the establishment of the prizes which bear his name.

There were chemists greater than he. Certainly the contributions to chemistry of Lavoisier, Berzelius, Cavendish, Berthelot, Mendeleyev and Priestley were greater than those of Nobel. And the world knows today that Rockefeller or Carnegie donated for educational and charitable purposes many more millions than Alfred Nobel did, though Nobel's millions were accumulated at an earlier time.

There was in Alfred Nobel something that cannot be found in other scientists, art patrons and philanthropists. His figure is picturesque and unique in the same sense as the figures of Franklin, Lincoln, Lafayette or Mazzini. Then too, his was a complex character with conflicting ideas and tendencies that ordinarily exclude one another.

He was a pacifist, yet he invented one of the most dreadful weapons of war. He was a millionaire many times over; yet in some of his utterances he supported socialism. He benefited thousands of men, yet he considered himself a misanthrope. He was an atheist, yet he contributed liberally to the Church.

Alfred Nobel hated publicity, particularly self-advertisement. At the time when he had already become a world celebrity, his brother suggested that he write an autobiography. Alfred categorically refused to do so, framing his objection in words full of sarcasm, so peculiar of any discussion of himself. He exclaimed:

Alfred Nobel? Why, a merciful physician should have put an end to his existence at the very moment of his birth. His principal virtues? He has clean fingernails, and he never sat on any one's neck. His principal vices? The absence of a family, a bad disposition and poor digestion. He has only one desire: not to be buried alive. His worst sin? He does not worship Mammon. Important events in his life? none.

He was a man of deep humility. Every November newspapers in all parts of the world publish columns on the potential candidates whose work has brought values of research and culture and peace to their fellow beings. On December tenth, the prizes are announced and the name of Alfred Nobel is printed in every publication, is flashed over the world by radio, is sounded on television and over telstar, is spoken in the tongues of all the men of this earth.

Perhaps Nobel's greatest achievement was in setting up a new kind of example for the world to acknowledge and follow. He replaced the idolized war heroes, the men of power and wealth and high position, with men who were endowed with high dedication and true inspiration. He honored the men who forfeited popularity and money to write from their hearts about the sufferings and hopes of all peoples; the scientists who searched, alone and ceaselessly, for knowledge; and those who defied the greed of nations and the cruelty of men to pursue the ideal of a world where all nations could live together in harmony and trust. The search for knowledge, compassion and love were Alfred Nobel's gifts to the world.

PART V

HIS AWARDS

The Nobel Prize

The Nobel awards in physics, chemistry and medicine are given to those persons who, in the opinion of the panel of judges, shall have made the most important discoveries, inventions or improvements in these fields. What is "most important" is a judgment based on available contemporary information, and necessarily involves an estimate of future worth. Only history can prove the validity of the judges' appraisals of the relative long-range significance of the work of the many candidates for the awards. It is interesting, for example, to note that Albert Einstein was awarded the Nobel prize in 1921 "for the photoelectric law and his work in the domain of theoretical physics." There is no evidence that the judges at that time had any thought whatever that an earlier Einstein discovery, $E = MC^2$, made in 1905, would far overshadow the photoelectric law in worldwide significance. Who could have foreseen then the vast technological, social and political changes this simple law of physics would initiate—nuclear power plants, the A-bomb, the hydrogen bomb and the threat of mass annihilation.

The judges for the Nobel awards have no crystal ball that enables them to peer into the future, yet their record to date is outstanding, and one has a comfortable feeling that the selection process works well, at least in science and medicine. Although the extent of practical usage is not necessarily a meaningful measure of importance, the fact that so many discoveries cited in Nobel awards in physics, chemistry and medicine have already led to the development of major new industries, revolutionary new drugs, etc. indicates that the Nobel award judges have been highly successful in the selection of "important" achievements in these fields.

The Nobel awards in literature are more difficult to evaluate. In light of the hot wars and the cold wars of the past several decades, one can question whether any of the activities for which the Nobel Peace Prizes were given have, in fact, been of any great value in bringing about peace to our world. This situation, of course, in no way detracts from the merits of the other Nobel prizes, which justifiably command the highest respect throughout the world and confer indeed, upon the recipients, the highest honors of our times.

ARNOLD O. BECKMAN

Baroness Bertha von Suttner
Peace, 1905

Ivan Petrovic Pavlov
Medicine, 1904

Rabindranath Tagore
Literature, 1913

Woodrow Wilson
Peace, 1919

Albert Einstein
Physics, 1921

277

Robert A. Millikan
Physics, 1923

Thomas Hunt Morgan
Medicine, 1933

278

Carl O. Anderson
Physics, 1936

Edward D. McMillan
Physics, 1951

Linus Pauling
Chemistry, 1954, Peace Award, 1962

William Shockley
Physics, 1956

George W. Beadle
Medicine, 1958

Arthur Kornberg
Medicine, 1959

Donald A. Glazer
Physics, 1960

Rudolph Mossbauer
Physics, 1961

Charles H. Townes
Physics, 1964

Richard Feynman
Physics, 1965

John Steinbeck
Literature, 1962

List of Nobel Laureates

Eligible for a Nobel Prize are only individuals except for the Peace Prize, which also may be awarded to institutions and associations.

The Nobel Committees start their preparatory work on February 1st and submit the ensuing recommendations in the early autumn of the same year to the respective prize-awarding bodies which have the sole right to decide. Even a unanimous committee recommendation can be overruled by the adjudicating prize-awarding institutions. The prize awards must be made not later than November 15; the decisions are final and without appeal. The deliberations as well as the votes are kept secret. Only the results are made public.

(NOTE: *Titles, data and places given below refer to the time of the prize-award.*)

I. PHYSICS

1901 RONTGEN, WILHELM CONRAD, Germany, Munich University, *1845, †1923: "in recognition of the extraordinary services he has rendered by the discovery of the remarkable rays subsequently named after him."

1902 The prize was awarded jointly to:
LORENTZ, HENDRIK ANTOON, the Netherlands, Leyden University, *1853, †1928; and

ZEEMAN, PIETER, the Netherlands, Amsterdam University, *1865, †1943: "in recognition of the extraordinary service they rendered by their researches into the influence of magnetism upon radiation phenomena."

1903 The prize was divided, one half being awarded to:
BECQUEREL, ANTOINE HENRI, France, Ecole Polytechnique Paris, *1852, †1908: "in recognition of the extraordinary services he has rendered by his discovery of spontaneous radioactivity";

*born †died

the other half jointly to:

CURIE, PIERRE, France, (Municipal School of Industrial Physics and Chemistry), Paris, *1859, †1906; and his wife.

CURIE, MARIE, née SKLODOWSKA, France, *1867 (in Warsaw, Poland), †1934; "in recognition of the extraordinary services they have rendered by their joint researches on the radiation phenomena discovered by Professor Henri Becquerel."

1904 RAYLEIGH, Lord (JOHN WILLIAM STRUTT), Great Britain, Royal Institution of Great Britain, London, *1842, †1919: "for his investigations of the densities of the most important gases and for his discovery of argon in connection with these studies."

1905 VON LENARD, PHILIPP EDUARD ANTON, Germany, Kiel University, *1862 (in Pressburg, then Hungary), †1947: "for his work on cathode rays."

1906 THOMSON, JOSEPH JOHN, Great Britain, Cambridge University, *1856, †1940: "in recognition of the great merits of his theoretical and experimental investigations on the conduction of electricity by gases."

1907 MICHELSON, ALBERT ABRAHAM, U. S. A., Chicago University, *1852 (in Strelno, then Germany), †1931: "for his optical precision instruments and the spectroscopic and metrological investigations carried out with their aid."

1908 LIPPMANN, GABRIEL, France, Sorbonne University, Paris, *1845 (in Hollerich, Luxembourg), †1921: "for his method of reproducing colours photographically based on the phenomenon of interference."

1909 The prize was awarded jointly to:
MARCONI, GUGLIELMO, Italy, Marconi Wireless Telegraph Co. Ltd., London, Great Britain, *1874, †1937; and

BRAUN, CARL FERDINAND, Germany, Strasbourg University, Alsace (then Germany), *1850, †1918: "in recognition of their contributions to the development of wireless telegraphy."

1910 VAN DER WAALS, JOHANNES DIDERIK, the Netherlands, Amsterdam University, *1837, †1923: "for his work on the equation of state for gases and liquids."

*born †died

286

1911 WIEN, WILHELM, Germany, Würzburg University, *1864, †1928: for his discoveries regarding the laws governing the radiation of heat."

1912 DALEN, NILS GUSTAF, Sweden, Swedish Gas-Accumulator Co., Lidingö-Stockholm, *1869, †1937: "for his invention of automatic regulators for use in conjunction with gas accumulators for illuminating lighthouses and buoys."

1913 KAMERLINGH-ONNES, HEIKE, the Netherlands, Leyden University, *1853, †1926: "for his investigations on the properties of matter at low temperatures which led, *inter alia,* to the production of liquid helium."

1914 VON LAUE, MAX, Germany, Frankfort-on-the-Main University, *1879, †1960: "for his discovery of the diffraction of X-rays by crystals."

1915 The prize was awarded jointly to:
BRAGG, Sir WILLIAM HENRY, Great Britain, London University, *1862, †1942; and his son

BRAGG, WILLIAM LAWRENCE, Great Britain, Victoria University, Manchester, *1890 (in Adelaide, Australia): "for their services in the analysis of crystal structure by means of X-rays."

1916 Reserved.

1917 The prize money for 1916 was allocated to the Special Fund of this prize section.
The prize for 1917: Reserved.

1918 The prize for 1917:
BARKLA, CHARLES GLOVER, Great Britain, Edinburgh University, *1877, †1944: "for his discovery of the characteristic Röntgen radiation of the elements."
The prize for 1918: Reserved.

1919 The prize for 1918:
PLANCK, MAX KARL ERNST LUDWIG, Germany, Berlin University, *1858, †1947: "in recognition of the services he rendered to the advancement of Physics by his discovery of energy quanta."

*born †died

The prize for 1919:
STARK, JOHANNES, Germany, Greifswald University, *1874, †1957: "for his discovery of the Doppler effect in canal rays and the splitting of spectral lines in electric fields."

1920 GUILLAUME, CHARLES EDOUARD, France, (International Bureau of Weights and Measures), Sèvres, *1861 (in Fleurier, Switzerland), †1938: "in recognition of the service he has rendered to precision measurements in Physics by his discovery of anomalies in nickel steel alloys."

1921 Reserved.

1922 The prize for 1921:
EINSTEIN, ALBERT, Germany, Kaiser-Wilhelm-Institut (now Max-Planck-Institut) für Physik, Berlin, *1879, †1955: "for his services to Theoretical Physics, and especially for his discovery of the law of the photoelectric effect."

The prize for 1922:
BOHR, NIELS, Denmark, Copenhagen University, *1885, †1962: "for his services in the investigation of the structure of atoms and of the radiation emanating from them."

1923 MILLIKAN, ROBERT ANDREWS, U. S. A., California Institute of Technology, Pasadena, Calif., *1868, †1953: "for his work on the elementary charge of electricity and on the photoelectric effect."

1924 Reserved.

1925 The prize for 1924:
SIEGBAHN, KARL MANNE GEORG, Sweden, Uppsala University, *1886: "for his discoveries and research in the field of X-ray spectroscopy."
The prize for 1925: Reserved.

1926 The prize for 1925 was awarded jointly to:
FRANCK, JAMES, Germany, Goettingen University, *1882, †1964; and

HERTZ, GUSTAV, Germany, Halle University, *1887: "for their discovery of the laws governing the impact of an electron upon an atom."

*born †died

288

The prize for 1926:
PERRIN, JEAN BAPTISTE, France, Sorbonne University, Paris, *1870, †1942: "for his work on the discontinuous structure of matter, and especially for his discovery of sedimentation equilibrium."

1927 The prize was divided equally between:
COMPTON, ARTHUR HOLLY, U. S. A., Chicago University, *1892, †1962: "for his discovery of the effect named after him"; and

WILSON, CHARLES THOMSON REES, Great Britain, Cambridge University, *1869 (in Glencorse, Scotland), †1959: "for his method of making the paths of electrically charged particles visible by condensation of vapour."

1928 Reserved.

1929 The prize for 1928:
RICHARDSON, OWEN WILLANS, Great Britain, London University, *1879, †1959: "for his work on the thermionic phenomenon and especially for the discovery of the law named after him."

The prize for 1929:
DE BROGLIE, Prince LOUIS-VICTOR, France, Sorbonne University, Institut Henri Poincaré, Paris, *1892: "for his discovery of the wave nature of electrons."

1930 RAMAN, Sir CHANDRASEKHARA VENKATA, India, Calcutta University, *1888: "for his work on the scattering of light and for the discovery of the effect named after him."

1931 Reserved.

1932 The prize money for 1931 was allocated to the Special Fund of this prize section.
The prize for 1932: Reserved.

1933 The prize for 1932:
HEISENBERG, WERNER, Germany, Leipzig University, *1901: "for the creation of quantum mechanics, the application of which has, *inter alia*, led to the discovery of the allotropic forms of hydrogen."

*born †died

The prize for 1933 was awarded jointly to:
SCHRODINGER, ERWIN, Austria, Berlin University, Germany, *1887, †1961; and

DIRAC, PAUL ADRIEN MAURICE, Great Britain, Cambridge University, *1902: "for the discovery of new productive forms of atomic theory."

1934 Reserved.

1935 The prize money for 1934 was with ⅓ allocated to the Main Fund and with ⅔ to the Special Fund of this prize section.

The prize for 1935:
CHADWICK, JAMES, Great Britain, Liverpool University, *1891: "for his discovery of the neutron."

1936 The prize was divided equally between:
HESS, VICTOR FRANZ, Austria, Innsbruck University, *1883, †1964: "for his discovery of cosmic radiation"; and

ANDERSON, CARL DAVID, U. S. A., California Institute of Technology, Pasadena, Calif., *1905: "for his discovery of the positron."

1937 The prize was awarded jointly to:
DAVISSON, CLINTON JOSEPH, U. S. A., Bell Telephone Laboratories, New York, N. Y., *1881, †1958; and

THOMPSON, GEORGE PAGET, Great Britain, London University, *1892: "for their experimental discovery of the diffraction of electrons by crystals."

1938 FERMI, ENRICO, Italy, Rome University, *1901, †1954: "for his demonstrations of the existence of new radioactive elements produced by neutron irradiation, and for his related discovery of nuclear reactions brought about by slow neutrons."

1939 LAWRENCE, ERNEST ORLANDO, U. S. A., University of California, Berkeley, Calif., *1901, †1958: "for the invention and development of the cyclotron and for results obtained with it, especially with regard to artificial radioactive elements."

1940-
-1942 The prize money was with ⅓ allocated to the Main Fund and with ⅔ to the Special Fund of this prize section.

*born †died

290

1943 Reserved.

1944 The prize for 1943:
STERN, OTTO, U. S. A., Carnegie Institute of Technology, Pittsburgh, Pa., *1888 (in Sorau, then Germany): "for his contribution to the development of the molecular ray method and his discovery of the magnetic moment of the proton."

The prize for 1944:
RABI, ISIDOR ISAAC, U. S. A., Columbia University, New York, N. Y., *1898 (in Rymanow, then Austria-Hungary): "for his resonance method for recording the magnetic properties of atomic nuclei."

1945 PAULI, WOLFGANG, Austria, Princeton University, N. J., U. S. A., *1900 (in Vienna), †1958: "for the discovery of the Exclusion Principle, also called the Pauli Principle."

1946 BRIDGMAN, PERCY WILLIAMS, U. S. A., Harvard University, Cambridge, Mass., *1882, †1961: "for the invention of an apparatus to produce extremely high pressures, and for the discoveries he made therewith in the field of high pressure physics."

1947 APPLETON, Sir EDWARD VICTOR, Great Britain, Department of Scientific and Industrial Research, London, *1892, †1965: "for his investigations of the physics of the upper atmosphere, especially for the discovery of the so-called Appleton layer."

1948 BLACKETT, PATRICK MAYNARD STUART, Great Britain, Victoria University, Manchester, *1897: "for his development of the Wilson cloud chamber method, and his discoveries therewith in the fields of nuclear physics and cosmic radiation."

1949 YUKAWA, HIDEKI, Japan, Kyoto Imperial University, Visiting Professor Columbia University, New York, N. Y., U. S. A., *1907: "for his prediction of the existence of mesons on the basis of theoretical work on nuclear forces."

1950 POWELL, CECIL FRANK, Great Britain, Bristol University, *1903: "for his development of the photographic method of studying nuclear processes and his discoveries regarding mesons made with this method."

°born †died

1951 The prize was awarded jointly to:
COCKCROFT, Sir JOHN DOUGLAS, Great Britain, Atomic Energy
Research Establishment, Harwell, Didcot, Berks., *1897; and

WALTON, ERNEST THOMAS SINTON, Ireland, Dublin University,
*1903: "for their pioneer work on the transmutation of atomic
nuclei by artificially accelerated atomic particles."

1952 The prize was awarded jointly to:
BLOCH, FELIX, U. S. A., Stanford University, Stanford, Calif.,
*1905 (in Zurich, Switzerland); and

PURCELL, EDWARD MILLS, U. S. A., Harvard University, Cambridge, Mass., *1912: "for their development of new methods
for nuclear magnetic precision measurements and discoveries
in connection therewith."

1953 ZERNIKE, FRITS (FREDERIK), the Netherlands, Groningen University, *1888, †1966: "for his demonstration of the phase contrast method, especially for his invention of the phase contrast
microscope."

1954 The prize was divided equally between:
BORN, MAX, Great Britain, Edinburgh University, *1882 (in
Breslau, then Germany): "for his fundamental research in
quantum mechanics, especially for his statistical interpretation
of the wave-function"; and

BOTHE, WALTHER, Germany, Heidelberg University,
Max-Planck-Institut (former Kaiser-Wilhelm-Institut) für
medizinische Forschung, Heidelberg, *1891, †1957: "for the
coincidence method and his discoveries made therewith."

1955 The prize was divided equally between:
LAMB, WILLIS EUGENE, U. S. A., Stanford University, Stanford,
Calif., *1913: "for his discoveries concerning the fine structure
of the hydrogen spectrum"; and

KUSCH, POLYKARP, U. S. A., Columbia University, New York,
N. Y., *1911 (in Blankenburg, then Germany): "for his precision determination of the magnetic moment of the electron."

1956 The prize was awarded jointly, one third each, to:
SHOCKLEY, WILLIAM, U. S. A., Semiconductor Laboratory of
Beckman Instruments, Inc., Mountain View, Calif., *1910 (in
London, Great Britain);

*born †died

BARDEEN, JOHN, U. S. A., University of Illinois, Urbana, Ill., *1908; and

BRATTAIN, WALTER HOUSER, U. S. A., Bell Telephone Laboratories, Murray Hill, N. J., *1902: "for their researches on semiconductors and their discovery of the transistor effect."

1957 The prize was awarded jointly to:
YANG, CHEN NING, China, Institute for Advanced Study, Princeton, N. J., U. S. A., *1922; and

LEE, TSUNG DAO, China, Columbia University, New York, U. S. A., *1926: "for their penetrating investigation of the so-called parity laws which has led to important discoveries regarding the elementary particles."

1958 The prize was awarded jointly to:
CERENKOV, PAVEL ALEKSEJEVIC, USSR, Physics Institute of USSR Academy of Sciences, Moscow, *1904;

FRANK, IL'JA MICHAJLOVIC, USSR, University of Moscow and Physics Institute of USSR Academy of Sciences, Moscow, *1908; and

TAMM, IGOR' JEVGEN'EVIC, USSR, University of Moscow and Physics Institute of USSR Academy of Sciences, Moscow, *1895: "for the discovery and the interpretation of the Cerenkov effect."

1959 The prize was awarded jointly to:
SEGRE, EMILIO GINO, U. S. A., University of California, Berkeley, Calif., *1905 (in Tivoli, Italy); and

CHAMBERLAIN, OWEN, U. S. A., University of California, Berkeley, Calif., *1920: "for their discovery of the antiproton."

1960 GLASER, DONALD A., U. S. A., University of California, Berkeley, Calif., *1926: "for the invention of the bubble chamber."

1961 The prize was divided equally between:
HOFSTADTER, ROBERT, U. S. A., Stanford University, Stanford, Calif., *1915: "for his pioneering studies of electron scattering in atomic nuclei and for his thereby achieved discoveries concerning the structure of the nucleons"; and

*born

293

MOSSBAUER, RUDOLF LUDWIG, Germany, Technische Hochschule, Munich, at present California Institute of Technology, Pasadena, California, U. S. A., *1929: "for his researches concerning the resonance absorption of gamma radiation and his discovery in this connection of the effect which bears his name."

1962 LANDAU, LEV DAVIDOVIC, USSR, Academy of Sciences, Moscow, *1908: "for his pioneering theories for condensed matter, especially liquid helium."

1963 The prize was divided, one half being awarded to:
WIGNER, EUGENE P., U. S. A., Princeton University, Princeton, N. J., *1902: "for his contributions to the theory of the atomic nucleus and the elementary particles, particularly through the discovery and application of fundamental symmetry principles";

and the other half jointly to:

GOEPPERT-MAYER, MARIA, U. S. A., University of California, La Jolla, Calif., *1906 (in Kattowitz, then Germany); and

JENSEN, J. HANS D., Germany, University of Heidelberg, *1907: "for their discoveries concerning nuclear shell structure."

1964 The prize was divided, one half being awarded to:
TOWNES, CHARLES HARD, U. S. A., Massachusetts Institute of Technology, Cambridge, Mass., *1915; and the other half jointly to:

BASOV, NIKOLAI GENNADIEVIC, USSR, Lebedev Institute for Physics, Akademija Nauk, Moscow, *1922; and

PROCHOROV, ALEKSANDRE MIKHAILOVIC, USSR, Lebedev Institute for Physics, Akademija Nauk, Moscow, *1916: "for fundamental work in the field of quantum electronics, which has led to the construction of oscillators and amplifiers based on the maser-laser principle."

1965 The prize was awarded jointly to:
TOMONAGA, SIN-ITIRO, Japan, Tokyo University of Education Tokyo, *1906;

*born

294

Schwinger, Julian, U. S. A., Harvard University, Cambridge, Mass., *1918; and

Feynman, Richard P., U. S. A., California Institute of Technology, Pasadena, Calif., *1918: "for their fundamental work in quantum electrodynamics, with deep-ploughing consequences for the physics of elementary particles."

1966 Kastler, Alfred, France, École Normale Supérieure, Université de Paris, Paris, *1902: "for the discovery and development of optical methods for studying hertzian resonances in atoms."

1967 Bethe, Hans A., U. S. A., Cornell University, Ithaca, N. Y., *1906: "for his contributions to the theory of nuclear reactions, especially his discoveries concerning the energy production in stars."

1968 Alvarez, Luis W., U. S. A., University of California, Berkeley, Calif. *1911: "for his decisive contributions to elementary particle physics, in particular the discovery of a large number of resonance states, made possible through his development of the technique of using hydrogen bubble chamber and data analysis."

2. CHEMISTRY

1901 van 't Hoff, Jacobus Henricus, the Netherlands, Berlin University, Germany, *1852, †1911: "in recognition of the extraordinary services he has rendered by the discovery of the laws of chemical dynamics and osmotic pressure in solutions."

1902 Fischer, Hermann Emil, Germany, Berlin University, *1852, †1919: "in recognition of the extraordinary services he has rendered by his work on sugar and purine syntheses."

1903 Arrhenius, Svante August, Sweden, Stockholm University, *1859, †1927: "in recognition of the extraordinary services he has rendered to the advancement of chemistry by his electrolytic theory of dissociation."

1904 Ramsay, Sir William, Great Britain, London University, *1852, †1916: "in recognition of his services in the discovery of the inert gaseous elements in air, and his determination of their place in the periodic system."

*born †died

1905 VON BAEYER, JOHANN FRIEDRICH WILHELM ADOLF, Germany, Munich University, *1835, †1917: "in recognition of his services in the advancement of organic chemistry and the chemical industry, through his work on organic dyes and hydroaromatic compounds."

1906 MOISSAN, HENRI, France, Sorbonne University, Paris, *1852, †1907: "in recognition of the great services rendered by him in his investigation and isolation of the element fluorine, and for the adoption in the service of science of the electric furnace called after him."

1907 BUCHNER, EDUARD, Germany, Landwirtschaftliche Hochschule (Agricultural College), Berlin, *1860, †1917: "for his biochemical researches and his discovery of cell-free fermentation."

1908 RUTHERFORD, ERNEST, Great Britain, Victoria University, Manchester, *1871 (in Nelson, New Zealand), †1937: "for his investigations into the disintegration of the elements, and the chemistry of radioactive substances."

1909 OSTWALD, WILHELM, Germany, Leipzig University, *1853 (in Riga, then Russia), †1932: "in recognition of his work on catalysis and for his investigations into the fundamental principles governing chemical equilibria and rates of reaction."

1910 WALLACH, OTTO, Germany, Goettingen University, *1847, †1931: "in recognition of his services to organic chemistry and the chemical industry by his pioneer work in the field of alicyclic compounds."

1911 CURIE, MARIE, née SKLODOWSKA, France, Sorbonne University, Paris, *1867 (in Warsaw, Poland), †1934: "in recognition of her services to the advancement of chemistry by the discovery of the elements radium and polonium, by the isolation of radium and the study of the nature and compounds of this remarkable element."

1912 The prize was divided equally between:
GRIGNARD, VICTOR, France, Nancy University, *1871, †1935: "for the discovery of the so-called Grignard reagent, which in recent years has greatly advanced the progress of organic chemistry"; and

*born †died

296

SABATIER, PAUL, France, Toulouse University, *1854, †1941: "for his method of hydrogenating organic compounds in the presence of finely disintegrated metals whereby the progress of organic chemistry has been greatly advanced in recent years."

1913 WERNER, ALFRED, Switzerland, Zurich University, *1866 (in Mulhouse, Alsace, then Germany), †1919: "in recognition of his work on the linkage of atoms in molecules by which he has thrown new light on earlier investigations and opened up new fields of research especially in inorganic chemistry."

1914 Reserved.

1915 The prize for 1914:
RICHARDS, THEODORE WILLIAM, U. S. A., Harvard University, Cambridge, Mass., *1868, †1928: "in recognition of his accurate determinations of the atomic weight of a large number of chemical elements."

The prize for 1915:

WILLSTATTER, RICHARD MARTIN, Germany, Munich University, *1872, †1942: "for his researches on plant pigments, especially chlorophyll."

1916 Reserved.

1917 The prize money for 1916 was allocated to the Special Fund of this prize section.
The prize for 1917: Reserved.

1918 The prize money for 1917 was allocated to the Special Fund of this prize section.
The prize for 1918: Reserved.

1919 The prize for 1918:
HABER, FRITZ, Germany, Kaiser-Wilhelm-Institut (now Fritz-Haber-Institut) für physikalische Chemie und Electrochemie, Berlin-Dahlem, *1868, †1934: "for the synthesis of ammonia from its elements."
The prize for 1919: Reserved.

1920 The prize money for 1919 was allocated to the Special Fund of this prize section.
The prize for 1920: Reserved.

*born   †died

297

1921 The prize for 1920:

NERNST, WALTHER HERMANN, Germany, Berlin University, *1864, †1941: "in recognition of his work in thermochemistry." The prize for 1921: Reserved.

1922 The prize for 1921:

SODDY, FREDERICK, Great Britain, Oxford University, *1877, †1956: "for his contributions to our knowledge of the chemistry of radioactive substances, and his investigations into the origin and nature of isotopes."

The prize for 1922:

ASTON, FRANCIS WILLIAM, Great Britain, Cambridge University, *1877, †1945: "for his discovery, by means of his mass spectrograph, of isotopes in a large number of non-radioactive elements, and for his enunciation of the whole-number rule."

1923 PREGL, FRITZ, Austria, Graz University, *1869, †1930: "for his invention of the method of micro-analysis of organic substances."

1924 Reserved.

1925 The prize money for 1924 was allocated to the Special Fund of this prize section.
The prize for 1925: Reserved.

1926 The prize for 1925:

ZSIGMONDY, RICHARD ADOLF, Germany, Goettingen University, *1865 (in Vienna, Austria), †1929: "for his demonstration of the heterogeneous nature of colloid solutions and for the methods he used, which have since become fundamental in modern colloid chemistry."

The prize for 1926:

SVEDBERG, THE (THEODOR), Sweden, Uppsala University, *1884: "for his work on disperse systems."

1927 Reserved.

1928 The prize for 1927:

WIELAND, HEINRICH OTTO, Germany, Munich University, *1877, †1957: "for his investigations of the constitution of the bile acids and related substances."

*born †died

298

The prize for 1928:
WINDAUS, ADOLF OTTO REINHOLD, Germany, Goettingen University, *1876, †1959: "for the services rendered through his research into the constitution of the sterols and their connection with the vitamins."

1929 The prize was divided equally between:
HARDEN, ARTHUR, Great Britain, London University, *1865, †1940; and

VON EULER-CHELPIN, HANS KARL AUGUST SIMON, Sweden, Stockholm University, *1873 (in Augsburg, Germany), †1964: "for their investigations on the fermentation of sugar and fermentative enzymes."

1930 FISCHER, HANS, Germany, Technische Hochschule (Institute of Technology), Munich, *1881, †1945: "for his researches into the constitution of haemin and chlorophyll and especially for his synthesis of haemin."

1931 The prize was awarded jointly to:
BOSCH, CARL, Germany, Heidelberg University and I. G. Farbenindustrie A. G. Heidelberg, *1874, †1940; and

BERGIUS, FRIEDRICH, Germany, Heidelberg, and I. G. Farbenindustrie A. G., Mannheim-Rheinau, *1884, †1949: "in recognition of their contributions to the invention and development of chemical high pressure methods."

1932 LANGMUIR, IRVING, U. S. A., General Electric Co., Schenectady, N. Y., *1881, †1957: "for his discoveries and investigations in surface chemistry."

1933 Reserved:

1934 The prize money for 1933 was with ⅓ allocated to the Main Fund and with ⅔ to the Special Fund of this prize section.

The prize for 1934:
UREY, HAROLD CLAYTON, U. S. A., Columbia University, New York., *1893: "for his discovery of heavy hydrogen."

1935 The prize was awarded jointly to:
JOLIOT, FREDERIC, France, Institut du Radium, Paris, *1900, †1958; and his wife

*born †died

JOLIOT-CURIE, IRENE, Institut du Radium, Paris, *1897, †1956: "in recognition of their synthesis of new radioactive elements."

1936 DEBYE, PETRUS (PETER) JOSPHUS WILHELMUS, the Netherlands, Berlin University, and Kaiser-Wilhelm-Institut (now Max-Planck-Institut) für Physik, Berlin-Dahlem, Germany, *1884, †1966: "for his contributions to our knowledge of molecular structure through his investigations on dipole moments and on the diffraction of X-rays and electrons in gases."

1937 The prize was divided equally between:
HAWORTH, WALTER NORMAN, Great Britain, Birmingham University, *1883, †1950: "for his investigations on carbohydrates and vitamin C"; and

KARRER, PAUL, Switzerland, Zurich University, *1889 (in Moscow, Russia): "for his investigations on carotenoids, flavin and vitamins A and B₂."

1938 Reserved.

1939 The prize for 1938:
KUHN, RICHARD, Germany, Heidelberg University, and Kaiser-Wilhelm-Institut (now Max-Planck-Institut) Heidelberg, *1900 (in Vienna, Austria): "for his work on carotenoids and vitamins." (caused by the authorities of his country to decline the award but later received the diploma and the medal.)

The prize for 1939 was divided equally between:
BUTENANDT, ADOLF FRIEDRICH JOHANN, Germany, Berlin University and Kaiser-Wilhelm-Institut (now Max-Planck-Institut) "for his work on sex hormones." (caused by the authorities of his country to decline the award but later received the diploma and the medal); and

RUZICKA, LEOPOLD, Switzerland, Eidgenössische Technische Hochschule (Federal Institute of Technology), Zurich, *1887 (in Vukovar, then Austria-Hungary): "for his work on polymethylenes and higher terpenes."

1940- The prize money was with ⅓ allocated to the Main Fund
-1942 and with ⅔ to the Special Fund of this prize section.

1943 Reserved.

*born †died

300

1944 The prize for 1943:

DE HEVESY, GEORGE, Hungary, Stockholm University, Sweden, *1885, †1966: "for his work on the use of isotopes as tracers in the study of chemical processes."

The prize for 1944: Reserved.

1945 The prize for 1944:

HAHN, OTTO, Germany, Kaiser-Wilhelm-Institut (now Max-Planck-Institut), *1879: "for his discovery of the fission of heavy nuclei."

The prize for 1945:

VIRTANEN, ARTTURI ILMARI, Finland, Helsinki University, *1895: "for his research and inventions in agricultural and nutrition chemistry, especially for his fodder preservation method."

1946 The prize was divided, one half being awarded to:

SUMNER, JAMES BATCHELLER, U. S. A., Cornell University, Ithaca, N. Y., *1887, †1955: "for his discovery that enzymes can be crystallized";

the other half jointly to:

NORTHROP, JOHN HOWARD, U. S. A., Rockefeller Institute for Medical Research, Princeton, N. J., *1891; and

STANLEY, WENDELL MEREDITH, U. S. A., Rockefeller Institute for Medical Research, Princeton, N. J., *1904: "for their preparation of enzymes and virus proteins in a pure form."

1947 ROBINSON, Sir ROBERT, Great Britain, Oxford University, *1886: "for his investigations on plant products of biological importance, especially the alkaloids."

1948 TISELIUS, ARNE WILHELM KAURIN, Sweden, Uppsala University, *1902: "for his research on electrophoresis and adsorption analysis, especially for his discoveries concerning the complex nature of the serum proteins."

1949 GIAUQUE, WILLIAM FRANCIS, U. S. A., University of California, Berkeley, Calif., *1895: "for his contributions in the field of chemical thermodynamics, particularly concerning the behaviour of substances at extremely low temperatures."

*born †died

301

1950 The prize was awarded jointly to:
DIELS, OTTO PAUL HERMANN, Germany, Kiel University, *1876, †1954; and

ALDER, KURT, Germany, Cologne University, *1902, †1958: "for their discovery and development of the diene synthesis."

1951 The prize was awarded jointly to:
McMILLAN, EDWIN MATTISON, U. S. A., University of California, Berkeley, Calif., *1907; and

SEABORG, GLENN THEODORE, U. S. A., University of California, Berkeley, Calif., *1912: "for their discoveries in the chemistry of the transuranium elements."

1952 The prize was awarded jointly to:
MARTIN, ARCHER JOHN PORTER, Great Britain, National Institute for Medical Research, London, *1910; and

SYNGE, RICHARD LAURENCE MILLINGTON, Great Britain, Rowett Research Institute, Bucksburn (Scotland), *1914: "for their invention of partition chromatograph."

1953 STAUDINGER, HERMANN, Germany, University of Freiburg (State Research Institute for Macromolecular Chemistry), Freiburg i Br., *1881, †1965: "for his discoveries in the field of macromolecular chemistry."

1954 PAULING, LINUS CARL, U. S. A., California Institute of Technology, Pasadena, Calif., *1901: "for his research into the nature of the chemical bond and its application to the elucidation of the structure of complex substances."

1955 DU VIGNEAUD, VINCENT, U. S. A., Cornell University, New York, N. Y., *1901: "for his work on biochemically important sulphur compounds, especially for the first synthesis of a polypeptide hormone."

1956 The prize was awarded jointly to:
HINSHELWOOD, Sir CYRIL NORMAN, Great Britain, Oxford University, *1897; and

SEMENOV, NIKOLAJ NIKOLAJEVIC, USSR, Institute for Chemical Physics of the Academy of Sciences of the USSR, Moscow, *1896: "for their researches into the mechanism of chemical reactions."

*born †died

302

1957 TODD, Sir ALEXANDER R., Great Britain, Cambridge University, *1907: "for his work on nucleotides and nucleotide co-enzymes."

1958 SANGER, FEDERICK, Great Britain, Cambridge University, *1918: "for his work on the structure of proteins, especially that of insulin."

1959 HEYROVSKY, JAROSLAV, Czechoslovakia, Polarographic Institute of the Czechoslovak Academy of Science, Prague, *1890, †1967: "for his discovery and development of the polarographic methods of analysis."

1960 LIBBY, WILLARD FRANK, U. S. A., University of California, Los Angeles, Calif., *1908: "for his method to use carbon-14 for age determination in archaeology, geology, geophysics, and other branches of science."

1961 CALVIN, MELVIN, U. S. A., University of California, Berkeley, California, *1911: "for his research on the carbon dioxide assimilation in plants."

1962 The prize was divided equally between:
PERUTZ, MAX FERDINAND, Great Britain, Laboratory of Molecular Biology, Cambridge, *1914 (in Vienna); and

KENDREW, JOHN COWDERY, Great Britain, Laboratory of Molecular Biology, Cambridge, *1917: "for their studies of the structures of globular proteins."

1963 The prize was divided equally between:
ZIEGLER, KARL, Germany, (Max-Planck-Institute for Carbon Research), Mülheim/Ruhr, *1898; and
NATTA, GIULIO, Italy, Institute of Technology, Milan, *1903: "for their discoveries in the field of the chemistry and technology of high polymers."

1964 HODGKIN, DOROTHY, CROWFOOT, Great Britain, Royal Society, Oxford University, Oxford, *1910: "for her determinations by X-ray techniques of the structures of important biochemical substances."

1965 WOODWARD, ROBERT BURNS, U. S. A., Harvard University, Cambridge, Mass., *1917: "for his outstanding achievements in the art of organic synthesis."

*born †died

1966 MULLIKEN, ROBERT S., U.,S. A., University of Chicago, Chicago, Ill., *1896: "for his fundamental work concerning chemical bonds and the electronic structure of molecules by the molecular orbital method."

1967 The prize was divided equally between:
EIGEN, MANFRED, Federal Republic of Germany, Max Planck Institute for Physical Chemistry, Göttingen, *1927;

NORRISH, R. G. W., Great Britain, Institute of Physical Chemistry, Cambridge, *1897, and

PORTER, GEORGE, Great Britain, Royal Institution, London, *1920: "for their studies of extremely fast chemical reactions, effected by disturbing the equilibrium by means of very short pulses of energy."

1968 ONSAGER, LARS, U. S. A., Yale University, New Haven, Conn., *1903: "for the discovery of the reciprocal relations bearing his name which are fundamental for the thermodynamics of irreversible processes."

3. PHYSIOLOGY OR MEDICINE

1901 VON BEHRING, EMIL ADOLF, Germany, Marburg University, *1854, †1917: "for his work on serum therapy, especially its application against diphtheria, by which he has opened a new road in the domain of medical science and thereby placed in the hands of the physician a victorious weapon against illness and death."

1902 Ross, Sir RONALD, Great Britain, University College, Liverpool, *1857 (in Almora, India), †1932: "for his work on malaria, by which he has shown how it enters the organism and thereby has laid the foundation for successful research on this disease and methods of combating it."

1903 FINSEN, NIELS RYBERG, Denmark, Finsen Medical Light Institute, Copenhagen, *1860 (in Thorshavn, Faroe Islands), †1904: "in recognition of his contribution to the treatment of diseases, especially lupus vulgaris, with concentrated light radiation, whereby he has opened a new avenue for medical science."

*born †died

1904 PAVLOV, IVAN PETROVIC, Russia, Military Medical Academy, St. Petersburg (now Leningrad), *1849, †1936: "in recognition of his work on the physiology of digestion, through which knowledge on vital aspects of the subject has been transformed and enlarged."

1905 KOCH, ROBERT, Germany, Institut för Infektionskrankheiten (Institute for Infectious Diseases), Berlin, *1843, †1910: "for his investigations and discoveries in relation to tuberculosis."

1906 The prize was awarded jointly to:
GOLGI, CAMILLO, Italy, Pavia University, *1843, †1926; and

RAMON Y CAJAL, SANTIAGO, Spain, Madrid University, *1852, †1934: "in recognition of their work on the structure of the nervous system."

1907 LAVERAN, CHARLES LOUIS ALPHONSE, France, Institut Pasteur, Paris, *1845, †1922: "in recognition of his work on the role played by protozoa in causing diseases."

1908 The prize was awarded jointly to:
MECNIKOV, IL'JA IL'JIC, Russia, Institut Pasteur, Paris, France, *1845, †1916; and

EHRLICH, PAUL, Germany, Goettingen University and Könnigliches Institut für experimentelle Therapie (Royal Institute for Experimental Therapy), Frankfort-on-the-Main, *1854, †1915: "in recognition of their work on immunity."

1909 KOCHER, EMIL THEODOR, Switzerland, Berne University, *1841, †1917: "for his work on the physiology, pathology and surgery of the thyroid gland."

1910 KOSSEL, ALBRECHT, Germany, Heidelberg University, *1853, †1927: "in recognition of the contributions to our knowledge of cell chemistry made through his work on proteins, including the nucleic substances."

1911 GULLSTRAND, ALLVAR, Sweden, Uppsala University, *1862, †1930: "for his work on the dioptrics of the eye."

1912 CARREL, ALEXIS, U. S. A., Rockefeller Institute for Medical Research, New York, N. Y., *1873 (in Saint-Foy-lès-Lyon, France), †1944: "in recognition of his work on vascular suture and the transplantation of blood-vessels and organs."

*born †died

305

1913 RICHET, CHARLES ROBERT, France, Sorbonne University, Paris, *1850, †1935: "in recognition of his work on anaphylaxis."

1914 BARANY, ROBERT, Hungary, Vienna University, *1876 (in Vienna, Austria), †1936: "for his work on the physiology and pathology of the vestibular apparatus."

1915 Reserved.

1916 The prize money for 1915 was allocated to the Special Fund of this prize section.
The prize for 1916: Reserved.

1917 The prize money for 1916 was allocated to the Special Fund of this prize section.
The prize for 1917: Reserved.

1918 The prize money for 1917 was allocated to the Special Fund of this prize section.
The prize for 1918: Reserved.

1919 The prize money for 1918 was allocated to the Special Fund of this prize section.
The prize for 1919: Reserved.

1920 The prize for 1919:
BORDET, JULES, Belgium, Brussels University, *1870, †1961: "for his discoveries relating to immunity."

The prize for 1920:
KROGH, SHACK AUGUST STEENBERGER, Denmark, Copenhagen University, *1874, †1949: "for his discovery of the capillary motor regulating mechanism."

1921 Reserved.

1922 The prize money for 1921 was allocated to the Special Fund of this prize section.
The prize for 1922: Reserved.

1923 The prize for 1922 was divided equally between:
HILL, ARCHIBALD VIVIAN, Great Britain, London University, *1886: "for his discovery relating to the production of heat in the muscle"; and

*born †died

306

MEYERHOF, OTTO FRITZ, Germany, Kiel University, *1884, †1951: "for his discovery of the fixed relationship between the consumption of oxygen and the metabolism of lactic acid in the muscle."

The prize for 1923 was awarded jointly to:
BANTING, FREDERICK GRANT, Canada, Toronto University, *1891, †1941; and

MACLEOD, JOHN JAMES RICHARD, Canada, Toronto University, *1876 (in Cluny, Scotland), †1935: "for the discovery of insulin."

1924 EINTHOVEN, WILLEM, the Netherlands, Leyden University, *1860 (in Semarang, Java then Dutch East Indies), †1927: "for his discovery of the mechanism of the electrocardiogram."

1925 Reserved.

1926 The prize money for 1925 was allocated to the Special Fund of this prize section.
The prize for 1926: Reserved.

1927 The prize for 1926:
FIBIGER, JOHANNES ANDREAS GRIB, Denmark, Copenhagen University, *1867, †1928: "for his discovery of the Spiroptera carcinoma."

The prize for 1927:
WAGNER-JAUREGG, JULIUS, Austria, Vienna University, *1857, †1940: "for his discovery of the therapeutic value of malaria inoculation in the treatment of dementia paralytica."

1928 NICOLLE, CHARLES JULES HENRI, France, Institut Pasteur, Tunis, *1866, †1936: "for his work on typhus."

1929 The prize was divided equally between:
EIJKMAN, CHRISTIAAN, the Netherlands, Utrecht University, *1858, †1930: "for his discovery of the antineuritic vitamin"; and

HOPKINS, Sir FREDERICK GOWLAND, Great Britain, Cambridge University, *1861, †1947: "for his discovery of the growth-stimulating vitamins."

*born †died

307

1930 LANDSTEINER, KARL, Austria, Rockefeller Institute for Medical Research, New York, N. Y., U. S. A., *1868, †1943: "for his discovery of human blood groups."

1931 WARBURG, OTTO HEINRICH, Germany, Kaiser-Wilhelm-Institut (now Max-Planck-Institut) für Biologie, Berlin-Dahlem, *1883: "for his discovery of the nature and mode of action of the respiratory enzyme."

1932 The prize was awarded jointly to:
SHERRINGTON, Sir CHARLES SCOTT, Great Britain, Oxford University, *1857, †1952; and

ADRIAN, EDGAR DOUGLAS, Great Britain, Cambridge University, *1889: "for their discoveries regarding the functions of neurons."

1933 MORGAN, THOMAS HUNT, U. S. A., California Institute of Technology, Pasadena, Calif., *1866, †1945: "for his discoveries concerning the role played by the chromosome in heredity."

1934 The prize was awarded jointly to:
WHIPPLE, GEORGE HOYT, U. S. A., Rochester University, Rochester, N. Y., *1878;

MINOT, GEORGE RICHARDS, U. S. A., Harvard University, Cambridge, Mass., *1885, †1950; and

MURPHY, WILLIAM PARRY, U. S. A., Harvard University, Cambridge, Mass., and Peter Brent Brigham Hospital, Boston, Mass., *1892: "for their discoveries concerning liver therapy in cases of anaemia."

1935 SPEMANN, HANS, Germany, University of Freiburg im Breisgau, *1869, †1941: "for his discovery of the organizer effect in embryonic development."

1936 The prize was awarded jointly to:
DALE, Sir HENRY HALLETT, Great Britain, National Institute for Medical Research, London, *1875; and

LOEWI, OTTO, Austria, Graz University, *1873 (in Frankfort-on-the-Main, Germany), †1961: "for their discoveries relating to chemical transmission of nerve impulses."

*born †died

1937 SZENT-GYORGYI VON NAGYRAPOLT, ALBERT, Hungary, Szeged University, *1893: "for his discoveries in connection with the biological combustion processes, with special reference to vitamin C and the catalysis of fumaric acid."

1938 Reserved.

1939 The prize for 1938:
HEYMANS, CORNEILLE JEAN FRANCOIS, Belgium, Ghent University, *1892: "for the discovery of the role played by the sinus and aortic mechanisms in the regulation of respiration."

The prize for 1939:
DOMAGK, GERHARD, Germany, Munster University, *1895, †1964: "for the discovery of the antibacterial effects of prontosil."
(caused by the authorities of his country to decline the award, but later received the diploma and the medal.)

1940- The prize money was with ⅓ allocated to the Main Fund
-1942 and with ⅔ to the Special Fund of this prize section.

1943 Reserved.

1944 The prize for 1943 was divided equally between:
DAM, HENRIK CARL PETER, Denmark, Polytechnic Institute, Copenhagen, *1895: "for his discovery of vitamin K"; and
DOISY, EDWARD ADELBERT, U. S. A., Saint Louis University, St. Louis, Mo., *1893: "for his discovery of the chemical nature of vitamin K."

The prize for 1944 was awarded jointly to:
ERLANGER, JOSEPH, U. S. A., Washington University, St. Louis, Mo., *1874, †1965; and

GASSER, HERBERT SPENCER, U. S. A., Rockefeller Institute for Medical Research, New York, N. Y., *1888, †1963: "for their discoveries relating to the highly differentiated functions of single nerve fibres."

1945 The prize was awarded jointly to:
FLEMING, Sir ALEXANDER, Great Britain, London University, *1881 (in Lochfield, Scotland), †1955;

*born †died

309

CHAIN, ERNST BORIS, Great Britain, Oxford University, *1906 (in Berlin, Germany); and

FLOREY, Sir HOWARD WALTER, Great Britain, Oxford University, *1898 (in Adelaide, Australia): "for the discovery of penicillin and its curative effect in various infectious diseases."

1946 MULLER, HERMANN JOSEPH, U. S. A., Indiana University, Bloomington, Indiana, *1890, †1967: "for the discovery of the production of mutations by means of X-ray irradiation."

1947 The prize was divided, one half being awarded jointly to: CORI, CARL FERDINAND, U. S. A., Washington University, St. Louis, Mo., *1896 (in Prague, then Austria), and his wife

CORI, GERTY THERESA, née RADNITZ, U. S. A., Washington University, St. Louis, Mo., *1896 (in Prague, then Austria), †1957: "for their discovery of the course of the catalytic conversion of glycogen"; and the other half being awarded to:

HOUSSAY, BERNARDO ALBERTO, the Argentine, Instituto de Biologia y Medicina Experimental (Institute for Biology and Experimental Medicine), Buenos Aires, *1887: "for his discovery of the part played by the hormone of the anterior pituitary lobe in the metabolism of sugar."

1948 MULLER, PAUL HERMANN, Switzerland Laboratorium der Farben-Fabriken J. R. Geigy A. G. (Laboratory of the J. R. Geigy Dye-Factory Co.), Basle, *1899, †1965: "for his discovery of the high efficiency of DDT as a contact poison against several arthropods."

1949 The prize was divided equally between:
HESS, WALTER RUDOLF, Switzerland, Zurich University, *1881: "for his discovery of the functional organization of the interbrain as a coordinator of the activities of the internal organs"; and

MONIZ, ANTONIO CAETANO DE ABREU FREIRE EGAS, Portugal, University of Lisbon, Neurological Institute, Lisbon, *1874, †1955: "for his discovery of the therapeutic value of leucotomy in certain psychoses."

1950 The prize was awarded jointly to:
KENDALL, EDWARD CALVIN, U. S. A., Mayo Clinic, Rochester, Minn., *1886;

*born †died

REICHSTEIN, TADEUS, Switzerland, Basle University, *1897 (in Wloclawek, Poland); and

HENCH, PHILIP SHOWALTER, U. S. A., Mayo Clinic, Rochester, Minn., *1896, †1965: "for their discoveries relating to the hormones of the adrenal cortex, their structure and biological effects."

1951 THEILER, MAX, Union of South Africa, Laboratories Division of Medicine and Public Health, Rockefeller Foundation, New York, N. Y., U. S. A., *1899: "for his discoveries concerning yellow fever and how to combat it."

1952 WAKSMAN, SELMAN ABRAHAM, U. S. A., Rutgers University, New Brunswick, N. J., *1888 (in Priluka, Ukraine, Russia): "for his discovery of streptomycin, the first antibiotic effective against tuberculosis."

1953 The prize was divided equally between:
KREBS, HANS ADOLF, Great Britain, Sheffield University, *1900 (in Hildesheim, Germany): "for his discovery of the critic acid cycle"; and

LIPMANN, FRITZ ALBERT, U. S. A., Harvard Medical School and Massachusetts General Hospital, Boston, Mass., *1899 (in Koenigsberg, then Germany): "for his discovery of coenzyme A and its importance for intermediary metabolism."

1954 The prize was awarded jointly to:
ENDERS, JOHN FRANKLIN, U. S. A., Harvard Medical School, Boston, Mass.; Research Division of Infectious Diseases, Children's Medical Center, Boston, *1897;

WELLER, THOMAS HUCKLE, U. S. A., Research Division of Infectious Diseases, Children's Medical Center, Boston, Mass., *1915; and

ROBBINS, FREDERICK CHAPMAN, U. S. A., Western Reserve University, Cleveland, Ohio, *1916: "for their discovery of the ability of poliomyelitis viruses to grow in cultures of various types of tissue."

1955 THEORELL, AXEL HUGO THEODOR, Sweden, Nobel Medical Institute, Stockholm, *1903: "for his discoveries concerning the nature and mode of action of oxidation enzymes."

*born   †died

1956 The prize was awarded jointly to:
Cournand, Andre Frederic, U. S. A., Cardio-Pulmonary Laboratory, Columbia University Division, Bellevue Hospital, New York, N. Y., *1895 (in Paris, France);

Forssmann, Werner, *Germany*, Mainz University and Bad Kreuznach, *1904; and

Richards Jr., Dickinson W., U. S. A., Columbia University, New York, *1895: "for their discoveries concerning heart catheterization and pathological changes in the circulatory system."

1957 Bovet, Daniel, Italy, Istituto Superiore di Sanità (Chief Institute of Public Health), Rome, *1907 (in Neuchâtel, Switzerland): "for his discoveries relating to synthetic compounds that inhibit the action of certain body substances, and especially their action on the vascular system and the skeletal muscles."

1958 The prize was divided, one half being awarded jointly to:
Beadle, George Wells, U. S. A., California Institute of Technology, Pasadena, Calif., *1903; and

Tatum, Edward Lawrie, U. S. A. Rockefeller Institute for Medical Research, New York, *1909: "for their discovery that genes act by regulating definite chemical events."
and the other half to:

Lederberg, Joshua, U. S. A., Wisconsin University, Madison, Wisconsin, *1925: "for his discoveries concerning genetic recombination and the organization of the genetic material of bacteria."

1959 The prize was awarded jointly to:
Ochoa, Severo, U. S. A., New York University, College of Medicine, New York, *1905 (in Luarca, Spain); and

Kornberg, Arthur, U. S. A., Stanford University, Stanford, Calif., *1918: "for their discovery of the mechanisms in the biological synthesis of ribonucleic acid and deoxiribonucleic acid."

*born

1960 The prize was awarded jointly to:

BURNET, Sir F. (FRANK) MACFARLANE, Australia, Walter and Eliza Hall Institute for Medical Research, Melbourne, *1899; and

MEDAWAR, PETER BRIAN, Great Britain, University College, London, *1915: "for the discovery of acquired immunological tolerance."

1961 VON BEKESY, GEORG, U. S. A., Harvard University, Cambridge, Mass., *1899 (in Budapest): "for his discoveries of the physical mechanism of stimulation within the cochlea."

1962 The prize was awarded jointly to:

CRICK, FRANCIS HARRY COMPTON, Great Britain, Institute of Molecular Biology, Cambridge, *1916;

WATSON, JAMES DEWEY, U. S. A., Harvard University, Cambridge, Mass., *1928; and

WILKINS, MAURICE HUGH FREDERICK, Great Britain, University of London, *1916: "for their discoveries concerning the molecular structure of nuclear acids and its significance for information transfer in living material."

1963 The prize was awarded jointly to:

ECCLES, Sir JOHN CAREW, Australia, Australian National University, Canberra, *1906;

HODGKIN, ALAN LLOYD, Great Britain, Cambridge University, Cambridge, *1914; and

HUXLEY, ANDREW FIELDING, Great Britain, London University, *1917: "for their discoveries concerning the ionic mechanisms involved in excitation and inhibition in the peripheral and central portions of the nerve cell membrane."

1964 The prize was awarded jointly to:

BLOCH, KONRAD, U. S. A., Harvard University, Cambridge, Mass. ,*1912 (in Neisse, Germany); and

LYNEN, FEODOR, Germany, Max-Planck-Institut für Zellchemie, Munich, *1911: "for their discoveries concerning the mechanism and regulation of the cholesterol and fatty acid metabolism."

*born

1965 The prize was awarded jointly to:
JACOB, FRANCOIS, France, Institut Pasteur, Paris, *1920;

LWOFF, ANDRE, France, Institut Pasteur, Paris, *1902; and

MONOD, JACQUES, France, Institut Pasteur, Paris, *1910: "for their discoveries concerning genetic control of enzyme and virus synthesis."

1966 The prize was divided equally between:
ROUS, PEYTON, U. S. A., Rockefeller University, New York, N. Y., *1879: "for his discovery of tumor-inducing viruses"; and

HUGGINS, CHARLES BRENTON, U. S. A., Ben May Laboratory for Cancer Research, University of Chicago, Chicago, Ill. *1901: "for his discoveries concerning hormonal treatment of prostatic cancer."

1967 The prize was divided equally between:
GRANIT, RAGNAR, Sweden, Royal Caroline Institute, Stockholm, *1900;

HARTLINE, HALDAN KEFFER, U. S. A., The Rockefeller University, New York, *1903, and

WALD, GEORGE, U. S. A., Harvard University, Cambridge, Mass., *1906; "for their discoveries concerning the primary chemical and physiological visual processes in the eye."

1968 The prize was divided equally between:
HOLLEY, ROBERT W., U. S. A., Cornell University, Ithaca, *1922;
KHORANA, H. GOBIND, U. S. A., University of Wisconsin, Madison, *1922;

NIRENBERG, MARSHALL W., U. S. A., National Institutes of Health, Bethesda, *1927: "for their interpretation of the genetic code and its function in protein synthesis."

4. LITERATURE

1901 SULLY PRUDHOMME (pen-name of PRUDHOMME, RENE FRANÇOIS ARMAND), France, *1938, †1907: "in special recognition of his poetic composition, which gives evidence of lofty idealism, artistic perfection and a rare combination of the qualities of both heart and intellect."

*born †died

314

1902 MOMMSEN, CHRISTIAN MATTHIAS THEODORE, Germany, *1817 (in Garding, Sleswick, then Denmark), †1903: "the greatest living master of the art of hisitorical writing, with special reference to his monumental work, *A history of Rome.*"

1903 BJORNSON, BJORNSTJERNE MARTINUS, Norway, *1832, †1910: "as a tribute to his noble, magnificent and versatile work as a poet, which has always been distinguished both for the freshness of its inspiration and its rare purity of spirit."

1904 The prize was divided equally between:
MISTRAL, FREDERIC, France, *1830, †1914: "in recognition of the fresh originality and true inspiration of his poetic production, which faithfully reflects the natural scenery and native spirit of his people, and, in addition, his significant work as a Provencal philologist"; and

ECHEGARAY Y EIZAGUIRRE, JOSE, Spain, *1833, †1916: "in recognition of the numerous and brilliant compositions which, in an individual and original manner, have revived the great traditions of the Spanish drama."

1905 SIENKIEWICZ, HENRYK, Poland, *1846, †1916: "because of his outstanding merits as an epic writer."

1906 CARDUCCI, GIOSUE, Italy, *1835, †1907: "not only in consideration of his deep learning and critical research, but above all as a tribute to the creative energy, freshness of style, and lyrical force which characterize his poetic masterpieces."

1907 KIPLING, RUDYARD, Great Britain, *1865 (in Bombay, Br. India), †1936: "in consideration of the power of observation, originality of imagination, virility of ideas and remarkable talent for narration which characterize the creations of this world-famous author."

1908 EUCKEN, RUDOLF CHRISTOPH, Germany, *1846, †1926: "in recognition of his earnest search for truth, his penetrating power of thought, his wide range of vision, and the warmth and strength in presentation with which in his numerous works he has vindicated and developed an idealistic philosophy of life."

*born †died

315

1909 LAGERLOF, SELMA OTTILIANA LOVISA, Sweden, *1858, †1940: "in appreciation of the lofty idealism, vivid imagination and spiritual perception that characterize her writings."

1910 HEYSE, PAUL JOHANN LUDWIG, Germany, *1830, †1914: "as a tribute to the consummate artistry, permeated with idealism, which he has demonstrated during his long productive career as a lyric poet, dramatist, novelist and writer of worldrenowned short stories."

1911 MAETERLINCK, Count, MAURICE (MOORIS) POLIDORE MARIE BERNHARD, Belgium, *1862, †1949: "in appreciation of his many-sided literary activities, and especially of his dramatic works, which are distinguished by a wealth of imagination and by a poetic fancy, which reveals, sometimes in the guise of a fairy tale, a deep inspiration, while in a mysterious way they appeal to the readers' own feelings and stimulate their imaginations."

1912 HAUPTMANN, GERHART JOHANN ROBERT, Germany, *1862, †1946: "primarily in recognition of his fruitful, varied and outstanding production in the realm of dramatic art."

1913 TAGORE, RABINDRANATH, India, *1861, †1941: "because of his profoundly sensitive, fresh and beautiful verse, by which, with consummate skill, he has made his poetic thought, expressed in his own English words, a part of the literature of the West."

1914 Reserved.

1915 The prize money for 1914 was allocated to the Special Fund of this prize section.
The prize for 1915: Reserved.

1916 The prize for 1915:
ROLLAND, ROMAIN, France, *1866, †1944: "as a tribute to the lofty idealism of his literary production and to the sympathy and love of truth with which he has described different types of human beings."

The prize for 1916:
VON HEIDENSTAM, CARL GUSTAF VERNER, Sweden, *1859, †1940: "in recognition of his significance as the leading representative of a new era in our literature."

*born †died

316

1917 The prize was divided equally between:
GJELLERUP, KARL ADOLPH, Denmark, *1857, †1919: "for his varied and rich poetry, which is inspired by lofty ideals"; and PONTOPPIDAN, HENRIK, Denmark, *1857, †1943: "for his authenic descriptions of present-day life in Denmark."

1918 Reserved.

1919 The prize money for 1918 was allocated to the Special Fund for this prize section.
The prize for 1919: Reserved.

1920 The prize for 1919:
SPITTELER, CARL FRIEDRICH GEORG, Switzerland, *1845, †1924: "in special appreciation of his epic, *Olympian Spring*."
The prize for 1920:
HAMSUN, KNUT PEDERSEN, Norway, *1859, †1952: "for his monumental work, *Growth of the Soil*."

1921 ANATOLE FRANCE (pen-name of THIBAULT, JACQUES ANATOLE), France, *1844, †1924: "in recognition of his brilliant literary achievements, which are characterized by nobility and vigour of style, great-hearted human sympathy, genuine charm and a true French temper."

1922 BENAVENTE, JACINTO, Spain, *1866, †1954: "for the happy manner in which he has continued the illustrious traditions of the Spanish drama."

1923 YEATS, WILLIAM BUTLER, Ireland, *1865, †1939: "for his always inspired poetry, which in a highly artistic form gives expression to the spirit of a whole nation."

1924 REYMONT (pen-name of Reyment), WLADYSLAW STANISLAW, Poland, *1868, †1952: "for his great national epic, *The Peasants*."

1925 Reserved.

1926 The prize for 1925:
SHAW, GEORGE BERNARD, Great Britain, *1856 (in Dublin, Ireland), †1950: "for his work which is marked by both idealism and humanity, its stimulating satire often being infused with a singular poetic beauty."
The prize for 1926: Reserved.

*born †died

1927 The prize for 1926:

GRAZIA DELEDDA (pen-name of MADESANI, GRAZIA, née DE-
LEDDA) Italy, *1871 (in Nuoro, Sardina), †1936: "for her
idealistically inspired writings which with plastic clarity picture the life on her native island and with depth and sympathy
deal with human problems in general."
The prize for 1927: Reserved.

1928 The prize for 1927:

BERGSON, HENRI, France, *1859, †1941: "in recognition of his
rich and vitalizing ideas and the brilliant skill with which they
have been presented."
The prize for 1928:

UNDSET, SIGRID, Norway, *1882 (in Kalundborg, Denmark),
†1949: "principally for her powerful descriptions of Northern
life during the Middle Ages."

1929 MANN, THOMAS, Germany, *1875, †1955: "principally for his
great novel, *Buddenbrooks,* which has won steadily increased
recognition as one of the classic works of contemporary literature."

1930 LEWIS, SINCLAIR, U. S. A., *1885, †1951: "for his vigorous and
graphic art of description and his ability to create, with wit
and humour, new types of characters."

1931 The prize was awarded to:
KARLFELDT, ERIK AXEL, Sweden, *1864, †1931: "The poetry
of Erik Axel Karlfeldt."

1932 GALSWORTHY, JOHN, Great Britain, *1867, †1933: "for his distinguished art of narration which takes its highest form in the
Forsyte Saga."

1933 BUNIN, IVAN ALEKSEJEVIC, stateless, domicile in France, *1870
(in Voronez, Russia), †1953: "for the strict artistry with which
he has carried on the classical Russian traditions in prose
writing."

1934 PIRANDELLO, LUIGI, Italy, *1867, †1936: "for his bold and ingenious revival of dramatic and scenic art."

*born †died

318

1935 Reserved.

1936 The prize money for 1935 was with ⅓ allocated to the Main Fund and with ⅔ to the Special Fund of this prize section. The prize for 1936:

O'NEIL, EUGENE GLADSTONE, U. S. A., *1888, †1953: "for the power, honesty and deep-felt emotions of his dramatic works, which embody an original concept of tragedy."

1937 MARTIN DU GARD, ROGER, France, *1881, †1958: "for the artistic vigour and truthfulness with which he has pictured human contrasts as well as some fundamental aspects of contemporary life in the novel-cycle *Les Thibault.*"

1938 PEARL BUCK (pen-name of WALSH, PEARL, née SYDENSTRICKER), U. S. A., *1892: "for her rich and truly epic descriptions of peasant life in China and for her biographical masterpieces."

1939 SILLANPAA, FRANS EEMIL, Finland, *1888, †1964: "for his deep comprehension and exquisite art in painting the peasant-life and nature of his country in their mutual relations."

1940- The prize money was with ⅓ allocated to the Main Fund
-1943 and with ⅔ to the Special Fund of this prize section.

1944 JENSEN, JOHANNES VILHELM, Denmark, *1873, †1950: "for the rare strength and fertility of his poetic imagination with which is combined and intellectual curiosity of wide scope and a bold, freshly creative style."

1945 GABRIELA MISTRAL (pen-name of GODOY Y ALCAYAGA, LUCILA), Chile, *1889, †1957: "for her lyric poetry, which is inspired by powerful emotions and which has made her name a symbol of the idealistic aspirations of the entire Latin-American world."

1946 HESSE, HERMANN, Switzerland, *1877 (in Calw, Wurttemberg, Germany, †1962: "for his inspired writings which, while growing in boldness and penetration, exemplify the classical humanitarian ideals and high qualities of style."

*born †died

319

1947 GIDE, ANDRE PAUL GUILLAUME, France, *1869, †1951: "for his comprehensive and artistically significant writings, in which human problems and conditions have been presented with a fearless love of truth and keen psychological insight."

1948 ELIOT, THOMAS STEARNS, Great Britain, *1888 (in St. Louis, Mo., U. S. A.), †1965: "for his outstanding, pioneer contribution to present-day-poetry."

1949 Reserved.

1950 The prize for 1949:
FAULKNER, WILLIAM, U. S. A., *1897, †1962: "for his powerful and artistically unique contribution to the modern American novel."

The prize for 1950:
RUSSELL, EARL (BERTRAND ARTHUR WILLIAM), Great Britain, *1872: "in recognition of his varied and significant writings in which he champions humanitarian ideals and freedom of thought."

1951 LAGERKVIST, PAR FABIAN, Sweden, *1891: "for his artistic vigour and true independence of mind with which he endeavours in his poetry to find answers to the eternal questions confronting mankind."

1952 MAURIAC, FRANCIOS, France, *1885: "for the deep spiritual insight and the artistic intensity with which he has in his novels penetrated the drama of human life."

1953 CHURCHILL, Sir WINSTON LEONARD SPENCER, Great Britain, *1874, †1965: "for his mastery of historical and biographical description as well as for brilliant oratory in defending exalted human values."

1954 HEMINGWAY, ERNEST MILLER, U. S. A., *1898, †1961: "for his powerful mastery—with its influence on contemporary style— of the art of story-telling most recently evinced in *The Old Man and the Sea*."

1955 LAXNESS, HALLDOR KILJAN, Iceland, *1902: "for his vivid epic power which has renewed the great narrative art of Iceland."

*born †died

1956 JIMENEZ, JUAN RAMON, Spain (domicile in Puerto Rico, U. S. A.), *1881, †1958: "for his lyrical poetry, which in Spanish language constitutes an example of high spirit and artistical purity."

1957 CAMUS, ALBERT, France, *1913 (in Mondovi, Algeria), †1960: "for his important literary production, which with clearsighted earnestness illuminates the problems of the human conscience in our times."

1958 PASTERNAK, BORIS LEONIDOVIC, USSR, *1890, †1960: "for his important achievement both in contemporary lyrical poetry and in the field of the great Russian epic tradition." (Declined the prize).

1959 QUASIMODO, SALAVATORE, Italy, *1901: "for his lyrical poetry, which with classical fire expresses the tragic experience of life in our own times."

1960 SAINT-JOHN PERSE (pen-name of LEGER, ALEXIS), France, *1887 (on Guadeloupe Island): "for the soaring flight and the evocative imagery of his poetry which in a visionary fashion reflects the conditions of our time."

1961 ANDRIC, Ivo, Yugoslavia, *1892 (in Travnik, Bosnia): "for the epic force with which he has depicted themes and human destinies drawn from the history of his country."

1962 STEINBECK, JOHN, U. S. A., *1902, †1968: "for his at one and the same time realistic and imaginative writings, distinguished as they are by a sympathetic humour and a social perception."

1963 SEFERIS, GIORGOS (pen-name of SEFERIADIS, GIORGOS), Greece, *1900 (in Smyrna, Turkey): "for his eminent lyrical writing, inspired by a deep feeling for the Hellenic world of culture."

1964 SARTRE, JEAN-PAUL, France, *1905: "for his imaginative writing, which by reason of its spirit of freedom and striving for truth has exercised a far-reaching influence on our age." (Declined the prize).

1965 SOLOCHOV, MICHAIL ALEKSANDROVIC, USSR, *1905: "for the artistic power and integrity with which in his epic of the Don he has given creative expression to a historic phase in the history of the Russian people."

*born †died

1966 The prize was divided equally between:
AGNON, SHMUEL YOSEF, Israel, *1888: "for his profoundly characteristic narrative art with motifs from the life of the Jewish people"; and

SACHS, NELLY, *1891 in Germany, domiciled in Sweden since 1940: "for her outstanding lyrical and dramatic writing, which interprets Israel's destiny with touching strength."

1967 ASTURIAS, MIGUEL ANGEL, Guatemala, *1899: "for his highly coloured writings rooted in a national individuality and Indian traditions."

1968 KAWABATA, YASUNARI, Japan, *1899: "for his narrative mastery, which with great sensibility expresses the essence of the Japanese mind."

5. PEACE

1901 The prize was divided equally between:
DUNANT, JEAN HENRI, Switzerland, Founder International Committee of the Red Cross (Comité International de la Croix-Rouge), Geneva, Originator Geneva Convention (Convention de Genève), *1828, †1910; and

PASSY, FREDERIC, France, Founder and President first French peace society (called Société Française), *1822, †1912.

1902 The prize was divided equally between:
DUCOMMUN, ÉLIE, Switzerland, Honorary Secretary Permanent International Peace Bureau, Berne, *1833, †1906; and

GOBAT, CHARLES ALBERT, Switzerland, Secretary General Inter-Parliamentary Union, Honorary Secretary Permanent International Peace Bureau, Berne, *1843, †1914.

1903 CREMER, Sir WILLIAM RANDAL, Great Britain, Member British Parliament, Secretary International Arbitration League, *1838, †1908.

1904 INSTITUT DE DROIT INTERNATIONAL (INSTITUTE OF INTERNATIONAL LAW), Ghent, scientific society, founded 1873.

*born †died

322

1905 VON SUTTNER, Baroness, BERTHA SOPHIE FELICITA, née Countess KINSKY VON CHINIC und TETTAU, Austria, Writer, Hon. President Permanent International Peace Bureau, Berne, Author "Lay Down Your Arms," *1843 (in Prague, then Austria), †1914.

1906 ROOSEVELT, THEODORE, U. S. A., President United States of America, Collaborator various peace treaties, *1858, †1919.

1907 The prize was divided equally between:
MONETA, ERNESTO TEODORO, Italy, President Lombard League of Peace, *1833, †1918; and

RENAULT, LOUIS, France, Professor International Law, Sorbonne University, Paris, *1843, †1918.

1908 The prize was divided equally between:
ARNOLDSON, KLAS PONTUS, Sweden, Writer, formerly Member Swedish Parliament, Founder Swedish Peace and Arbitration League, *1844, †1916; and

BAJER, FREDRIK, Denmark, Member Danish Parliament, Honorary President Permanent International Peace Bureau, Berne, *1837, †1922.

1909 The prize was divided equally between:
BEERNAERT, AUGUSTE MARIE FRANCOIS, Belgium, ex-Prime Minister, Member Belgian Parliament, (International Court of Arbitration) at the Hague, *1829, †1912; and

D'ESTOURNELLES DE CONSTANT, PAUL HENRI BENJAMIN BALLUET, Baron DE CONSTANT DE REBECQUE, France, Member French Parliament (Sénateur), Founder and President French Founder, parliamentary group for voluntary arbitration, Committee for the defense of national interests and international conciliation, *1852, †1924.

1910 PERMANENT INTERNATIONAL PEACE BUREAU, Berne, founded 1891.

1911 The prize was divided equally between:
ASSER, TOBIAS MICHAEL CAREL, the Netherlands, Prime Minister, Member Privy Council, Originator International Conferences of Private Law at the Hague, *1838, †1913; and

*born †died

323

FRIED, ALFRED HERMANN, Austria, Journalist, Founder "Die Friedenswarte," a peace publication, *1864, †1921.

1912 Reserved.

1913 The prize for 1912:
ROOT, ELIHU, U. S. A., i. a. ex-Secretary of State, Originator various treaties of arbitration, *1845, †1937.

The prize for 1913:
LA FONTAINE, HENRI, Belgium, Member Belgian Parliament (Sénateur), President Permanent International Peace Bureau, Berne, *1854, †1943.

1914 Reserved.

1915 The prize money for 1914 was allocated to the Special Fund of this prize section.
The prize for 1915: Reserved.

1916 The prize money for 1915 was allocated to the Special Fund of this prize section.
The prize for 1916: Reserved.

1917 The prize money for 1916 was allocated to the Special Fund of this prize section.

The prize for 1917:
INTERNATIONAL COMMITTEE OF THE RED CROSS, Geneva, founded 1863.

1918 Reserved.

1919 The prize money for 1918 was allocated to the Special Fund of this prize section.
The prize for 1919: Reserved.

1920 The prize for 1919:
WILSON, THOMAS WOODROW, U. S. A., President United States of America, Founder of Société des Nations (the League of Nations), *1856, †1924.

The prize for 1920:
BOURGEOIS, LEON VICTOR AUGUSTE, France, i. a. ex-Secretary of State, President French Parliament (Sénat), President Conseil de la Société des Nations (Council of the League of Nations), 1851, †1925.

*born †died

324

1921 The prize was divided equally between:
BRANTING, KARL HJALMAR, Sweden, Prime Minister, Swedish Delegate Council of the League of Nations, *1860, †1925; and

LANGE, CHRISTIAN LOUS, Norway, Secretary General Inter-Parliamentary Union, Brussels, *1869, †1938.

1922 NANSEN, FRIDTJOF, Norway, Scientist, Explorer, Norwegian Delegate League of Nations, Originator "Nansen passports" (for refugees), *1861, †1930.

1923 Reserved.

1924 The prize money for 1923 was allocated to the Special Fund of this prize section.
The prize for 1924: Reserved.

1925 The prize money for 1924 was allocated to the Special Fund of this prize section.
The prize for 1925: Reserved.

1926 The prize for 1925 was awarded jointly to:
CHAMBERLAIN, JOSEPH, Sir AUSTEN, Great Britain, Foreign Secretary, Part-originator Locarno Pact, *1863, †1937; and

DAWES, CHARLES GATES, U. S. A., Vice-President of United States of America, Chairman Allied Reparation Commission (Originator "Dawes Plan"), *1865, †1951.

The prize for 1926 was awarded jointly to:
BRIAND, ARISTIDE, France, Foreign Minister, Part-originator Locarno Pact, Briand-Kellogg Pact, *1862, †1932; and

STRESEMANN, GUSTAV, Germany, ex-Lord High Chancellor, Foreign Minister, Part-originator Locarno Pact, *1878, †1929.

1927 The prize was divided equally between:
BUISSON, FERDINAND, France, Formerly Professor Sorbonne University, Paris, Founder and President, League for Human Rights, *1841, †1932; and

QUIDDE, LUDWIG, Germany, Professor Berlin University, Member German Parliament, Participant various peace conferences, *1858, †1941.

1928 Reserved.

*born †died

1929 The prize money for 1928 was allocated to the Special Fund of this prize section.

The prize for 1929: Reserved.

1930 The prize for 1929:
KELLOGG, FRANK BILLINGS, U. S. A., ex-Secretary of State, Part-originator Briand-Kellogg Pact, *1856, †1937.

The prize for 1930:
SODERBLOM, LARS OLOF NATHAN (JONATHAN), Sweden, Archbishop, Leader in the ecumenical movement, *1866, †1931.

1931 The prize was divided equally between:
ADDAMS, JANE, U. S. A., Sociologist, International President Women's International League for Peace and Freedom, *1860, †1935; and

BUTLER, NICHOLAS MURRAY, U. S. A., President Columbia University, Promoter Briand-Kellogg Pact, *1862, †1947.

1932 Reserved.

1933 The prize money for 1932 was allocated to the Special Fund of this prize section.

The prize for 1933: Reserved.

1934 The prize for 1933:
ANGELL (RALPH LANE), Sir NORMAN, Great Britain, Writer, Member Commission Exécutive de la Société des Nations (Executive Committee of the League of Nations) and of National Peace Council, Author "The Great Illusion," *1874.

The prize for 1934:
HENDERSON, ARTHUR, Great Britain, ex-Foreign Secretary, President Disarmament Conference 1932, *1863, †1935.

1935 Reserved.

1936 The prize for 1935:
VON OSSIETZKY, CARL, Germany, Journalist, Pacifist, *1889, †1938.

The prize for 1936:
SAAVEDRA LAMAS, CARLOS, the Argentine, Secretary of State, President League of Nations, Mediator in a conflict between Paraguay and Bolivia, *1878, †1959.

*born †died

326

1937 CECIL OF CHELWOOD, Viscount, (Lord EDGAR ALGERNON ROBERT GASCOYNE CECIL), Great Britain, Writer, i. a. ex-Lord Privy Seal, Founder and President International Peace Campaign, *1864, †1958.

1938 OFFICE INTERNATIONAL NANSEN POUR LES REFUGIES, Geneva, an international relief organization, started by Fridtjof Nansen, 1921.

1939- The prize money was allocated to the Main Fund.
1940-

1943 Reserved.

1944 The prize money for 1943 was allocated with ⅓ to the Main Fund and with ⅔ to the Special Fund of this prize section. The prize for 1944: Reserved.

1945 The prize for 1944:
INTERNATIONAL COMMITTEE OF THE RED CROSS, Geneva, founded 1863.

The prize for 1945:
HULL, CORDELL, U. S. A., ex-Secretary of State, Prominent part-taker in originating the United Nations, *1871, †1955.

1946 The prize was divided equally between:
BALCH, EMILY GREENE, U. S. A., formerly Professor of History and Sociology, Honorary International President Women's International League for Peace and Freedom, *1867, †1961; and

MOTT, JOHN RALEIGH, U. S. A., Chairman International Missionary Council, President World Alliance of Young Men's Christian Associations, *1865, †1955.

1947 The prize was awarded jointly to:
THE FRIENDS' SERVICE COUNCIL (The Quakers), London, founded 1647; and

THE AMERICAN FRIENDS' SERVICE COMMITTEE (The Quakers), Washington, first official meeting 1672.

1948 Reserved.

1949 The prize money for 1948 was allocated with ⅓ to the Main Fund and with ⅔ to the Special Fund of this prize section.

*born †died

The prize for 1949:

BOYD ORR OF BRECHIN, Lord, JOHN, Great Britain, Physician, Alimentary Politician, Prominent organizer and Director General Food and Agricultural Organization, President National Peace Council and World Union of Peace Organizations, *1880 (in Kilmaurs, Scotland).

1950 BUNCHE, RALPH, U. S. A., Professor Harvard University, Cambridge, Mass., Director div. of Trusteeship U. N., Acting Mediator in Palestine 1948, *1904.

1951 JOUHAUX, LEON, France, President Trade Union Confederation "C. G. T.-Force Ouvière." President Conseil National économique and International Committee of the European Council, Vice President International Confederation of Free Trade Unions, Vice President Fédération Syndicale Mondiale, Member Council of I. L. O. (International Labour Organization), Delegate U.N., *1879, †1954.

1952 Reserved.

1953 The prize for 1952:

SCHWEITZER, ALBERT, France, Missionary Surgeon, Founder Lambaréné Hospital (République du Gabon), *1875 (in Kaysersberg, Alsace, then Germany), †1965.

The prize for 1953:

MARSHALL, GEORGE CATLETT, U. S. A., General, President American Red Cross, ex-Secretary of State and of Defense, Delegate U. N., Originator "Marshall Plan," *1880, †1959.

1954 Reserved.

1955 The prize for 1954:

OFFICE OF THE UNITED NATIONS' HIGH COMMISSIONER FOR REFUGEES, Geneva, an international relief organization, founded by U. N. in 1951.

The prize for 1955: Reserved.

1956 The prize money for 1955 was allocated with ⅓ to the Main Fund and with ⅔ to the Special Fund of this prize Section. The prize for 1956: Reserved.

1957 The prize money for 1956 was allocated with ⅓ to the Main Fund and with ⅔ to the Special Funnd of this prize Section.

*born †died

328

The prize for 1957:
PEARSON, LESTER BOWLES, Canada, former Secretary of State, Foreign Department in Canada, President 7th Session of the United Nations General Assembly, *1897.

1958 PIRE, GEORGES, Belgium, Father of the Dominican Order, Leader of the relief organization for refugees, *1910.

1959 NOEL-BAKER, PHILIP J., Great Britain, Member of Parliament, lifelong ardent worker for international peace and cooperation, *1889.

1960 Reserved.

1961 The prize for 1960:
LUTULI, ALBERT JOHN, South Africa, formerly President of the African National Congress in S. A., *1898 (in Southern Rhodesia).

The prize for 1961:
HAMMARSKJOLD, DAG HJALMAR AGNE CARL, p. m., Sweden, formerly Secretary General of the U.N., *1905, †1961.

1962 Reserved.

1963 The prize for 1962:
PAULING, LINUS CARL, U. S. A., California Institute of Technology, Pasadena, Calif., *1901.

The prize for 1963 was divided equally between:
INTERNATIONAL COMMITTEE OF THE RED CROSS, Geneva, founded 1863; and

LEAGUE OF RED CROSS SOCIETIES, Geneva.

1964 KING, MARTIN LUTHER JR., U. S. A., leader of "Southern Christian Leadership Conference," *1929, †1968.

1965 UNITED NATIONS CHILDREN'S FUND (UNICEF), New York, an international relief organization, founded by U.N. in 1946.

1966 Reserved.

1967 Reserved.

1968 CASSIN, RENE, France, President of the European Court for Human Rights, *1887.

*born †died

Table 1968

showing the distribution of prizes between different countries based on the nationality of the prize-winner at the time of the award.

Country	Phys.	Chem.	Med.	Lit.	Peace	Total
Argentine	—	—	1	—	1	2
Australia	—	—	2	—	—	2
Austria	3	1	3	—	2	9
Belgium	—	—	2	1	3	6
Canada	—	—	2	—	1	3
Chile	—	—	—	1	—	1
China	2	—	—	—	—	2
Czechoslovakia	—	1	—	—	—	1
Denmark	1	—	4	3	1	9
Finland	—	1	—	1	—	2
France	8[1]	6[1]	6	11[1]	9	40
Guatemala	—	—	—	1	—	1
Germany	14	22	10	6[7]	3	55
Great Britain	15	17	15	6	7	60
Greece	—	—	—	1	—	1
Hungary	—	1	2[2]	—	—	3
Iceland	—	—	—	1	—	1
India	1	—	—	1	—	2
Ireland	1	—	—	1	—	2
Israel	—	—	—	1	—	1
Italy	2	1	2	4	1	10
Japan	2	—	—	1	—	3
The Netherlands	5	2	2	—	1	10
Norway	—	—	—	3	2	5
Poland	—	—	—	2	—	2
Portugal	—	—	1	—	—	1

Table 1968 (Continued)

Country	Phys.	Chem.	Med.	Lit.	Peace	Total
Spain	—	—	1	3	—	4
Sweden	2	4	2	4	4	16
Switzerland	—	3	4	2	3	12
Union of S. Africa	—	—	1[4]	—	1	2
U. S. A.	34	15[5]	30	6	14[5]	98
U. S. S. R. (before 1922 Russia)	6	1	2	3[3]	—	12
Yugoslavia	—	—	—	1	—	1
Institutions	—	—	—	—	9[6]	9
Grand total	88	71	92	62	61	388

[1]Marie Curie counted twice as she received half of the physics prize jointly with her husband Pierre Curie in 1903, and later, the whole chemistry prize in 1911. Literature: Sartre 1964, prize declined.

[2]One of them Bárány, born in Vienna, of Hungarian family.

[3]Bunin, Russian-born stateless; Pasternak, prize declined.

[4]Theiler, citizen both of Switzerland (whence his family originated) and of South Africa; scientific work achieved in the U.S.A.

[5]Linus Pauling counted twice as having received both a prize in chemistry in 1954 and in peace in 1963.

[6]The International Committee of the Red Cross is counted as one institution, although it has received a prize three times, in 1917, in 1944 and a divided prize in 1963.

[7]One of them Nelly Sachs, a naturalized Swedish citizen, born in Germany and writing in the German language.

Epilogue

That Alfred Nobel was a talented physical scientist, that he was a genius at business organization and administration, and that, as a consequence, he became one of the richest men of his time is not now important to us; his abilities and successes were perhaps not even important to him. What mattered to him then and to us now was his concern and compassion for mankind *and* what he did about it. While he lived, the advancement of learning—for the sake of itself and because he believed knowledge would aid in the cause of world peace—received his enthusiastic support. Also, Nobel fully appreciated the personal satisfaction of philanthropy both during his lifetime and in legacy. The greater gratification of giving compared to getting was well known to him and he set an incomparable example for others to follow.

Many men alive today have great wealth, yet use it unwisely during their lifetimes and do damage with it in their wills. Thus, it is the continuing value to mankind of the annual Nobel awards and the example of wise philanthropy which he set which make Alfred Nobel's sometimes lonely life important to us now.

Alfred Nobel used his wealth with wisdom and compassion, for the Nobel awards have provided incentive and have brought recognition in the cause of greater knowledge in the sciences, greater understanding of man, and the betterment of the human race. For these things he is remembered.

HENRY T. MUDD

INDEX

334

DATE DUE

Map by Daniel R. DeChaine

61116